Kinship Care

Also of interest from the Urban Institute Press:

Clearing the Way: Deconcentrating the Poor in Urban America,
by Edward G. Goetz

Federalism and Health Policy,
edited by John Holahan, Alan Weil, and Joshua M. Wiener

*Choosing a Better Life: Evaluating the Moving to Opportunity Social
Experiment,* edited by John Goering and Judith D. Feins

Welfare Reform: The Next Act,
edited by Alan Weil and Kenneth Finefold

*Who Speaks for America's Children? The Role of Child Advocates in
Public Policy,* edited by Carol J. De Vita and Rachel Mosher-Williams

Kinship Care

Making the most of a valuable resource

Edited by Rob Geen

THE URBAN INSTITUTE PRESS
WASHINGTON, DC

THE URBAN INSTITUTE PRESS
2100 M Street, N.W.
Washington, D.C. 20037

Library of Congress Cataloging in Publication Data

Kinship care: making the most of a valuable resource / edited by Rob
Geen.
      p. cm.
Includes bibliographical references and index.
   ISBN 0-87766-718-7 (paper, alk. paper)
  1. Kinship care—United States I. Geen, Rob.
   HV881.K553 2003
   362.73'3—dc22

                                                2003020519

Printed in the United States of America

THE URBAN INSTITUTE is a nonprofit policy research and educational organization established in Washington, D.C., in 1968. Its staff investigates the social, economic, and governance problems confronting the nation and evaluates the public and private means to alleviate them. The Institute disseminates its research findings through publications, its web site, the media, seminars, and forums.

Through work that ranges from broad conceptual studies to administrative and technical assistance, Institute researchers contribute to the stock of knowledge available to guide decisionmaking in the public interest.

Conclusions or opinions expressed in Institute publications are those of the authors and do not necessarily reflect the views of officers or trustees of the Institute, advisory groups, or any organizations that provide financial support to the Institute.

*This book is dedicated to
my wife, Linda, and our children, Cece and Danny,
whom I missed greatly during my travels
to collect information for this book, and
to all our kin who helped out while I was away.
This book is also dedicated, with special appreciation,
to the memory of Tillye, whom we miss every day.*

Contents

Acknowledgments ix

1   Kinship Foster Care: An Ongoing,
     Yet Largely Uninformed Debate 1
     Rob Geen

2   Identifying and Recruiting Kin to Act as
     Foster Parents 25
     Karin Malm and Roseana Bess

3   Licensing and Payment of Kinship Foster Parents 63
     Amy Jantz Templeman

4   Casework Practices with Kinship Foster Parents 95
     Rob Geen and Karin Malm

5   Providing Services to Kinship Foster Care Families ... 129
     Rob Geen

6   Permanency Planning with Kinship Foster Parents ... 153
     Rob Geen

7 Voluntary Placement or Foster Care Diversion? 179
Karin Malm and Rob Geen

8 In Their Own Words: Kin Speak Out about Their
Caregiving Experiences 201
Victoria Russell and Karin Malm

9 Kinship Care: Paradigm Shift or
Just Another Magic Bullet? 231
Rob Geen

Appendix: Study Description 261
Rob Geen and Cynthia Andrews Scarcella

References 275

About the Editor 283

About the Contributors 285

Index 287

Acknowledgments

This book and the research upon which it is based could not have been completed without the assistance of literally hundreds of individuals. We would like to thank all of the kinship caregivers who so openly and eloquently shared their experiences so that we could better understand the challenges they face and appreciate the commitment they have made to their related children. We also thank all of the child welfare caseworkers, supervisors, service providers, administrators, and court personnel who generously gave their time. In addition, our data collection site visits would not have been successful without the assistance of key staff persons at the local child welfare agencies charged with handling the logistics of our visits. We would like to acknowledge the hard work of these individuals: Susan Altman, Kathy Bahe, Rogest Carstarphen, Kim Clarke, Karen Crabtree, Alfred Fisher, Jorge Gonzalez, Jodi Harris, Sharon Hayes, Myra Helt, Jaime Horta, Vickie Jones, Robert LaFarge, Kim McAlister, and Clarence Rowe.

We also thank Jennifer Ehrle and Amy Billing, who participated in the study design, data collection, and data analysis, and David Berns, Donna Butts, and Mark Courtney for providing excellent comments on earlier drafts of the book. We also wish to recognize the fine work of the Urban Institute Press, especially the assistance provided by Scott Forrey and Suellen Wenz.

Finally, we are grateful to Lucy Salcido Carter and the David and Lucile Packard Foundation for financially supporting the research upon which this book is based.

1

Kinship Foster Care

An Ongoing, Yet Largely Uninformed Debate

Rob Geen

When public child welfare agencies find it necessary to remove children from their parents' homes due to abuse or neglect, these agencies seek to place children with foster parents. When the Adoption Assistance and Child Welfare Act of 1980 was passed, forming the basis of federal foster care policy, it was very rare for a child's relative to act as a foster parent. Today, child welfare agencies increasingly consider kin as the first placement choice when foster care is needed and kin are available and able to provide a safe home. Being separated from a parent, even an abusive or neglectful one, is traumatic for a child. By placing a child with someone he or she already knows, child welfare agencies hope to minimize this trauma.

Since the early 1980s, states' use of kin as foster parents has grown rapidly, yet very little information is available on how and when local child welfare agencies use kin as foster parents, how agencies' approach to kinship care differs from their approach to traditional foster care, and how local kinship care policies and practices vary across states. Thus, it has been difficult for federal and state policymakers, as well as advocates and practitioners, to evaluate how well kinship care ensures children's safety, promotes permanency in their living situation, and enhances their well-being—three basic goals of the child welfare system. Nonetheless, both federal and state governments continue to implement kinship care policies—both explicitly and implicitly.

Defining Kinship Care

In its broadest sense, kinship care is any living arrangement in which children live with neither of their parents but instead are cared for by a relative or someone with whom they have had a prior relationship. Note that the term *kin* is often used interchangeably with *relative*. However, many state child welfare agencies define *kinship care* to include persons beyond blood relatives—for example, godparents, family friends, or others with a strong emotional bond to a child (Jantz et al. 2002). Almost half of the states (24, including the District of Columbia) include only those related by blood, marriage, or adoption in their definition of kin. Almost as many states (22) define kin as those related beyond blood, marriage, or adoption. The remaining states (5) report having no definition of kin. The way states define kin is important, because all states treat kin in a different way than they treat non-kin, whether through preference, licensing, payment, and so on. In this book, the authors use the words *kin* and *relative* interchangeably, but they note when policies or practices for blood relatives differ from those for broader kin.

Kinship care arrangements are not a new phenomenon. Anthropologists have documented the role that extended families play in raising children in cultures and communities around the world (Korbin 1991; Young 1970). Extended family members and other persons with a bond to the family have been particularly important in African-American families dating back to the time of slavery when parents and children were often separated. In fact, the phrase *kinship care* was coined by Stack (1974) in work documenting the importance of kinship networks in the African-American community.

Traditionally, kinship care has been described as either "informal," meaning that such caregiving arrangements occur without the involvement of a child welfare agency, or "formal," meaning that kin act as foster parents for children in state custody. Unfortunately, the use of the terms *informal* and *formal* to describe the range of kinship care arrangements may be misleading and inaccurate. For example, referring to kinship caregiving outside the purview of the child welfare system as informal may incorrectly imply that such arrangements are short term or tenuous. Some informal kinship caregivers have legal custody of children through adoption or guardianship, and others have legal decision-making authority through a power of attorney. In short, some informal kinship care arrangements are more formal than others. Likewise, kinship care arrangements designated as "formal" vary in the extent to which they are publicly supported and monitored. Most earlier researchers have used formal kinship care to refer to arrangements in which children have been adjudicated as abused or neglected and placed in foster care with kin. However, child welfare may be involved in other kinship care placements. There are instances in which child welfare agencies help arrange the placement of a child with a relative but do not seek court action to obtain custody of the child. For example, during or after a child protective services investigation, a caseworker may advise a parent to place a child with a relative; both the parent and the relative know that if the parent refuses a "voluntary" kinship placement, the agency may petition the court to obtain custody of the child.

Given the limitations of the terms *formal* and *informal*, the authors in this book refer to all kinship care arrangements that occur without the child welfare agency's involvement as private kinship care and all kinship care arrangements that occur with child welfare contact as either kinship foster care (if the child is in state custody) or voluntary kinship care. As discussed at length in later chapters, kinship foster care may or may not be licensed in the same way as traditional non-kin foster care. And voluntary kinship care arrangements may or may not receive any on-going supervision from child welfare authorities or the juvenile court.

Children in Kinship Care

In 2002, approximately 2.3 million children lived with relatives without a parent present in the home.[1] The vast majority of these children, approximately 1.8 million, were in private kinship care. Between the periods 1983–85 and 1992–93,[2] the number of children in private kinship care grew slightly faster than the number of children in the United States as a whole—8.4 versus 6.6 percent (Harden, Clark, and Maguire 1997). Many researchers argue that during this period such social ills as increased homelessness, drug and alcohol abuse, juvenile delinquency, HIV/AIDS, and child abuse and neglect placed great pressure on the nuclear family and caused this increase (Hornby, Zeller, and Karraker 1996; Spar 1993). Since 1994, however, both the number and prevalence of children in private kinship care appear to have declined slightly.[3]

In contrast, available evidence suggests that kinship foster care increased substantially during the late 1980s and early 1990s (Boots and

Geen 1999; Harden et al. 1997; Kusserow 1992). Based on data from 25 states, the U.S. Department of Health and Human Services reported that the proportion of all children in state custody placed with kin increased from 18 percent in 1986 to 31 percent in 1990 (Kusserow 1992). Moreover, there is evidence that kinship care continued to increase through 1993 in California, Illinois, and New York, the three states that accounted for the great majority of the 1986–90 growth (Harden et al. 1997).

Several factors contributed to the growth in kinship foster care. While the number of children requiring placement outside the home increased (the foster care population doubled between 1983 and 1998), the number of non-kin foster parents declined. In addition, child welfare agencies developed a more positive attitude toward the use of kin as foster parents. By 1996, almost all states had policies giving family members preference when children required placement (Boots and Geen 1999). Finally, several federal and state court rulings have recognized the rights of relatives to act as foster parents and to be compensated financially for doing so.

In some states, the proportion of children in kinship care is far higher than the national average. For example, in California and Illinois, kinship care accounts for 43 percent and 47 percent of the caseloads, respectively (Needell et al. 2001; Wulczyn and Hislop 2001). While kinship care is unevenly used across the states, it continues to be the placement of choice for states with some of the highest caseloads in the country; it is also common in large urban centers, where placement rates are high and ethnic diversity prevails (Wulczyn, Brunner, and Goerge 1997).

Available data suggest that states' use of kinship foster care has leveled off. From March 1998 to September 2001, the portion of children in out-of-home care placed with relatives declined from 29 percent to 24 percent, and the number of children in kinship foster care decreased from 151,000 to 131,000. Since data show that children in kinship care tend to remain in out-of-home care longer than children placed in non-kin settings, the proportion of children *entering* foster care who are placed with kin is lower than this. Based on data from 25 states, only 20 percent of children entering foster care between April and September 1997 and still in placement on September 30, 1997, were in kinship care (HHS 2003).

It is important to note that the national data above on kinship care may underestimate the true number of foster children placed with kin.

Some states do not include in their kinship care data children placed with kin who are not licensed or who do not receive foster care payments. At the same time, some states cannot differentiate kin who have become licensed as foster parents from non-kin foster parents, especially when the kin are not related by blood to the children in their care. Data from the National Survey of America's Families (NSAF), a nationally representative household survey, suggests that the number of children in kinship foster care may be as high as 200,000 (Ehrle and Geen 2002a).

The apparent leveling off of states' use of kin as foster parents does not necessarily mean that states are not seeking out kin, but instead may be using kin in different ways. Almost all states report giving preference to and actively seeking out kin when children cannot remain with their biological parents (Jantz et al. 2002). However, it appears that child welfare agencies are frequently using kin as an alternative to foster care (i.e., voluntary kinship care). NSAF was also the first national survey to estimate the number of children in voluntary kinship care. According to NSAF data, approximately 285,000 children were living with relatives in 1997 as a result of child welfare involvement but were not in the custody of the state (Ehrle, Geen, and Clark 2001). While researchers had previously identified this group (Hornby, Zeller, and Karraker 1996; Takas 1992), this estimate was considerably higher than previously believed.

Several studies have identified differences between children in kin and non-kin arrangements in terms of their age, race or ethnicity, and other background characteristics.[4] Prior research has shown that children in kinship foster care are younger than children in non-kin foster care (Berrick, Needell, and Barth 1995; Chipungu et al. 1998; Cook and Ciarico 1998; Dubowitz, Feigelman, and Zuravin 1993; Iglehart 1994; Landsverk et al. 1996; LeProhn and Pecora 1994). These children are far more likely to be black than children in non-kin foster care (Berrick et al. 1995; Bonecutter and Gleeson 1997; Cook and Ciarico 1998; Dubowitz 1990; Grogan-Kaylor 1996; Iglehart 1994; Landsverk et al. 1996; Scannapieco, Hegar, and McAlpine 1997). For example, one study found that 60 percent of children in kinship foster care were African American, compared with 45 percent of children in non-kin foster care (Cook and Ciarico 1998). There appear to be no significant differences between the proportion of kin and non-kin foster children who are Hispanic[5] (Chipungu et al. 1998; Cook and Ciarico 1998). In addition, kinship care appears to be far more common in the South than in other regions (Harden et al. 1997).

Children in kinship care are also more likely than non-kin foster children to have been removed from their parents' homes due to abuse or neglect as opposed to other family problems, such as a parent-child conflict or behavioral problems (Cook and Ciarico 1998). Several small-scale studies have also found that kinship care children are more likely than children in non-kin foster care to be removed due to neglect as opposed to other forms of maltreatment (Gleeson, Bonecutter, and Altshuler 1995; Grogan-Kaylor 1996; Iglehart 1994; Landsverk et al. 1996).

Children in kinship care are more likely to come from homes in which the birth parents had a drug or alcohol problem (AFCARS 1998; Altshuler 1998; Beeman et al. 1996; Benedict, Zuravin, and Stallings 1996; Cook and Ciarico 1998; Gleeson et al. 1995). In addition, it appears that the birth parents of kinship care children are more likely to be young and never married than the birth parents of children in non-kin foster care (Altshuler 1998; Cook and Ciarico 1998).

Kinship Foster Parents

Kinship foster parents differ from non-kin foster parents in several important ways. Almost all of these differences illustrate that kinship foster parents face numerous challenges that most non-kin foster parents do not encounter. Moreover, these challenges suggest that substantial numbers of children in kinship foster care face various socioeconomic risks to their healthy development and illustrate the supports needed by kinship foster parents (Ehrle, Geen, and Clark 2001).

Almost all the studies that have collected data on the income of kinship caregivers have found that they are significantly poorer than non-kin foster parents (Barth et al. 1994; Berrick, Barth, and Needell 1994; Brooks and Barth 1998; Chipungu et al. 1998; Ehrle and Geen 2002b; Gebel 1996; Harden et al. 1997; LeProhn 1994; Zimmerman et al. 1998). For example, one study found that 39 percent of children in kinship foster care live in households with income below the federal poverty level, compared with 13 percent of children in non-kin foster care (Ehrle and Geen 2002b).

A few key factors may contribute to these caregivers' poverty. First, kinship caregivers have less formal education than non-kin caregivers (Barth et al. 1994; Beeman et al. 1996; Berrick et al. 1994; Chipungu et al.

1998; Gebel 1996; LeProhn 1994; Zimmerman et al. 1998). Approximately 32 percent of children in kinship foster care live with a caregiver who has less than a high school education, compared with only 9 percent of children in non-kin foster care (Ehrle and Geen 2002b). Second, kinship caregivers appear to be much more likely than non-kin foster parents to be single (Barth et al. 1994; Bonecutter and Gleeson 1997; Chipungu and Everett 1994; Chipungu et al. 1998; Dubowitz 1990; Gaudin and Sutphen 1993; Gebel 1996; LeProhn 1994; Pecora, LeProhn, and Nasuti 1999; Scannapieco et al. 1997). Between 48 and 62 percent of kinship foster parents are single, compared with 21 to 37 percent of non-kin foster parents (Berrick et al. 1994; Chipungu et al. 1998; Gebel 1996; LeProhn 1994). Third, kinship caregivers appear to be more likely to care for large sibling groups, although there is no difference in the average number of foster children in kinship care compared with non-kin foster homes (Berrick et al. 1994).

Kinship caregivers also tend to be older than non-kin foster parents, with a sizable difference in the number of caregivers over 60 years of age (Barth et al. 1994; Berrick et al. 1994; Chipungu et al. 1998; Davis et al. 1996; Gaudin and Sutphen 1993; Gebel 1996; Harden et al. 1997; LeProhn 1994). Between 15 and 21 percent of kinship foster parents are over age 60, compared with less than 9 percent of non-kin foster parents (Chipungu et al. 1998; Gebel 1996). These differences are not surprising, given the fact that kin foster parents are most often the grandparents of the children in their care (Brooks and Barth 1998; Dubowitz 1990; Ehrle and Geen 2002b; Gebel 1996; Gleeson et al. 1995; Harden et al. 1997; LeProhn 1994; Link 1996; Testa 1999). Studies have also shown that kinship caregivers are more likely to report being in poorer health than non-kin foster parents (Barth et al. 1994; Berrick et al. 1994; Chipungu et al. 1998), which may be due to their older age. It could be very challenging for an older caregiver in poor health to adequately care for a young child.

The research on kinship caregivers' employment is conflicting. Some studies have found that kinship caregivers are more likely to be employed than non-kin foster parents (Barth et al. 1994; Berrick et al. 1994; Chipungu et al. 1998) and to be employed full-time (Barth et al. 1994; Chipungu et al. 1998). In contrast, other studies have found that kin are less likely to be employed or employed full-time (Beeman et al. 1996; Gebel 1996). Employment clearly affects the time a caregiver has available to spend with the child, but it may also affect the resources a caregiver can offer to the child.

In addition to the socioeconomic challenges that many kin foster parents face, they, unlike non-kin foster parents, usually receive little, if any, advanced preparation in assuming their role as caregivers. They may not have time to prepare mentally for their new roles and may not have adequate space, furniture (e.g., a crib), or other child-related necessities (such as toys or a car seat). Since most kinship caregivers are grandparents, they may not have had parenting duties for some time and may be apprehensive about raising a child at this stage in their lives.

Few researchers have examined the impact of caregiving on kin. Those that have studied this issue have focused on differences between custodial and noncustodial grandparents. Solomon and Marx (2000) found that 45 percent of custodial grandparents reported being in fair to poor physical health, compared with 24 percent of noncustodial grandparents. Moreover, by most measures, the emotional health and life satisfaction of custodial grandparents is lower than that of their noncustodial counterparts. Minkler, Roe, and Price (1992) found that one-third of their sample of 72 African-American grandmothers indicated that their health had worsened since beginning caregiving and many directly attributed this to their caregiving responsibilities. Another study found that caregiving was directly associated with high levels of depression among grandparent caregivers (Minkler et al. 2000).

While most of the research on kin caregiving has focused on the negative effects that caregiving may have on kin, some researchers have explored the positive rewards from this experience. Caregiving can provide a meaningful role for kin, leading them to feel more useful and productive (Emick and Hayslip 1996). Caring for a child may also be intrinsically rewarding (Giarrusso et al. 1996).

The Evolution of Federal and State Policies

Federal policies affecting kinship caregivers fall under the domain of both income assistance and child welfare. Federal income assistance policies have acknowledged the role of kin caregivers, while federal child welfare policies have historically been vague regarding the financial support of kin. With limited federal guidance and sometimes-unclear congressional intent, states' child welfare policies have developed in ways that treat kinship foster care differently from non-kin foster care.

Federal Policy Development

An early income assistance policy that affected kin was the 1950 amendment to the Social Security Act. It allowed for relatives, if eligible, to receive payment for themselves and the children they were caring for under the Aid to Families with Dependent Children (AFDC) program, thus treating relatives like members of the nuclear family. However, if relatives were not eligible for assistance, they could receive payments for the child only. In this second scenario, because relatives were not legally required to care for the child, the relatives were not considered part of the assistance unit. Under current federal policy, states can provide Temporary Assistance for Needy Families (TANF) child-only grants to any relative caring for a child in a kinship care arrangement, regardless of the relative's income, provided that the relative meets the state's TANF definition of a relative caretaker.[6]

In the child welfare policy area, amendments to Title IV of the Social Security Act in 1962 authorized federally reimbursed payments to licensed foster parents. However, at that time, most kinship caregivers were kept out of the child welfare system and did not become licensed foster parents or receive foster care payments. Most kinship caregivers were referred to income assistance programs for support. However, welfare grants were and are smaller than foster care payments, sometimes significantly, depending on the state as well as the number of children being cared for (Boots and Geen 1999).

In 1979, the Supreme Court ruled in *Miller v. Youakim* that relative foster parents caring for children who are eligible for federally reimbursed foster care payments (i.e., Title IV-E–eligible) are entitled to the same federal benefits as non-relative foster parents if they meet the same licensing standards. However, the case did not address what support should be provided to kin caring for children who are not eligible for federal foster care funds, or to those kin who do not meet certain state foster care licensing requirements.

The Indian Child Welfare Act of 1978 and the Adoption Assistance and Child Welfare Act of 1980 were viewed as giving tacit preference to relative foster parents. The Indian Child Welfare Act (P.L. 96-272) stated that Native American children in foster care should be placed near their home and with their extended family if possible. The Adoption Assistance and Child Welfare Act required that when placing children in foster care, the state should use the "least restrictive, most family-like setting available in close proximity to the parent's home, consistent with the best interests and special needs of the child." The 1996 Personal Responsibility and Work Opportunity Reconciliation Act (P.L. 104-193)—legislation that significantly altered the federal cash assistance program—also addressed kinship care, requiring states to "consider giving preference to an adult relative over a non-related caregiver when determining a placement for a child, provided that the relative caregiver meets all relevant State child protection standards."

Recent federal child welfare policy also promotes kinship placements. In 1997, concerned about the length of time children spent in foster care, Congress passed the Adoption and Safe Families Act (ASFA). While promoting more timely permanency for all children, the act acknowledges the unique circumstances of kinship care and permits states to treat kinship care and non-kin foster children differently. ASFA requires states to seek termination of parental rights (TPR) after a child has been in foster care for 15 of 22 consecutive months. However, ASFA allows states to extend this time frame if "the child is being cared for by a relative." ASFA is also the first federal legislation to address kinship care as a potential permanent placement by indicating that "a fit and willing relative" could provide a "planned permanent living arrangement."

While each state sets its own foster care licensing standards, the federal government provides financial reimbursement to states to cover certain costs associated with foster care placements. There are certain minimum procedural guidelines that states must meet to receive financial reimbursement. ASFA clarified conditions under which the federal government would provide financial reimbursement. The Act, and the ASFA final rule of January 2000 that documented how the Department of Health and Human Services (HHS) would implement the Act, included a number of provisions that affected or clarified the federal reimbursement of foster care payments made to children placed with kin. States may not collect federal reimbursement for all kin caring for IV-E–eligible children. Instead, "relatives must meet the same licensing/ approval standards as non-relative foster family homes." Waivers for certain licensing standards may only be issued on a case-by-case basis, not for kin as a group. No waivers can be granted for safety issues. In addition, the final rule prohibits states from claiming IV-E reimbursement for provisionally licensed or emergency placement kin homes.

While the federal government will not reimburse states for foster care payments made to kin who are not licensed the same as non-relative foster homes, neither ASFA nor the final rule prohibit states from assessing kin differently than non-kin. Some argue that kinship care is a unique situation and should not be held to the same standards as non-kin placements. Traditional foster care requirements, especially those not related to safety, may be irrelevant in a kinship care placement. The potential benefits of living with a family member or close family friend may outweigh the need for safety checks, such as space requirements. However, safety is the most important concern to child welfare agencies, which may be reluctant to waive requirements or hold kin to less stringent standards than those non-kin foster parents must meet.

The cumulative impact of the ASFA final rule is that kin may be less likely to receive foster care payments and may be forced to make do with the significantly less generous support provided by TANF child-only grants. Given the financial pressures that many kin already experience, these changes may make fewer kin able to care for a child needing placement.

State Kinship Care Policies

States have historically had considerable flexibility in determining how to assess and pay kinship caregivers. While the federal government has carefully regulated states' foster care practices and set guidelines for the types of non-kin foster families that may receive federal reimbursement, until recently it remained silent on how states may treat kin differently from non-kin foster parents. With limited federal guidance, state kinship care policies have evolved in such a way that there is significant variation in the ways in which states assess and support kinship caregivers, and many states have multiple licensing or approval options for kin.

In 1993, Gleeson and Craig were among the first to examine the differences among state kinship care policies. As part of their study, they requested written documentation of kinship care policies, obtaining responses from 32 states. They found that while many states use the same approval standards for kin as for non-kin foster parents, 17 states had developed approval standards specifically for kin or waived certain non-kin foster care requirements. Gleeson and Craig also found a link between the assessment and payment of kin, reporting that "some states use foster home licensing standards as criteria for whether a relative home will be eligible for foster care boarding rates, but not as a criteria for child safety" (1994, 18). Sixteen of the 32 states' documents stated that relatives could receive foster care payments if they met the foster home licensing or relative approval standards.

In 1997, 1999, and 2001, the Urban Institute conducted national surveys of states' kinship care policies. These surveys found that while state policies were still evolving (27 states changed their licensing policies between 1999 and 2001), most states provided flexibility to allow kin to act as foster parents (Jantz et al. 2002). Only 15 states required kin to meet all the same licensing criteria as non-kin foster parents. All but nine states would place children with kin before they meet all of the assessment criteria required of them, sometimes referred to as provisional licensing or approval.

Because kin may be unable or choose not to be licensed as foster parents, they may not be eligible to receive monthly foster care payments on behalf of the children in their care. In 26 states, at least some kin are not eligible to receive foster care payments (Jantz et al. 2002). A few states (six) provide state-funded foster care payments to kin who meet standards that are different from non-kin foster parents, which makes these states ineligible for federal reimbursement of the payments.

Most states also offer kin flexibility in permanency planning. Almost all states (43) have implemented the ASFA option and allow children to remain in long-term foster care with kin under certain circumstances. In addition, 35 states offer subsidies to kin who are not interested in adopting but are willing to become permanent legal guardians.

Services for Families

Child welfare agencies are responsible for ensuring that the children they place in foster care are cared for appropriately. Agencies may provide or refer children for a variety of services to meet their needs, including services that address issues arising from the abuse or neglect the children have suffered. Agencies also provide a variety of supports to foster care parents in their effort to care for children.

While state policies indicate that kin are generally eligible to receive the same services as non-kin foster parents, past research has clearly shown that in practice, kin foster parents and the children in their care receive fewer services. Kin are offered and request fewer services (Barth et al. 1994; Berrick et al. 1994; Chipungu and Everett 1994; Chipungu et al. 1998; Cook and Ciarico 1998).

Experts have offered several explanations for these disparities. These variations may reflect differences in the service needs of kin and non-kin foster parents. Child welfare caseworkers may also treat kin and non-kin foster parents differently. A few studies have shown that kin foster parents were less likely to receive services they requested (Chipungu et al. 1998; LeProhn and Pecora 1994).

Kin also fail to receive the assistance they are eligible for from non–child welfare agencies. While all kin who do not receive foster care payments from the child welfare agency are eligible to receive TANF assistance from an income assistance agency,[7] many fail to receive either TANF or foster care payments. Similarly, many kin who are eligible for assistance fail to receive Medicaid health insurance coverage for the children in their care, food stamps, child care subsidies, or housing assistance (Ehrle and Geen 2002a).

At the same time, many states have recently developed programs to better meet the needs of kinship caregivers, designed as alternatives to either TANF or foster care programs (Geen et al. 2001). Some of these programs provide greater financial assistance than kin would otherwise be eligible to receive through TANF; some offer a range of supportive services, such as child or respite care, support groups, education and mentoring services, transportation, and recreation; and others seek to link kin to available community resources.

The Ongoing Debate

In spite of explicit federal and state preference for kinship care and states' continued heavy reliance on kin as foster parents, kinship care remains a field of policy and practice that is mired in controversy and complexity. Policymakers, for example, are still ambivalent about the appropriate responsibilities of kin caring for children in the child welfare system. Whether kin should play a role in child welfare that corresponds to that of traditional foster parents, or whether they should be considered family providing informal supports (Berrick and Needell 1999; Testa 2001) remains a tension that is yet to be resolved. This tension plays out in debates about how child welfare agencies should financially support kin, as well as in how policymakers assess how well kinship care meets the child welfare goals of safety, permanency, and well-being (Shlonsky and Berrick 2001). Moreover, discussions about kinship care practice, as well as child welfare practices more generally, are intertwined with the issues of race and class. Finally, our knowledge of kinship foster care is severely limited; much of the existing research is either narrow in focus or lacking in methodological rigor.

Payment

Some may argue that kin should not be paid for caring for a related child because such care is part of a family's responsibility. Moreover, some experts have argued that the higher foster care payment rates (compared with TANF) may provide an incentive for private kinship caregivers to become part of the child welfare system (Berrick, Minkler, and Needell 1999; Johnson 1994). These arguments, however, view kinship care from the perspective of the caregiver rather than that of the maltreated child. Indeed, Testa and Slack (2002) found that placement stability is enhanced when kinship caregivers receive the full foster care subsidy. Geen and Berrick (2002) suggest that arguments concerning kinship care payments should turn on government's responsibility for children in state custody rather than on the licensing status or family ties between caregiver and child. They argue that states assume the same level of responsibility for children in state custody regardless of where a child is placed and that it makes no sense for states to provide less financial assistance on behalf of a child in kinship care solely because the caregiver is unable to meet certain licensing criteria.

The ASFA final rule also prohibits kin who are provisionally licensed from receiving federally reimbursed foster care payments. Almost all kinship caregivers are provisionally licensed, since they typically begin caring for a related child with little advance warning. Since the licensing process in many states takes six months or more, kin may lose considerable financial assistance by being denied foster care and supplemental payments until they are licensed.

At the same time, the ASFA final rule allows states, under certain circumstances, to recoup foster care expenses for children who were already living with kin when child welfare became involved. These placements are often called constructive or paper removals, since the child is not physically removed from the home but taken into state custody. Child welfare agencies face a difficult decision in determining the circumstances under which they should take a child into custody, particularly when the child may already be in a safe and stable home. If only

15 percent of the children living in private kinship care arrangements were brought into child welfare systems, the kinship foster care population would double. And Illinois's experience has taught us that making foster care payments available to private kin can lead to significant increases in kinship foster care (Testa 1997).

A related concern centers on when it might be appropriate for child welfare agencies to divert children from the foster care system by using voluntary kinship care placements. The aforementioned issues relating to equity in financial assistance apply in these cases, but just as important, these children may effectively be excluded from public agency supervision, from the specialized health and mental health and school-related services that might be available through foster care, and their parents are denied the services they may need in order to effectively reunify with their children. At the same time, voluntary kinship care placements may benefit children and caregivers by preventing the stigma and intrusion of child welfare system and juvenile court involvement. Not a single study to date has examined voluntary kinship care placements in depth.

Safety

Kinship care advocates have had to fight for years to overcome the negative perception among many child welfare workers and administrators that "the apple does not fall far from the tree"—in other words, parents who are abusive were probably abused themselves. Persons who subscribe to this notion suspect that kin abused the parent whose child is being removed by a child welfare agency. While some studies lend credence to the theory of an intergenerational cycle of abuse, it appears that most children in kinship care are placed there because of parental neglect rather than abuse (Gleeson et al. 1995; Grogan-Kaylor 1996; Iglehart 1994; Landsverk et al. 1996). Despite this fundamental concern, few studies have directly assessed the safety of kinship care placements. Two studies that compared the rate of abuse by kin and non-kin foster parents had conflicting results, with one finding children in kinship care more likely to suffer abuse (Dubowitz, Feigelman, and Zuravin 1993) and the other finding them less likely to suffer abuse (Zuravin, Benedict, and Somerfield 1993).

Concern about the safety of kinship care placements led HHS in the ASFA final rule to mandate that "relatives must meet the same licensing standards as non-relative family foster homes" for states to receive federal foster care reimbursement. HHS notes that "given the emphasis in ASFA on child safety . . . we believe that it is incumbent upon us, as part of our oversight responsibilities, to fully implement the licensing and safety requirements specified in the statute." However, it seems hypocritical for federal policy to suggest that kin must be licensed for states to receive federal reimbursement because of safety concerns, but not require states to license those kinship care homes for which they do not seek federal reimbursement. Moreover, the federal government allows states great flexibility in setting foster care home licensing standards, and the stringency in standards varies greatly among states. Thus, kin meeting a licensing standard in one state may actually meet more stringent standards than licensed foster parents in another state.

In addition to the policy conundrums associated with kin care, practitioners encounter many challenges in their work with kin as they struggle to respect both kin as the principal decisionmakers in children's lives and their own professional judgment about the best interests of children (Gleeson and Hairston 1999). Several studies have shown that child welfare workers tend to supervise kinship care families less closely than non-kin foster families (Beeman et al. 1996; Berrick et al. 1994). Concerns have also been raised because studies have shown birth parent visitation of children in kinship care is often unsupervised and thus parents may have inappropriate access to children they have abused or neglected (Barth et al. 1994; Berrick et al. 1994; Chipungu et al. 1998).

Permanency

The new federal law also reflects ambivalence about kin in its policy approach to permanency. Whereas ASFA clearly encourages permanency (i.e., adoption or legal guardianship) for children in non-kin care who cannot be reunified and specifically disallows long-term foster care for non-kin, it includes explicit provisions for long-term care for children placed with relatives. Indeed, placement stability is much greater for children placed with kin than with non-kin (Beeman et al. 1996; Benedict et al. 1996; Berrick 1998; Cook and Ciarico 1998; Courtney and Needell 1997), but it is hardly guaranteed, and according to recent work by Testa (2001), extended kinship care placements may be as likely to break down as long-term placements with non-kin.

Conflicting views about the potential for permanency with kin have developed, in part, because of child welfare workers' attitudes and expectations (Beeman and Boisen 1999; Berrick, Needell, and Barth 1999), presumptions about the role of blood and culture in some communities (Burnette 1997), and some research suggesting that kin may be disinclined to adopt (Gleeson 1999; Thornton 1991). More recent work by Testa (in press; Testa et al. 1996) suggests that many kin can and will adopt if they are provided accurate information and if they are reassured about ongoing payment subsidies, the continued role of birth parents in the lives of children, and the option to leave children's birth names intact.

Still, concerns remain about whether placement with relatives dampens birth parents' efforts toward reunification. Children remain in kin placements for relatively long periods and are less likely to be reunified with their parents (Benedict and White 1991; Berrick et al. 1995; Chipungu et al. 1998; Courtney 1994; Testa 1997). Testa and Slack (2002) examined reunification rates for children in kin care and found that—not unlike findings for children in non-kin care (Hess 1987)— regular visitation and parents' active efforts toward reunification are strongly associated with the child's return home. While critics of ASFA have suggested that the new, shortened time frames available for permanency may reduce opportunities for reunification for all children (whether in kin or non-kin care), the effects for children in kinship care may be especially profound since they are less likely than children in non-kin care to have moved toward reunification within the allotted 12-month period.

Well-Being

Despite the challenges faced by kin caregivers, advocates of kinship care argue that children fare better when placed with relatives. Since children are more likely to be familiar with a kin caregiver, many experts suggest that these placements are less traumatic and disruptive for children than placements with non-kin (Gleeson and Craig 1994; Johnson 1994; Zwas 1993). Many argue that placement with kin is less psychologically harmful to children than placement with strangers (National Commission on Family Foster Care 1991). Further, studies of children's experiences in care suggest that the vast majority of children feel "loved" by their kin caregivers and "happy" with their living arrangements (Wilson and Conroy 1999).

In addition, children may maintain a stronger family bond in kinship foster care because they are more likely to be placed with siblings than are children in non-kin foster care (Berrick et al. 1994; Gleeson, O'Donnell, and Bonecutter 1997; Testa and Rolock 1999). Kinship foster care also helps children maintain a connection with their community—research has indicated that they are more frequently placed close to the homes from which they were removed (DiLeonardi, n.d.; Testa 1997; Testa and Rolock 1999). In addition, kinship foster care helps maintain family continuity. Children in kinship foster care have much more frequent and consistent contact with both birth parents and siblings than do children in non-kin foster care (Barth et al. 1994; Berrick et al. 1994; Chipungu et al. 1998; Davis, Landsverk et al. 1996; GAO 1999; LeProhn and Pecora 1994). Prior research has also shown that children in kinship foster care are significantly less likely than children in non-kin foster care to experience multiple placements (Beeman et al. 1996; Benedict et al. 1996; Berrick et al. 1995; Chipungu et al. 1998; Courtney and Needell 1997; Goerge 1990; Iglehart 1994; LeProhn and Pecora 1994; Zimmerman et al. 1998).

One of the only studies examining outcomes from kinship care (Benedict et al. 1996) suggested that as young adults, children placed with kin do as well as children placed in non-kin family foster care. The study only included kin providers licensed as foster parents, however, so the study is of limited utility, given the diversity of kinship foster care arrangements. A larger body of literature has developed to examine children's health and mental health while in kin care (Dubowitz et al. 1994; Sawyer and Dubowitz 1994). These studies all point to rough comparability between children in both settings. Shore et al. (2002) found that children in kin and non-kin care have rates of internalized and externalized behavior problems that are higher than rates for the general population, but that there are few differences in behavior problems between children in kin and non-kin care. Because all of the studies to date examine children's behavior while in care, issues remain as to whether the similarities we see are largely due to patterns of behavior associated with out-of-home care, or whether children present with similar problems at initial placement.

Race and Class

Issues of race and class have been and continue to be intertwined with child welfare and kinship care policy and practices. Nationally, African-American children are overrepresented in reports of abuse or neglect and in the number of children living in foster care (Leashore, McMurray, and Bailey 1997). Further, the majority of children living in kinship care arrangements are children of color. Thus, policies that affect families in the child welfare system, in kinship care, or both have an especially strong impact on African-American families. Many researchers have argued that child welfare practices do not reflect the cultural norms of minority groups and that changes in child welfare policies, especially those related to kinship care, "should be based on a deliberate and conscious recognition of the cultural patterns of various racial and ethnic groups" (Everett, Chipungu, and Leashore 1997). When looking at race and kinship care, it is important to consider the argument that "African Americans, for example, have relied on extended family and other informal systems of care not only because these informal systems are cultural strengths, but because African-American children for many years were excluded from public and private sector child welfare programs" (Bonecutter and Gleeson 1997).

Issues of race and class also play out in the values surrounding kinship definitions, in determining whether a potential kin caregiver is appropriate for an abused or neglected child, and in deciding what permanency options are appropriate for children in kinship care. It can be argued, for example, that "a lack of understanding of family as defined by non-Western culture has created most of the current debate over what role, if any, kinship care should have in child welfare. The extended family structure has been viewed as a variant family form because its structure is different from what has traditionally been considered the ideal structure of the nuclear family" (Johnson 1994). Moreover, many observers argue that current foster parent home licensing criteria, such as the number of rooms in the foster parent's home (which some states waive for kin), are not related to safety or quality of care but instead reflect middle-class values regarding proper homes (Kinship Care Advisory Panel 1998). Similarly, while the child welfare system has traditionally considered permanence to be either reunification or adoption, reunification is not always possible, and adoption may not be consistent with the values of some communities. In Native American communities, for example, the legal status afforded by adoption has little relevance or meaning. Instead, "the responsibility to assume care of relatives' children was both implied and expressly stated in the oral traditions and spiritual teachings of most tribes" (Johnson 1994).

Limits of Existing Research

This chapter has attempted to introduce the topic of kinship foster care by presenting a summary of the existing research. In addition to the obvious research gaps, it is important to understand that much of the research that is presented suffers from methodological limitations that raise questions about the generalizability of the findings. Many of the studies cited are based on small, idiosyncratic samples or surveys with low response rates. Almost all of the studies cited are based on bivariate analyses, addressing the relationship between a particular type of foster care and a variety of characteristics and experiences of families and children, based on point-in-time data. These analyses do not take into account the multitude of differences before placement that might influence these characteristics and experiences. Moreover, studies generally have not taken into account differences in state kinship care policies and practices that may affect comparison with other studies. Additional limitations and a discussion of research gaps are presented at greater length in chapter 9.

Purpose and Overview of the Book

While a great deal of information has been collected about the characteristics of kinship care children and foster parents as well as federal and state kinship care policies, little research has focused on "frontline" kinship care practices. This book seeks to fill this void. Using results from a study involving 96 focus groups of child welfare workers and kinship caregivers, in addition to interviews with local administrators, advocates, and service providers (a detailed description of the study is included in the appendix), it describes frontline kinship care practices and provides an in-depth understanding of how and why child welfare agencies approach kin and non-kin foster care differently.

The following chapters present the results of intensive case studies conducted by the Urban Institute of local kinship care policies and frontline practices in 13 locations in four states during the spring and summer of 2001. The case study sites included Jefferson (Birmingham), Mobile, and Talladega counties in Alabama; Los Angeles, San Diego, Santa Clara (San Jose), and Santa Cruz counties in California; Bridgeport, Hartford, and Torrington municipalities in Connecticut; and Lake

(Gary), LaPorte, and Marion (Indianapolis) counties in Indiana. Four states with different state policies for licensing and paying kinship foster parents were purposely selected. In each state, sites that placed large numbers of children in kinship foster care were chosen. These sites were the larger, more urban counties in the states. In addition, in each state researchers selected one rural county or municipality (Talladega, Santa Cruz, Torrington, and LaPorte) to assess whether kinship care practices might be different in these communities.

In each of the 13 study sites, we interviewed child welfare administrators and/or court personnel or judges and conducted focus groups with child welfare supervisors, caseworkers, and kinship caregivers. In all, we conducted 41 focus groups with 235 caseworkers and 30 focus groups with 137 supervisors. In addition, we conducted 25 focus groups with 157 kinship caregivers. All focus groups were recorded and the audiotapes were transcribed. The transcribed notes from the focus groups, as well as notes from the other interviews, were coded for analysis using Nud*ist content analysis software. Direct quotes from administrators, workers, and caregivers included in this book were selected to be representative of the opinions voiced. Moreover, we present caseworker opinions and caregivers' experiences based on their perspective. Thus, the information they provided about such things as eligibility for services or agency procedures may not be accurate, but it is what they believe to be true.

The study has a number of additional limitations that limit the generalizability of the results. The samples of workers and kinship caregivers participating in the focus group, while large and varied, were not necessarily representative of the jurisdictions in which the study collected data, and certainly not representative of the nation as a whole. All interviews and focus groups were conducted in English, so the number of Hispanic kinship caregivers that participated was less than we would expect had groups also been held in Spanish. In only a few locations was child care made available, which may have affected participation in the focus groups. Most of the focus groups were held at child welfare agency offices, which may have limited respondents' comfort in providing candid comments. The rural sites selected for the study were all relatively close to urban areas and thus are not representative of all rural areas. Data collection focused on worker and caregiver perceptions; findings were not validated with empirical evidence.

The book is organized chronologically in terms of child welfare involvement. Thus, chapter 2 focuses on agency efforts to identify and recruit kin to act as foster parents when the agency determines that a child cannot remain in his or her parents' home. The chapter examines how local child welfare agencies interpret the federal and state policy that they should give preference to relatives over non-relatives when a child must be placed in foster care. Chapter 2 also assesses how and when child welfare workers actively seek out relatives to be foster parents, how they choose a relative to act as a foster parent when multiple relatives come forward to care for a child, and the extent to which the desires of the child and the birth parent affect this decision. Chapter 3 examines how local child welfare agencies assess kin before placing a child in their care and how this assessment differs from the licensing of non-kin foster parents. Because financial assistance provided to kin is intimately linked with licensing procedures, this chapter also examines the payments that kin may receive.

Chapters 4, 5, and 6 examine agency practices once a child has been placed with kin. Chapter 4 examines how well kin understand what is expected of them as foster parents, as well as the role of the child welfare agency and court. This chapter describes how caseworker supervision of kin and non-kin foster parents differs and why. Chapter 4 also documents how birth parent visitation is different when children are placed with kin instead of non-kin foster parents. Chapter 5 compares the service needs of kin and non-kin foster parents and children, documents and explains why kin are offered and request fewer services, and identifies barriers kin face in gaining access to services. Chapter 6 examines the different way that local agencies approach permanency planning when children are in kin rather than non-kin foster care. This chapter assesses the impact of ASFA on permanency planning practices, documents local agency efforts to increase adoptions by kin, and identifies reasons why kin may not want to adopt, including financial disincentives created by local policies.

Chapter 7 explores child welfare agencies' use of voluntary kinship care. It identifies factors caseworkers consider in deciding whether to help arrange voluntary placements and how agency staff members assess, monitor, and support these placements. This chapter also describes how child welfare agencies respond when private kin seek out assistance.

Chapter 8 offers the experiences of 25 kinship foster parents. It seeks to convey the passion with which kin spoke about how their caregiving affected, and was affected by, larger family issues, the issues faced by the children in their care, their own issues and challenges, and their interaction with the child welfare agency and the courts.

Chapter 9 concludes by summarizing the findings from the book; providing recommendations for policy, program development, caseworker training, and kinship caregiver training; and identifying issues for future research.

NOTES

1. Urban Institute analysis of 2002 National Survey of America's Families.

2. Census Bureau Current Population Survey (CPS) data. Data are provided based on two- or three-year averages because the number of children in kinship care in a single year's CPS sample is relatively small and provides unreliable estimates. In addition, because of the introduction of improved data collection and processing procedures, data before 1994 are not comparable with later years.

3. According to Urban Institute analysis of Current Population Survey data, the number of children in kinship care declined from an average of 2.16 million in 1995–97 to an average of 2.14 million in 1998–2000 and the proportion declined from 3.05 to 2.98 percent.

4. There are no significant differences in gender between kinship care and non-kin foster care children (Beeman et al. 1996; Berrick et al. 1994; Dubowitz et al. 1993; Harden et al. 1997; Iglehart 1994; LeProhn and Pecora 1994).

5. Data on other ethnic groups are not available.

6. Under AFDC, relatives were entitled to child-only payments. Under TANF, states are not obligated to provide assistance to kinship caregivers, although currently all states except Wisconsin provide payments to all relative caregivers who seek assistance. Wisconsin's Kinship Care program provides a TANF-funded kinship care benefit to kin caring for related children at risk of abuse or neglect.

7. They can receive assistance for themselves and the children in their care if they are poor enough to qualify for benefits. Relative caregivers (though not unrelated kin), regardless of their income, can generally receive assistance for related children in their care.

2

Identifying and Recruiting Kin to Act as Foster Parents

Karin Malm and Roseana Bess

It was extremely rare for a child's relative to act as a foster parent when the Adoption Assistance and Child Welfare Act of 1980 mandated that when placing children in foster care, states should find the "least restrictive, most family-like setting available located in close proximity to the parent's home." Many states interpreted this as an unstated preference for the use of kin as foster parents, and several states began to enact laws that explicitly gave preference to kin. In 1996, Congress, as part of the welfare reform legislation, went even further, requiring states to "consider giving preference to an adult relative over a non-related caregiver when determining a placement for a child." Today, almost all child welfare agencies seek out and give preference to kin when foster care is needed and kin are available to provide a safe home (Jantz et al. 2002).

In addition to giving preference to kin, child welfare agencies are active in identifying and recruiting kin to act as foster parents, when appropriate. In doing so, child welfare workers must assess and work through complicated and often hostile family dynamics. Kin often have a long history of trying to help, and being disappointed by, abusive birth parents. Similarly, birth parents may not want to allow kin, who may even have reported them for abuse or neglect, to care for their children. Thus, workers often have the difficult tasks of convincing birth parents to identify kin, assessing whether kin can be effective foster parents, and convincing appropriate kin to take on the care of a child.

This chapter examines how local child welfare agencies identify and recruit kin to act as foster parents. It assesses the extent to which caseworkers actively recruit relatives, including how they search for an appropriate relative. It discusses how workers choose a relative to act as a foster parent when multiple relatives come forward to care for a child, including how the desires of the child and the birth parent affect this decision. Finally, this chapter examines the factors that influence kin's willingness to act as foster parents.

We find that when a child must be removed from his or her parent's home, caseworkers first look to see whether there is a noncustodial parent that can safely care for the child. Caseworkers report making greater efforts in recent years to identify, locate, and assess noncustodial fathers. The next preferred placement is with another relative. Agencies are actively seeking out relatives to act as foster parents; several factors have spurred caseworkers' efforts. At the same time, a number of factors influence whether kin will be willing to take on the role of caregiver. When kin express willingness to do so, caseworkers must assess whether that person or couple can provide an adequate level of protection and appropriate care. In addition, caseworkers identify a number of reasons why children may initially be placed with non-kin foster parents.

State Policies for Identifying Kin

According to a 2001 Urban Institute survey of state kinship care policies, in all but two states child welfare agencies require caseworkers to seek out kin when it is determined that a child cannot remain in his or her parents' home following a child abuse and neglect investigation.[1] One of the other two states gives preference to kin who come forward, and the other determines preference for kin on a case-by-case basis.

Thirty-five states report policies that discuss how workers should identify potential kinship care providers. These 35 state policies mention several sources of information about possible placement options. The most common method of identification is asking the parents, cited in six state policies. Five states ask the parents, child, and others, including other relatives, in addition to neighbors, witnesses to the child's removal, and family friends. Three state policies recommend holding family group conferences to identify placement options for children.

Twenty-nine states report that their policy instructs workers how to prioritize between kin if more than one wishes to take the child. Nine state policies instruct workers to prioritize kinship caregivers by suitability. Six state policies prioritize kin by relationship. For example, California gives preferential treatment only to adults who are the grandparents or an aunt, uncle, or sibling of a child. Three states leave the setting of priorities to the family and instruct workers to use a family group conference to decide which kin would be the most appropriate caregivers.

The way states define kin is important, because all states treat kin and non-kin differently with respect to preference, licensing, payment, and other factors. Many states have historically defined kinship care to include persons beyond blood relatives—that is, anyone with a strong emotional bond to a child. While just under half of the states (24, including the District of Columbia) include only those related by blood, marriage, or adoption in their definition of kin, almost as many states (22) define kin as those related beyond blood, marriage, or adoption (grandparents, family friends). The remaining states (5) report having no definition of kin.

Placement with Fathers and Paternal Relatives

While interviews with child welfare caseworkers and administrators at sites in four states focused on kinship care practices, we found that agencies' first priority and preference is to determine whether the child can be placed with a noncustodial or nonoffending parent. While in practice searching for a noncustodial parent and relatives often occurs simultaneously, the parent is the first placement preference. Recent data suggests that at least half of the children in foster care come from single-parent families headed by a female (Sonenstein, Malm, and Billing 2002). Thus, most of the parent search work is directed at locating noncustodial fathers.

A number of shifts in child welfare policies and practices have made the involvement of noncustodial fathers in child welfare case planning more likely. These include the provisions of the Adoption and Safe Families Act (ASFA) of 1997, the nationwide movement of the child welfare field toward concurrent case planning, and the growing popularity of family group decisionmaking (a case planning practice that seeks to involve extended family members in decisions). ASFA reduces the time in which child welfare agencies must make permanency decisions for children in custody from 18 months to 12 months, making early identi-fication and location of noncustodial fathers more important. In addi-tion, ASFA both allows and encourages states to use the Federal Parent Locator Service (FPLS), which is employed by child support enforce-ment programs to locate fathers and other relatives.

ASFA also supports the practice of concurrent planning, requiring caseworkers simultaneously to pursue both reunification with the parent and alternative permanency placement. Again, efforts to achieve perma-nency earlier means that agencies need to identify noncustodial parents as early as possible to facilitate appropriate involvement and possible placement or swift relinquishment or termination of parental rights, when needed. It is important to resolve paternity issues early to avoid court delays later. The resolution of paternity issues is also important to locating and recruiting paternal kin with whom a child can be placed. The increased use of family group decisionmaking may also lead to greater involvement of fathers. The wider the circle of relatives with knowledge of the case, the greater likelihood the child's father will be identified, located, and involved in the case. According to interviewees, agencies' practices appear to be changing regarding absent fathers as they look more to fathers for potential placement and do so earlier in the case process. Respondents noted one of the reasons for a lack of infor-mation on fathers is the reluctance of many mothers to provide such information.

"There was also, until recently, a distaste for absent fathers. An alleged father coming into court and the case is coming toward TPR [termination of parental rights] and the father didn't have much of a chance [of getting custody]. That is beginning to change more and more." (Alabama administrator)

"I think we're also exploring dads more than we used to, that's again something fairly recent. I think we used to dismiss dads years ago, didn't really track them down and see if they were placement options. Again, the legal system forces us to do diligent searches in a much more thorough way than we ever used to. So once you have a name and an address, you have to show reasonable efforts to reunite." (Connecticut ongoing supervisor)

"I don't think our mothers have, by and large, a good relationship with the absent parent, for whatever reason. It's very hard, even at intake, to pull that information out." (California investigative supervisor)

"[We have] a lot of moms that try to keep dad out of the kids' lives." (California investigative worker)

"My experience has always been really positive, because once we find them, like I said, it's the mother keeping them [children] away from the father and they don't know where they are. Then it turns out that this man, the father of this kid, has been looking for him since he was born and is appropriate and has a family of his own and took in this child that otherwise would end up in foster care." (California investigative supervisor)

Often the putative nature or noncustodial relationship of many fathers of children in care means that agencies cannot simply place the child in his custody. When a father does not have custodial rights to his child, he is assessed like other relatives. Also, many times siblings have different fathers, so placing children with fathers may result in splitting siblings up. Another problem is that birth fathers and mothers often live in different counties or states, which may make the child's later reunification with the birth mother more difficult. This situation may also complicate service delivery for the children placed if there are cross-jurisdictional issues.

"Dads need to LifeScan [undergo a criminal background check] before we can place the children there, unless he has joint custody. We don't know what his background is. . . . If there is no joint custody, he has to wait for the results before we can place the children there." (California investigative supervisor)

"Nonadjudicated fathers [fathers who have not established paternity]. . . . A lot of them come forth but they haven't done what they needed to do. They [children] can't go home with these nonadjudicated dads. That kind of stops a lot of stuff because they don't have that relationship there. Stops [the] paternal grandmother." (Indiana assessment supervisor)

"A lot of times in those cases when they ask us to contact the father, we'll find out he's not adjudicated, so we can't use him." (Indiana assessment worker)

Though practices toward fathers appear to be changing, some interviewees criticized the efforts of child welfare agencies to identify and locate fathers. Caregivers and court officials were especially critical of these agencies.

"The county does a horrendous job of finding fathers. [I'd] like to move to a policy where we look at dads first; [we] must find them and talk to them before placing elsewhere." (Indiana court contact)

"Last year was the first time the agency asked me about where my nieces' and nephews' father was. I have had them since 1996 and that was the first time they ever asked." (Connecticut caregiver)

"My youngest nephew's father is in the picture and a year after I had him the father gained custody. Even then the agency didn't ask about the other children's father." (Connecticut caregiver)

Preference for Relatives

When agencies are unable to locate the noncustodial parent, or when the parent is unable or unwilling to care for the child, efforts to identify and recruit other relatives become of paramount concern. While almost all states give preference to kin and are actively pursuing placements with relatives, a number of factors influence the level of effort agencies and workers make to find and place children with their kin. Respondents noted that local agency preference for kin varied and was influenced by a number of factors, including the extent to which agencies and workers value the extended family, specific agency policies, the courts, and a lack of non-kin foster homes.

Respondents at each site noted that preference for kin was warranted because of the familial bond and the continuity that kin provide. They noted how traumatic foster care can be for a child and how much placement with a relative can help mitigate this trauma.

"But I think there is more recognition of the value of extended family for kids. I think we're recognizing up front that to completely separate a child not only from the biological family, immediate biological family, but the whole extended family, they [children] lose so much over the years . . . and I think kids, years and years ago, completely lost that. I don't think we recognized that an extended family was to be searched out. I'm talking about a long time ago, we just placed kids and made whatever permanent plan and they just completely lost the connection. There's been so much about what happens to those kids when they become adults and have no connection to anyone that they have a biological relationship to." (Connecticut administrator)

"I think that I like to consider relative placements really seriously because of watching so many kids fail in foster care. A foster parent has a certain level of investment in a child, but it's not—there's no bond there. So, if a child gets suspended or the child hits a foster sibling or the child's behavior gets out of control—which is normal after placement—then foster parents are more likely to get stressed out and have the child removed. Rather than a relative, who can't do that to the kid. A relative is bonded." (Connecticut investigative worker)

"The court believes the family understands the family dynamics and that it is a rarer case when the family contributes to the pathology." (Indiana court contact)

"Stranger foster care is developmentally damaging. This proposition is beyond controversy. It gets worse and worse over time as child moves from caretaker to caretaker. The bond the child makes is broken; you are training them not to trust. Once they have developed a relationship, earned trust, then the trust is broken. Foster care can last a long time. You create adolescents that don't trust anyone." (California judicial contact)

Child welfare agencies are required by federal law to make "reasonable efforts" to maintain children with their parents before placing them in foster care. In Alabama, child welfare agencies extend this reasonable-efforts protection to the maintenance of families, which means that the agency must make efforts to place children with relatives before they can consider taking custody of a child. Respondents in Alabama noted that relatives are thus used as alternatives to foster care for children. The use of such "voluntary placements" is the subject of chapter 7.

"The county's policy is that 'reasonable efforts' must be explored for the placement of each child, and that means relative placement must be sought. Before we would file a petition [for child custody], we have to show reasonable efforts to prevent the child from coming into care; that's when a large part of our relatives come in." (Alabama administrator)

"[The courts] prefer the child to be with kin. They try to keep the child stable and out of foster care. Guardians *ad litem* really like relative care, too. It feels so much better placing a child with people he knows." (Alabama administrator)

"It is required that we seek relative resource placement initially as part of the RC [consent decree] guidelines to try and keep families together. We work towards this first, basically what we call 'reasonable efforts' to keep a child within their own home environment." (Alabama investigative worker)

Caseworkers in all sites were quick to point out that while relatives are given preference, a caseworker's primary responsibility is the safety of the child. Thus, while caseworkers look to kin first, preference for relatives is contingent on their ability to safely care for a child.

"Relative status does not preclude a good assessment. Hopefully it's going to work out in the best interests of the child." (Connecticut administrator)

"Very much so [agency has policy giving preference to kin], I'd say that's foremost in finding a relative that's appropriate. So, finding a relative placement and right along side of that is that safety issue. So it's not 'let's find a relative,' it's 'let's find a safe environment beginning with a relative.'" (California administrator)

Many respondents noted that the courts influence agency practice. While in many of the 13 study communities the courts mirrored the agencies' recommendations and approach to kinship care, there were times when the agency's philosophy toward kinship care differed from that of the court. Somewhat surprisingly, more often than not the court was more favorable toward kin than was the agency.

"The court sees it as a bad relative is better than a stranger, so there are times when the court wants to place with a relative and the agency doesn't agree." (Connecticut court liaison)

"They [the court] would rather have a bad relative versus a good foster parent." (California investigative supervisor)

Prior research has examined the extent to which child welfare agencies' preference for kin is the result of a limited number of non-kin foster homes. While data are limited, it appears that at the time that states began to increase their reliance on kin as foster parents, the number of children needing foster care placements was increasing and the number of non-kin foster parents was declining (HHS 2000). Moreover, foster care managers report that it is increasingly difficult to find families for the children now entering the foster care system—children who are older and more often face mental, emotional, or behavioral challenges than in the past (HHS-IG 2002). Recruiting non-kin foster parents may have also become more difficult due to a variety of social, demographic, and economic changes, including increases in single parenting, dual-income couples, older parenting couples, and the scarcity of affordable family housing. Those critical of kinship care sometimes question whether states are relying on kin not because it is better for children, but because the states are finding that their traditional foster parent recruitment efforts are less successful than they were previously, and states do not want to invest the time and resources needed to explore new recruitment strategies.

Overwhelmingly, respondents noted a lack of non-kin foster homes and expressed concern about the degree to which it affects kinship care.[2] Some respondents acknowledged that the lack of non-kin homes and the pressure to use kin and keep children out of shelter care (i.e., emergency care) can lead agencies to use and maintain even marginal kin placements.

"[There is] definitely a lack of non-kin foster homes. [I] would like to think that relatives were always the first preference for placement but always in the context of a lack of foster homes." (California administrator)

"If all those kids [in relative homes] had to be in an approved foster home, we would be in bad shape. There wouldn't be anywhere to put them." (Alabama foster care supervisor)

"We have more children than we ever have enough foster parents to care for. That has necessitated the relative placements." (California continuing worker)

"We have such a shortage of foster parents. We hesitate to push foster parents and relatives to do much, because we don't have a lot of options [placement alternatives for children]." (California on-going worker)

"We are under constant, unrelenting pressure to get children out of [the shelter] into foster homes. There are no foster homes, so [we must find a] relative, any relative . . . constant pressure to do that." (California investigative supervisor)

"[The supply of foster parents] is diminishing daily. The fewer foster parents we have, the more relatives we use. If there was a surplus of foster homes and we could match according to children's needs, workers probably wouldn't be scouring for relatives." (Connecticut licensing supervisor)

"I think there's a percentage of relatives we feel a little shaky about . . . [but] with the shortage of foster homes we're going to try that relative and see if we can't make it work. And that's a clear message to staff, that unless there's a clear issue of safety, you will look at the relative. But I think we have some [relative placements] that we worry a little about." (California administrator)

Identifying Relatives

Central to our discussions were descriptions of how, specifically, relatives are identified by child welfare staff. We wanted to know which workers identify relatives, for how long relatives are sought, and how workers perform this task. For the most part, the task of identifying relatives fell to investigative or intake workers. In one local office in California, a special investigative unit searches for absent parents and relatives and does criminal background checks. In Alabama, workers in an emergency after-hours program find relatives. Another local office in California noted that, in theory, it should be the emergency response worker who identifies and places children with kin, but because of the time needed to conduct criminal and child abuse background checks, it often is left to the next worker who gets the case—the dependency or intake worker.

Most agencies reported looking for kin throughout the case; however, responses differed depending on the type of worker. For example, investigative workers noted that they focus on examining the child abuse and neglect allegation and—unless the parent or child is forthcoming with relatives' names—may let the ongoing worker do more of the legwork of finding relatives.

> "'Reasonable efforts' policy requires that the agency continue its efforts to locate relatives throughout the life span of the case." (California administrator)

> "You always look [for relatives]. Children may be in a foster home and all of a sudden here comes grandma." (Indiana administrator)

> "No difficulty finding relatives, but I don't know how long I would look for them." (Indiana ongoing worker)

> "We don't spend much time looking for relatives. We spend more time doing the investigation, taking the time to place the child in protective custody; then we have these time frames to move the case. The option is, in the moment of trauma—when I'm removing the child—are you [the birth parent] going to give me the information. If you don't give it to me, I can't get it." (Indiana investigative worker)

> "We always continue to seek out relatives when kids are in state custody." (Alabama investigative worker)

Interviewees in the 13 localities described many ways in which relatives are identified. The most frequently cited method was to ask the birth parents. From there, workers noted asking the child, siblings, and other relatives. Neighbors and day care providers were also mentioned as sources. In addition, respondents noted that they check with former caseworkers if the family is known to the agency. In addition, they mentioned checking child abuse and neglect registries, Temporary Assistance for Needy Families (TANF) and food stamps records, and the child's school records.

While workers routinely ask birth parents to identify relatives, the practice is often fraught with difficulties. First, many parents are reluctant to identify relatives. Parents may not want the relative to know about the abuse or neglect incident or may not believe the relative would want to care for the children. Some parents are hostile toward relatives or feel isolated from their families. Some parents may initially refuse to identify relatives, thinking that the child will not be removed if the agency cannot locate a relative.

> "Sometimes we find that the appropriate relatives [are the ones] they [the parents] won't tell us about. Sometimes the relatives they hate the most are the most appropriate." (California investigative supervisor)

> "Birth parents have often burned all of their bridges, and they are in a state of crisis and feel no one cares or will help them. So I often tell them, 'You tell me who your family is and I'll take it from there.'" (California ongoing supervisor)

> "It happens a lot that birth parents won't give you relatives' names. Parents will say, 'They don't want them.'" (Alabama ongoing supervisor)

> "Most people, I would imagine, if they're having tough times, before their electric service is discontinued, they're gonna call their relative to seek help. And after time and time again the relative is saying, 'Find a job, manage your money better, get rid of the alcohol or drug problem, I can't do it anymore' . . . the parents who've undergone the removal [of children] do not want to see the children with those relatives. The anger is so great that they will specifically forbid it. They would prefer to see the children placed with strangers, so great is the hate for a brother or sister." (Indiana investigative worker)

> "With the exception of a few parents, no one is going to be cooperative with the removal of their child. [They're] impacted by the loss of welfare benefits, housing, beyond that of just [loss of] children." (Connecticut investigative supervisor)

> "The mother may not have a good relationship with her family. When you ask her, she may say she doesn't have anybody." (Indiana administrator)

> "[In] a case example of a drug raid with four kids involved . . . parents don't want relatives to know children were involved in the drug raid, so they won't give us any information on the relatives." (Indiana assessment worker)

Workers also routinely *ask the children* for the names of relatives they know and think could take care of them. However, workers noted, children often identify relatives who may not be appropriate, and older children often want to go to the relative least likely to enforce rules.

> "Depending on the age of the child . . . if they're a teen you can ask them if they have a relative." (Indiana ongoing worker)

> "We get a lot of calls from schools at 4:30 when parents have not picked up kids or parents have been arrested. We get children to identify a relative for placement." (Alabama investigative supervisor)

> "Almost immediately when we talk to the children, we ask them about grandma." (Alabama investigative worker)

> "You can also ask the kid if there's a relative they have a good relationship with, but usually they want to go with the more lax relative." (California investigative worker)

> "Many adolescents can tell you themselves, because of their age, about relatives. Sometimes these kids have already been through a lot of relatives, and they're different, too, because they're older kids and they have a lot more problems." (Connecticut ongoing worker)

Respondents noted that, frequently, children being removed come from families with prior involvement with the agency. If the family is known to the agency, its prior case history will list relatives by name. Caseworkers also said that they ask TANF caseworkers and schools for names of relatives.

> "Check case records. The case record's got a name of a relative the kid used to live with; we'll have that in our history. The school might have somebody on the emergency card." (Connecticut investigative supervisor)

> "A lot of times there is a record of past involvement for things that were minor and did not require removal of the child, and that involvement in the past should have identified relatives of the family." (Alabama investigative worker)

"Sometimes the person is receiving TANF assistance and you can talk to the caseworker and they can tell you, 'Well, her sister is so and so.'" (Indiana assessment worker)

"Other DHR [Department of Human Resources] computer assets, Food Stamps, [and] public assistance sometimes [have] relatives identified." (Alabama investigative worker)

Motivation and Willingness of Relatives to Care for Kin

Once a child's relatives have been identified by the child welfare agency, the next step involves determining whether or not a relative is willing to care for the child. Agency staff discussed their experiences related to the willingness and motivation of relatives to care for their kin. In addition, kin caregivers were asked to describe why they became involved in caring for these children.

Several factors appear to influence a kin's willingness to care for a child: the relationship with the birth parent, the characteristics or number of children, the obligation felt to family, expected length of stay, services offered initially, the kin caregiver's relationship with the child, and pressure from family or the child welfare agency. Some birth parents struggle for years with the issues that underlie the cause for their child's removal. Kin often have long histories with the birth parents of children needing placement, and this past history may affect whether they are willing to take the children.

The problems birth parents live with, such as domestic violence, drug addiction, or mental illness, often affect kin's willingness to get involved once a child is removed. Respondents (including kin caregivers) in all states except Alabama spoke about kin's unwillingness to care for children if the birth parent had such a history. Kin expressed fear that a birth parent or her partner would come to their home and make threats or be violent, or make harassing phone calls.

"No one wants [children of] the violent parents . . . [in] a case where the father had actually murdered the mother . . . none of the relatives wanted the children because they were afraid he [the father] would come after them." (California investigative supervisor)

"If there is a mother who is mentally ill, relatives don't want to have that come into their lives. Some of the people we have are really significantly disturbed. Harassing phone calls at all hours of the night, coming by the house banging on the door, calling the police. I had one relative where the mom would call the police and say the relative had kidnapped the kid. And the police come to the house. . . . Sometimes it becomes more than they [caregivers] can deal with." (California investigative worker)

"My concerns were the dads. They were criminals, in prison. I say dads because we don't know who the biological father is." (Indiana caregiver)

"The fear issue is real, though. We've had a couple of families that are very violent—gang related, severe domestic violence, assault. That's not the usual, but they [caregivers] do need to protect themselves sometimes." (Connecticut supervisor)

Respondents also noted that a relative's history with the birth parent influences his or her willingness to act as a foster parent. If a relative has a close relationship with the parent, that relative is more likely to be willing to care for the child. If the potential caregiver has intentionally kept a distance from the parent, that relative may not be willing to care for the child. Some respondents stated that many kin—aware of the problem in the birth parent's home—were either caring for the children intermittently or had washed their hands of the birth parent. Some reported that kin were more willing to step in once the child welfare agency was involved because they felt something might actually improve or the agency would protect them from the birth parent.

"I find that sometimes they don't have a close relationship with the child because the parent has kept them away. That doesn't mean that they don't want to help or be a caretaker. It depends—they do come out of the woodwork—somehow the word gets out and they come out and you interview them and try and do what's best for the children. And these people that don't have any relationship with them can turn out to be appropriate." (California investigative supervisor)

"Sometimes kin may have been burned by the birth parent, but with us [the child welfare agency] in the case and with some control over certain boundaries, [they feel better]." (California supervisor)

"Some relatives won't take the child because they don't want the birth parents to get lazy. Relatives feel like if they took them, the parent wouldn't do anything else, they wouldn't work towards their goals, they would get comfortable." (Alabama foster care worker)

"Some of these families are tired of this mother always getting in trouble and then always having to bail her out, and then always having to take her kids for a few months so that DHR can get her clean and then they just keep putting her back. I have had some relatives that just say, 'Forget it, I'm not doing it anymore. You clean her up and then send her back and then it happens again.' They get tired of the children going back and forth." (Alabama investigative worker)

"And a lot of time families know what's going on. They know mom and dad are substance abusers. And a lot of times they [the relatives] just sit back and that's just something that's known to the family, and it's only when DCF [Department of Children and Families] steps in to say 'This is an issue' [that] they're more quick to say, 'Okay, I know, I'll take the child.' But a lot of times they won't be the ones calling in the reports to say mom is using. It's not until DCF is involved, because they don't want to step forward, they don't want to stir up the family." (Connecticut foster care supervisor)

When a child is removed from his or her parent's home, there may not be a clear time frame within which the child will be returned to the parent. Respondents in all states spoke about kin's willingness to care for such children, believing the situation to be temporary even when told at the outset that it would be as long as six months. Most caregivers spoke about how at first they were in denial and believed the birth parent would "straighten up" quickly.

"I thought it would be temporary until the mother got her act together. When the second and third [child] came, then I was thinking about permanency." (California kinship caregiver)

"I was concerned. I thought I was helping out the parents. I thought it would be short-term. That the mother would go to a program and get her life together and I'd get to be the grandmother. And I'd visit them from time to time, and live my life. But the mother was in denial. She said she didn't use drugs and couldn't explain why they found drugs in the baby. She made a big production and said it wasn't her urine, that they probably switched urines. Then she said they only found a little bit. She [the birth mother] just made lots of excuses, but my son was determined to stay with her." (California kinship caregiver)

"We're all in denial for the first couple of years. We think they'll get it together and we can be 'grandma' again." (California kinship caregiver)

"Many times they [the relatives] think of it as temporary. They think the mother is going to get in this program and it's not going to be forever, and then it turns out to be much longer than expected. Wishful thinking." (Connecticut supervisor)

"I think they go in wanting to help their family, but they are thinking short-term. I think they're thinking, 'Okay I'll help them for three months and then they'll be back in the home.' And even though it's explained to them that this may be a six-month process, in the back of their minds they're still thinking he [the child] will be back in the home in three months." (Indiana investigative worker)

"I think if they heard that in the beginning—that they may be caring for this child until the child is coming of age or an adult—they would never get involved." (Alabama in-home worker)

On the other hand, some kin will specify to the worker how long they can care for a child, regardless of how long the worker suspects the child will need a placement. Supervisors and workers in all states spoke of potential caregivers who immediately state that they are willing and able to care for the child, but will only do so for a specified time period. Workers face a dilemma if they suspect that a child will need to remain in care longer than kin are willing to commit to. While kin may initially help minimize the trauma children experience upon being taken from their parents, if children cannot remain with kin, then they will experience two separations.

"Some relatives do state that they will only keep the child for a specific amount of time." (Alabama supervisor)

"Sometimes you know from the onset, they clearly tell you that this is temporary and they can only keep the child for three or four months." (California investigative supervisor)

Caseworkers noted that, just as with non-kin foster parents, they have difficulty convincing kin to care for teenagers or children with behavior problems. Workers in all states overwhelmingly reported that kin were much more willing to take infants and young children than adolescents. This is not to say that kin would not take teenagers or that all kin were willing to take infants and young children. But many workers believed that kin, especially older kin, did not want to deal with disrespectful or misbehaving teens. At the same time, some kin were not willing to take infants or young children, because they were concerned about the need for child care or preschool arrangements. Caseworkers reported that most kin were willing to take in sibling groups, more so than non-kin foster parents.

"Almost always a relative is stepping forward for a newborn." (Connecticut investigative supervisor)

"I think the latency-age children we don't have as much trouble placing with relatives as we do placing babies, toddlers, and teens. Each of those have their special needs that the extended family may not be willing or able to provide." (California investigative supervisor)

"Everyone wants a baby, no one wants a teenager." (Indiana investigative worker)

"Teenagers are the hardest to place, they have already burned many of the family ties." (Indiana licensing worker)

"Relatives are very willing to accept babies. They are more than willing to have the babies come home with them, more so than the older, school-age children." (Alabama investigative worker)

"Sex of the child may affect [willingness]. Some do not want to deal with a 15-year-old male with behavior problems, but might take a 15-year-old girl. Boys are harder [to place]." (California investigative worker)

While some respondents believed kin were reluctant to take children with behavior problems or special needs, many caseworkers suggested that relatives were more likely than non-kin foster parents to care for difficult children. In some cases, placing a child with kin is an alternative to placing the child in a group home or institution.

"This manager is constantly amazed at the types of children relatives come forward to take care of . . . children with severe mental health problems or physical disabilities. They are often the types of children that regular foster parents don't want to take. Relatives take care of these kids because they are family—if only for that reason, incentive that they are family." (Connecticut supervisor)

"Oftentimes relatives won't take children with significant psychiatric needs or those who are behaviorally too difficult." (Connecticut supervisor)

"Relatives are often willing to take kids with emotional problems longer—don't give up as easy [as non-kin]." (California supervisor)

"Many relatives are not resources because they don't want the aggressive, difficult child. We have to look at other resources like independent living or group homes." (Connecticut foster care worker)

Workers and supervisors reported difficulty placing sibling groups together in non-kin foster homes; however, many caregivers reported caring for sibling groups. Workers and supervisors discussed the flexibility non-kin foster parents have, to some extent, in determining which children they will foster. They found non-kin foster parents less willing than kin to take in sibling groups. In some localities, this is a significant problem because the birth parents they serve tend to have three or more children. Even when kin are willing to accept sibling groups, they may not be able to meet the licensing criteria for several children. Some agencies noted that when it comes to space requirements, they can make exceptions more easily for relatives than for non-kin, but acknowledged this was still a problem.

"If the child has siblings, it is hard to place many siblings together in regular foster homes. Many relatives do not want to break the children up, so they [the relatives] will take all the children." (Connecticut investigative worker)

"Relatives are usually the ones saying they'll take the whole gang." (California investigative supervisor)

"[For] most of my relatives, all of their children already have gone through childhood; they are either out or in college, and they [the relatives] were not ready to take any small children in. Many couldn't take all five . . . would volunteer to take only one. But the children, they have only been with their mother, so if you take them away from each other, the built foundation that they have is going to break. That is why I volunteered to take them." (Alabama kinship caregiver)

"We're only able to license a [foster] family for up to three kids. It takes an administrative exception to overload the home. We will try very hard to keep siblings together. We do overload homes, over capacity, over their license limit. If we have to separate siblings, what we do is take a look at the sibling group and figure out who really needs to be with whom." (Connecticut administrator)

Even amongst kin, some are more willing than others to care for children. Many workers felt grandparents—grandmothers, more specifically—were more willing to care for children than other kin. This may be because grandparents are closest to the children and may have cared for them in the past, because they have a greater sense of obligation given that the abusive parent is their child, or because they may have more available time and resources.

"I had a grandmother that wanted to take her grandson, but couldn't because her son [the father], who was addicted to drugs, was living in her house. She kicked her son out so she could take care of her grandson. That is a difficult decision to make; she had to choose between her child and her grandchild. From there I always knew that she had her grandson's best interest at heart." (Connecticut foster care worker)

"Sometimes these grandmothers are also caring for multiple siblings from more than one of their own children. They [grandmothers] can get overloaded and overburdened." (Connecticut investigative worker)

"Any relative really is willing, but grandparents are more determined to keep kids in the home." (California investigative worker)

"With [the] paternal side, my history is that you get these dads that have not been involved with the family, so the paternal grandmother has not had the opportunity to interact with these children. Maternal grandparent probably [has] already been raising [the] children and views these children as her own." (Indiana investigative worker)

"Grandparents and aunts are most often the ones coming forward to care for the child." (Alabama investigative worker)

Many caregivers noted that they felt they had no choice but to care for the children. They could not refuse, simply because they were related. As workers saw it, kin believed they did not have a choice because foster care was not a suitable option for the children. In addition, some caregivers had been raised by a family member other than their birth parent and saw this as their obligation because someone had kept them out of foster care. Moreover, various respondents in all states reported that kin are willing because of their upbringing—they were raised to care for each other. Caregivers themselves stated that the values they were taught would not allow them to refuse to take care of their kin.

"My theory on all this has always been that a lot of relatives don't really look at the factors that impact their taking the children. They operate on their gut—'it's blood'—a phrase I don't like to hear— 'it's family, it's blood, we can't let the children live in the foster care system.' And they don't look in their own lives at how taking the children can impact them. You get 18-, 19-year-old girls with two babies wanting to take babies that belong to their sister when they're barely able to keep their head above water as it is—'it's my blood, it's my sister's kids, I've gotta take 'em.' " (California investigative supervisor)

"We say, 'It is a choice, you can do this or you can do that.' But I think for a lot of them, it is not a choice. It is an obligation. They say, 'This is my family. I'm not going to see them somewhere else.' We have to take a different stand in saying to them that they can say no. Or if they are not going to take the children, we have to work with them around saying no. . . . I don't think it is a choice for a lot of them. A lot of times they have already been raising that child, they have been the caretaker." (Connecticut licensing worker)

"We're calling it a sense of responsibility, but it's more 'that's my brother, and I might not want to help him out, and I might not want his kid here, but how do I say no? How do I tell him in his time of crisis, no . . . how do I look him in the face and say no?'" (Indiana investigative worker)

"What they [DHR workers] do is they figure you love your blood this much, until you'll take the sacrifice, or whatever it takes, to hold onto them. And we do it! Once you take that first step to take that one, they've already broke you down, 'cause they know what you coming from, and when you take that one, they call before they call the doctor and say, 'Here come another.'" (Alabama kinship caregiver)

"When I heard that this girl had given up someone that was related to me, it was just something that I wouldn't be able to live with." (Alabama kinship caregiver)

"I think most of us think, 'How can you say no?' If you have a home, how can you turn down a child? The child didn't do anything wrong. It is just so difficult to think that the child is going to suffer, cast out into the unknown." (California kinship caregiver)

Many supervisors, workers, and caregivers felt kin were willing because they wanted to keep the children out of traditional foster care. Many kin illustrated this, discussing their beliefs that someone who is not family will not take as good care of the child or that foster parents are only in it for the paycheck. A few caregivers had been in foster care themselves and did not want this next generation of children to experience what they had gone through. Supervisors and workers referred to media stories highlighting isolated incidents of abuse in foster care and the image this may leave in the public's mind.

"I don't think, sometimes, foster parents understand what it means to be a foster parent. A foster parent is defined as a pseudo-parent. That means that you're taking the role of that parent. I should never come into your house and be able tell the difference between your foster child and your regular child. If I am able to tell that, then you are not doing what you are supposed to do. Some non-kin treat it as a career. Because they see it as a support payment coming in, they can get four or five children, about $1200 [per month] in income." (Alabama caseworker)

"Placed with family, he is treated like family. A foster parent is paid to care for the child; family will give better care because they're not in it for the money." (Alabama kinship caregiver)

"There is a big difference between a relative and a foster parent. The foster parent's doing [it] for years; it's income to them. They count children, some of them like they are dollars. They'll tell you, 'Can you send me another kid?' That's their mortgage payment. I'm not trying to be funny. Well, sometimes to a relative, that may be additional money, but its going to be short-term, short-lived. But this is the foster parent's livelihood, and that does make a difference to a great extent." (Indiana investigative worker)

"I had a neighbor who had a foster home. I saw what went on next door. Girls were sexually abused by her sons. That is why I did not want them to go into foster care. As long as I am alive, I will not let them go to a foster home." (California kinship caregiver)

"Relatives often have a negative feeling about the way kids are treated in foster care—they feel that kids are mistreated in regular foster care, sexually abused. So relatives will take kids, so they don't have to be in the system." (Connecticut supervisor)

Some would argue that kin are pressured into caring for children because it is a rushed decision and kin may be driven by their emotions and not think through the ramifications of caring for a related child or children. While a few kin expressed this sentiment, most caregivers felt they were pressured neither by the agency nor by other family members. Any pressure they felt was internal, their own guilt or desire to help the child.

"Years ago I think we used to sometimes 'dump' kids on relatives when it wasn't always the best thing, when the laws were a little looser, and I think we're more careful now. We used to try to talk people into taking kids." (Connecticut supervisor)

"I tell my workers that you have to talk to them [relative caregivers] and make sure they know that they don't have to do this. . . . First of all, we're not supposed to be putting out her [the caregiver's] own family to take care of these other kids where they don't fit—altogether four kids under five years old. . . . Family pressure is number one—the guilt, you know, and all of the relatives say, 'We'll help you.'" (California investigative supervisor)

"When we interact, negotiate with relatives, they're enthusiastic. . . . They don't realize how tough it's going to be. We are very pushy. We're trying to get the relative to take the child." (California investigative worker)

"I didn't feel any pressure at all. I felt it would be a good thing to get them out of the situation they were in and put them in a situation that would be stable." (Indiana kinship caregiver)

"Because of the way I was raised, you look out for your kin. I think I should take care of my own. I could not sit back and ignore that I had a home and these children were just out there and they were my relatives. I felt a commitment. So I feel pressure." (Alabama kinship caregiver)

Workers said that the availability of supports might also influence kin's willingness to care for a child. In particular, workers noted that the availability of financial assistance affected kin's willingness to accept a child. In some instances, workers and supervisors told anecdotes about kin who said they were not willing until an offer of financial assistance was made. Anecdotes like these raise concerns among kinship critics that birth parents are giving children to relatives so that they (the kin and the parents) can get financial support. However, according to many other workers, the availability of money was not a factor in kin's decision to care for a child; indeed, when offered financial assistance, kin often refused it.

"[It is a] financial hardship on the grandparents to take three to four children if the only assistance they can get is TANF [cash assistance] or to become licensed, and each of those takes a while. If there is something they could get when they get these children, I think we would see more relatives step forward." (Indiana supervisor)

"Sometimes they sincerely want to help, other times we run into cases where it's an issue of money. The child's getting SSI [Supplemental Security Income] or something like that, and that's the first thing they want to get transferred over. But normally I think it's family wanting to take care of family. . . . Sometimes I don't think it's as much greed as it is 'I can barely survive taking care of my family. I'd like to take these two to three extra kids, but I can't.' Sometimes it's just out of necessity." (Indiana investigative worker)

"There is a little bit of an unrealistic expectation edge to that. Because it often starts that way, 'No, no, I don't need any financial help. I love this child.' Then after the emergency of getting them out of the shelter and out of foster care, it's over and they're in the home. Sometimes within a week or two, it's like, 'This child is more expensive to take care of than I anticipated, and there's more behavior problems than I expected, and I do need help.' When you try to explain that there is funding available—'You should go down and apply'—they say, 'No, no, no, no, no.' That initial anxiety of getting the child out of the home can sometimes mislead you [kin] to what's going to happen when they're with you." (California investigative worker)

"My caseworker . . . that was all he threw in my face was money. When I first got this child, the first thing I said was 'I will take care of him. I have a job, my husband has a job.' [The caseworker] told me, 'Don't say that, you tell them [the welfare agency] you want money.' I said this is not a money issue, this child needs a roof over his head. . . . I already have to feed four people in my house. It is not going to cost me one penny more to take a little bit from each one of them four and make a fifth plate." (Connecticut caregiver)

The availability of child care was also a factor in most counties examined, especially the rural ones. Although most caregivers who participated in this study were grandparents, many were still working and needed child care. Assistance with the cost, through vouchers or subsidies, was an issue for many caregivers. Lack of assistance forced some caregivers to quit working, because they did not earn enough to afford child care.

"DCFS [Department of Children and Family Services] does not allow you to leave the kids with people that are not licensed. You have to be real careful with whom you leave the kids. Me and my husband, we work. It was hard at the beginning. I did a whole year without working . . . staying with her until she be a year old." (Connecticut kinship caregiver)

"I was making $4,000 a month, but I needed a babysitter. They told me I had to get into the system to get child care, but how can I get into the system—they would laugh at me. But it was okay that the worker would pay child care ($800 a month) for other people. They wanted me to pay the same amount. I could not do it . . . I had to drop out of those jobs. . . . They didn't care about all the sacrifices." (California kinship caregiver)

"One thing I've seen over time is money for child care. Many of them [the relatives] are working and they have to pay for child care next week. As soon as the child comes in they have to pre-pay for child care. [There is a] lack of money up front. A lot of these child care agencies . . . we're talking about hundreds of dollars up front. And if you don't have a savings or a credit card . . . sometimes relatives may not have immediate cash. Payment is usually a reimbursement, so it's after the fact. Our respite care funds are limited, so many times we don't have that quick jumpstart. Many times relatives will say they can't take the child because there is no immediate answer to these needs. We have relatives that would, but can't." (California investigative supervisor)

"Relatives are up front. They say, 'I will take child, but I need the following things. I work, I need child care, etc.'" (Alabama investigative supervisor)

Placement Decisions

Even if relatives have been identified by the agency and are willing to care for a child, it does not mean that kin will necessarily be given this responsibility. Caseworkers noted a range of factors that influence both their decision of whether to place children with kin and their choice of which kin to place a child with if more than one is willing and able. Kin generally cannot care for a child unless they pass licensing standards, including criminal and child protective services background checks. Workers also noted that their placement decisions were based on an assessment of how well the relative could protect and care for the child and the strength of the bond between the relative and the child. Other factors workers consider are the preferences of the birth parent and child, the relative's ability to care for a sibling group, and the proximity of the relative's home to the child's neighborhood.

According to interviewees, central to decisions to place a child with kin is the *level of protection* the relative can provide. Agency staff noted a range of characteristics they look for with regard to a relative's ability to protect the child, including willingness to believe the child's claims of abuse and prior knowledge of the abuse and neglect. The kind of abuse-neglect allegation or degree of injury to the child also affect a worker's decision to place a child with a relative. The protection issue was often discussed in the context of parent-child visitation. Many agency staff expressed concern that kin may allow birth parents inappropriate access to children they abused. This issue is discussed at length in chapter 4.

"We want to make sure relatives will protect the child and keep them safe, and don't tell the child that nothing happened. In this community, there are relatives that help each other out [tell child that he or she was not abused]." (California investigative worker)

"If relatives knew of prior domestic violence, we don't look at them for placement." (California investigative worker)

"[Workers must establish] believability . . . that they [relatives] are willing to work with us . . . that they have a certain belief that it actually happened and that they are going to be supportive of the child as a result of that. Sometimes you get kin who are so enmeshed with the family that they don't believe it happened." (California investigative supervisor)

"A lot of time when ER [the emergency response unit] is detaining children, it's for sexual abuse and the investigators find out everybody knew this was what was going on, but nobody did anything. Relatives did not protect before, why should they protect in the future? [We] have to take that into consideration." (California investigative worker)

"We are told to look at family, for the initial placement as well as for permanency. It depends upon the case. In serious cases of abuse or neglect, we will not look to relatives. We almost automatically exclude them if they knew what was going on and did nothing, and most often they do know. If they do not know, how well connected are they to the child in the first place?" (Connecticut supervisor)

The *standard of care* provided by relatives is another consideration in placing children with kin and in choosing between more than one relative. As discussed in chapter 1, kin often face significant challenges that most other foster parents do not. Given these challenges, agency respondents expressed concern about whether or not kin can provide appropriately for the child. Financial concerns and the age of the caregiver are also issues, along with kin's ability to care for children with special needs.

"If the child has special needs, can that relative handle therapy twice a week, school problems, tutoring? Special needs children take extra care. Is the relative willing and able to devote extra time and effort?" (California investigative worker)

"It's going to come back to who's able to provide for the needs of the child. It's got to be child focused in any placement, but in the case of a relative, we're going to hear from the kids and we're going to hear from the family, but we're going to identify some needs and we'll be looking at the relatives that are going to best be able to provide for those needs." (California administrator)

"I think we also need to look at the financial situation of the family [relative caregiver] too, because if they barely meet their own needs, [and] if they hear that $700 is coming their way for this child, sometimes that is the reason they come forward. I make it clear that that money is intended for the child's needs." (Connecticut investigative worker)

"Don't look at finances; poverty should not be a factor." (Indiana court contact)

"If the child has income, it becomes an issue for some families because they want the money. Even if they are on public assistance, that becomes an issue sometimes. We try to determine if that's a motivating factor for the relative; it weighs in the decisionmaking. If that's the overriding reason, you wonder if it's going to be good. It still may be okay." (Indiana investigative worker)

"I've found that even though you present everything, the more affluent person comes out better. I've had the court twice go with the more affluent relative and sure enough, down the road, we end up removing." (California investigative supervisor)

"Through an accurate financial picture at the beginning, we can realistically tell if the person is going to be able to care for the child." (Alabama supervisor)

"They [relatives] can apply for non-needy relative [TANF child-only] right away, but the topic of Miller-Youakim [foster care payments] won't come up until after placement. You want to be careful you're not putting that out there as a bait, 'cause that's what they're gonna go after, and you really want them to care for the child." (California intake worker)

It was clear from the responses that there is wide variation in frontline practice as far as placing children in the homes of older relatives. Some workers are concerned about the ability of an older caregiver to adequately care for a needy child, particularly if the older person faces health challenges. Other workers did not worry about older kin's current capacity, but questioned whether an older kin would be able to care for a child in the long term.

"Age of the relative has a lot to do with it. If I remove a child who is 15 or 16 and is very promiscuous or has a behavioral problem, there's no way I'm going to place her with her 78-year-old grandmother who can't monitor, control, or supervise her. I would try to find another relative." (Indiana assessment worker)

"Yes, there's ageism. I had a worker that went out today and said, 'Yeah, I have to go try and talk these 65-year-old grandparents out of taking this newborn, because mom's a heroin addict and dad's on methadone. The child's not going to reunify with these people and she [the mother] has a bunch of other kids in the house. Now we've got these 65-year-old-grandparents squawking and want the baby. Just how long do they think they're going to live?' This is something that comes up time and time again." (California investigative supervisor)

"Well, if you open up and say they're too old, the court accuses you of being ageist. I try and talk to them and say, 'You're 65 now. When this kid is 15, you're going to be 80. Do you really want to be chasing after a 15-year-old when you're 80?'" (California investigative supervisor)

"There are times also when we have older and younger family members who want to make that commitment. We would have the two relatives be coguardians. This way if grandma is 75 years old and in poor health, [and] if something should happen to her, we have a younger relative who can step in and they don't have to go back to court. It's all been done. That planning ahead is important." (California investigative supervisor)

Also of importance to workers in deciding whether to place a child with relatives is the *degree of bonding* between the relative and child. This is given special consideration when more than one relative is willing to step in. Respondents noted frequently that just because a person is related to the child does not mean that he or she has a relationship with that child. Workers also noted concern about relatives who, though well known to the child, have done nothing to alleviate the abusive or neglectful situation.

"Among a pool of relatives, the one with the closest bond gets priority . . . also closest blood relative. Usually child will tell you; we can tell when there is a real bond." (Alabama investigative supervisor)

"You look at the relationship between the grandmother and the child. If there's not a relationship there, you might explore something else." (Indiana investigative worker)

"If the relative was always around and hadn't done anything to prevent the abuse or neglect, we don't place there." (California investigative supervisor)

Interestingly, though the degree of bonding between the relative and child was a consideration in placement decisions, most agencies studied could not easily arrange placements with non-related kin. It seems clear that while respondents thought it beneficial to a child to be placed with a godparent or neighbor, agencies have a difficult time embracing these placements due to licensing requirements and eligibility guidelines for financial assistance. While Alabama's kinship program uses the term *kin* very loosely, other states appear to adhere to a stricter definition.[3]

"Food stamps and TANF look narrowly at relatives, child welfare looks very broadly." (Alabama investigative supervisor)

"Establishing relationship is loose; basically, if they are recognized by family, they are considered kin. No verification of relationship is required, though this may create problems getting support from TANF. Even if there is a relationship, there may not be financial support without written verification of relationship to prove that it falls within TANF [definition]." (Alabama foster care worker)

While respondents mentioned a more inclusive definition of kin beyond blood relatives (fictive kin), most noted the difficulties in placing a child with non-related kin. Some said that they simply do not place with non–blood relatives.

"Where the agency gets hung up is when someone in the community wants to take the child. Then it's very difficult to license them. It's still a special study, but it becomes much more involved." (Connecticut supervisor)

"We don't recognize everyone as a relative and that's a barrier. In a lot of cultures and even in mine, we recognize auntie because she's mom's best friend from high school, and we recognize auntie because 'She's my godmother—she's looking out for me.' They [DCF] don't recognize that [type of relationship] right now. They are not considered relatives." (Connecticut ongoing supervisor)

"Defining a relationship is difficult when talking about licensing. I think for licensing purposes, it is family—mother, father, extended family. Family as defined as being friends, or neighbors, is a whole different licensing thing for us. That's hard." (Connecticut supervisor)

"[Fictive kin] is more of a licensing issue that restrains us [the agency]. So for us they're not relatives—there's a very concrete list of who fits into the relative category. These others are considered a licensing issue, so we'd say let's give them a foster parent license." (California administrator)

"We had an incident where the grandmother was married to a man who is not the biological relative. Grandmother dies. He was declared not eligible for TANF. We could license him as a foster parent but not as an approved relative." (Indiana administrator)

"[The definition of kin] can extend beyond blood in some circumstances. Very rare but it has happened." (Indiana ongoing supervisor)

Other factors workers consider in placement decisions include the proximity of the relative to the child's school and to the birth parent's home and community. Workers noted that while placing a child with kin may reduce the trauma of being separated from a parent, if that means removing the child from his or her school or community, the child may be better off with a non-kin foster parent in the child's own neighborhood. Workers also noted concerns about birth parents having an adequate opportunity to visit their children and work toward reunification if the children are placed far away. Due to these concerns, workers said that out-of-state placements, while sometimes made, are not usually the best option.

> "And I think too that you would look at school. If school is going to end in two or three weeks, you wouldn't be disrupting and uprooting. School is a big problem for these kids. They've been moved around a lot." (California administrator)

> "We do attempt to keep the child in the same school, because enough changes are happening, being pulled out of their homes. We want to at least keep them with their friends and stuff. If there are relatives in that district, it makes it a whole lot easier. It is a consideration that we can't always fulfill." (Indiana investigative worker)

> "The newest thing is that we have to try to keep the child in the same neighborhood, keep them in the same school. Sometimes this is unsafe, especially in molest cases." (California investigative worker)

> "Our state policy is to be in the same community and school district. We have to justify why we can't do that, if it's not possible." (Alabama investigative worker)

> "Depends upon age [of the child]. If 5 years old, go with relative. If 14 years old, stay in community, if that's what child wants." (Connecticut supervisor)

> "We will place the child with the closest relative who clears the criminal check. Sometimes we have relatives out of state. Has to go

through the court . . . even if in another county. We will choose the closest location . . . easily accessible to the parent for visitation." (California investigative supervisor)

Respondents noted that both parents and children's preferences are taken into consideration, though they are typically not a deciding factor in a placement decision. Objections by birth parents and children to a specific relative would be factored into a decision. Unlike non-kin foster homes, relatives frequently have an ongoing relationship with the child's birth parent, and this relationship often is of concern to caseworkers. Since reunification is the primary goal at the onset of most cases, relative-parent interactions are important, and the relative must be willing to work toward the goal of reunification.

> "We listen to birth parents, but we're not bound by their opinion." (California administrator)

> "You don't do it [if birth parent objects] sometimes. A lot of times if they don't want the child with kin, they'll have a reason, and when you do the research, sometimes you find it's a valid reason." (Indiana assessment worker)

> "Sometimes you can tell. I've had parents say they don't want child with their mother. I've met the grandmother and see what the problem really is, the grandmother is just too strict and the birth parent wants the child in a setting [the birth parent] can manipulate." (Indiana assessment worker)

> "Usually we'll try to abide by mom's wishes. Because we do not have custody [of the child], it's a voluntary placement and mom must agree." (Alabama investigative supervisor)

> "A lot of times, too, if there is a lot of friction in the family, that [relative's home] may not be the best place to put the child. Then we're looking at the child being put in the middle [between] grandma and mom." (Indiana investigative worker)

While caseworkers will not always place a child with the relative they want to live with, workers take children's objections to possible placements seriously. The degree to which agencies consider a child's objections depends a great deal on the child's age. Respondents noted that if a teenager objects to a relative, he or she is likely to run from the home.

> "If a 14-year-old is saying no, the more we talk to them and try and explain this and they still say no, you can't force them to go. They'll run away." (Connecticut investigative worker)

> "If the children are 10 years or older, we ask them where they want to go, if the relative is appropriate." (California investigative worker)

> "Also, we would ask the child. They may have a close relationship. One of the issues they [current and former foster care youth involved in a support group] brought up was that they didn't always agree with relative placements. And they thought that not enough care went into it, and that just because they're a relative doesn't mean they're a better placement." (California administrator)

> "We don't encounter that [child objection] much. Some kids want to go to foster care, don't want to follow the rules of the [relative's] house, but after they see what shelter care is like, they want to live with kin." (Alabama investigative supervisor)

Initial Placements with Non-Kin

Since advocates of kinship foster care stress how such placement can reduce the trauma to children removed from their homes, it was somewhat surprising to hear respondents in all study locations say that frequently children are not immediately placed with relatives. To a large extent, the delays relate to licensing requirements, specifically criminal and child abuse and neglect background checks. However, interviewees also pointed to other issues that may affect whether or not a child can be placed directly with relatives or whether the agency may first want the child placed elsewhere.

In some cases, there may not be a relative close by who is prepared to take the child right away. In other cases, the parent is not forthcoming about identifying relatives. In addition, in some situations the agency wants the child to be in a non-kin home, at least initially. For example, if there is severe abuse and injuries, a worker may place the child with licensed foster parents well known to the agency. Workers noted that the program supervisor plays a large role in deciding whether the initial placement is with a relative. In some situations in Alabama, the birth parent refused to allow the child to be placed with a particular relative.[4] When the relationship between the birth parent and relative appears volatile, staff members said they place the child in a non-relative foster home until they become fully aware of the situation or it is resolved.

"I can't say I've placed with any relatives. Not right at the beginning." (California investigative supervisor)

"The best case scenario is 10 days, if they've [the relatives] got their act together. Sometimes the court releases [the child to the relatives] at the detention hearing, if they're doing what they are supposed to do." (California investigative supervisor)

"There may be lots of relatives up front and you may opt not to use any of them until the 'dust can clear' and we can see, because it's not always safe for the child at the relative's house, even if the relative is appropriate. Sometimes it's a violent situation where the parent is not incarcerated." (Connecticut administrator)

"[In] a case that has significant abuse factors and the kid is significantly injured, we tend to want to take that child into our custody with people that we know, non-kin foster parents . . . then pursue other options at a later point after further assessment." (Connecticut investigative worker)

"I don't think it has anything to do with abuse factors. I will be far more honest and say it has to do with the program supervisor involved; that is my opinion. The supervisor is who makes the actual decision whether or not the child gets placed with a relative. But I think some supervisors are resistant to that." (Connecticut investigative worker)

"If there are a lot of people at the scene arguing, then we, or I, would utilize the foster care home to have time to figure out the best situation, then take that to the judge. Each situation is so different from the next." (Indiana investigative worker)

Summary and Discussion

It is clear that in each of the child welfare agencies we visited, caseworkers, supervisors, and administrators as well as family court judges are making a concerted effort to identify and recruit kin to act as foster parents. In addition, respondents noted increased efforts to identify and assess noncustodial fathers. ASFA's emphasis on timely permanency appears to be a significant factor in the increased attention agencies are giving to identifying kin and noncustodial fathers early in the case planning process.

Worker practices in identifying and recruiting kin were fairly consistent. While a few counties studied pursued innovative strategies, for the most part, workers identified kin by asking birth parents, children, school officials, neighbors, or others with knowledge of the family. In contrast, how workers decide whether or not to place a child with an identified relative appears to vary considerably. Workers mentioned two key factors in their decision—the level of protection and the standard of care that kin can provide. However, workers noted little or no agency guidance on how they should assess kin based on these factors. They appear to be using their best judgment based on the facts of individual cases without the benefit of a structured risk assessment instrument or other agency protocol. So it should not be surprising that workers differ on the way they determine if kin can provide adequate protection.

A clear example of this was the different views expressed by workers on whether a kin who was older and financially disadvantaged could provide adequate care for a child (regardless of whether the kin could pass licensing requirements). Some workers argued that placing children in such environments was not acceptable, while others felt that these placements were still preferable to non-kin foster care because of the bond between the kin and the child.

Another area of contention was whether it was better for children to be placed with non-kin than kin if it meant that the children could remain in the same school. Some workers argued that the most important influence on many children's lives was school and maintaining the stability of school was more important than maintaining a family bond. Determining factors for workers included the child's age and how far the school year had proceeded.

While child development research cannot provide definitive answers to questions about when it is best to place a child with kin, the research can help agencies develop guidance to help workers make an informed decision. To begin with, research suggests that attachments to consistent and stable caregivers are important to a child's healthy development (Ainsworth 1985; Bowlby 1988). The formation and maintenance of these attachments are important factors to consider when making placement decisions for children separated from their parents (Grigsby 1994). For example, if a child is attached to particular relative or schoolteacher, the continuance of that relationship may be vital to the child's healthy development. Decisions about where to place a child need to be made on a case-by-case basis by workers and supervisors, but agencies can identify factors that should be considered in the decisionmaking process.

Acknowledging the benefits that kinship care can provide and actively seeking out available kin do not diminish the need for child welfare agencies to continue and to improve efforts to recruit non-kin foster parents. Several workers and administrators acknowledged that sometimes children are placed with marginal kin who may not be able to provide a high standard of care or protection because non-kin foster parents are not available.

Many workers noted that birth parents are often reluctant to identify their kin at the time when caseworkers remove a child from the home and that this often leads to children being initially placed with other foster parents. As a result, children experience the trauma of being removed from their parents' home, being placed with strangers, and then being moved again. In addition to the emotional toll, the child may be forced to change schools twice.

Because birth parents cannot be counted on to identify their kin, child welfare agencies should take advantage of any available resource to identify, locate, and assess kin early in the process. These resources include the Federal Parent Locator Service developed as part of the child support enforcement system, a child's school records, and neighbors, clergy, or other members of the community with whom the child or family has a connection.

NOTES

1. Data presented in this section are based on the Urban Institute 2001 Kinship Care Survey. See Jantz et al. 2002.

2. Respondents identified several reasons for the lack of foster homes. Those in California and Connecticut noted the high cost of living and that there were more two-

income families, making it difficult for parents to find the time needed to care for foster children. Specific to California was the lack of housing units large enough to accommodate foster children. In addition, in Connecticut, it was noted that an increasing number of foster homes are investigated due to allegations of abuse or neglect. Several sites noted that increasingly, non-kin foster parents are adopting the children in their care, often deciding not to foster any additional children. Respondents noted difficulties finding foster homes for particular types of children, including large sibling groups, extremely disturbed children, Spanish-speaking children, and children not yet of school age.

3. Alabama generally does not license relative placements and does not generally retain custody of the child. Thus, it can afford to be flexible in whom it identifies as kin.

4. Since the parent usually retains custody of the child in Alabama, the agency could not place the child in the home of the relative without the parent's agreement.

3

Licensing and Payment of Kinship Foster Parents

Amy Jantz Templeman

ll kin who want to care for a child in state custody must complete a formal assessment process, though as discussed below, it may not be the same as the one that non-kin foster parents must complete. While states refer to the assessment process by various names, such as an approval process or a foster care licensing process, for ease the process that kin must complete is referred to here as "licensing." This chapter discusses licensing and payment together, because they are intrinsically linked—how kin caregivers are licensed determines what type of financial support they are eligible to receive.

Both the licensing and payment of kin as foster parents have been vigorously debated. One side argues that all children in state custody are entitled to a minimum level of safety and the states' foster care licensing standards hold foster parents to this minimum. Thus, holding kin to a standard beneath the foster care licensing standard may deny children their right to a safe placement. On the other side of the licensing debate, kinship care advocates argue that many existing foster parent regulations (for example, a minimum number of bedrooms or square feet in a home) do not reflect safety concerns but rather "middle-class values" of what a home should look like. Thus, holding kin to foster care licensing standards may deny children the opportunity to be cared for by relatives who could ensure their safety, but who may not be able to meet foster care licensing standards. On the issue of payment, some argue that kin who act as foster parents should not be paid for caring for a related child, because such care is part of a family's responsibility. Moreover, higher foster care payment rates (compared with TANF) may provide an unintended incentive for kinship caregivers who have been caring for children on their own to seek out child welfare assistance (Berrick, Minkler et al. 1999; Johnson 1994). On the other hand, some maintain states assume the same level of responsibility for children in their custody regardless of where a child is placed, and there is no reason why states should provide less financial assistance on behalf of a child in kinship care solely because the caregiver cannot meet certain licensing criteria (Geen and Berrick 2002).

Federal policies allow states great discretion in determining how to license and support kinship foster parents. As a result, states' kinship care policies have developed in such a manner that they treat kinship foster care and non-kin foster care differently. While there is significant variation among states in their approaches to kinship care, most states have developed kinship care policies that seek to allow as many kin as possible to care for children placed in state custody because of abuse or neglect. At the same time, states' kinship care policies are still evolving— many states have changed their policies within the past few years.

This chapter begins by providing a brief history of financial assistance available to kinship caregivers, and then documents federal and state policies for the licensing and payment of kinship foster parents. The chapter then focuses on implementation of kinship care policies by frontline child welfare workers. It examines instances in which kin are not licensed as foster parents, licensing requirements that kin have difficulty meeting, and local practices that allow kin to receive waivers from licensing requirements. The chapter also examines how these licensing practices affect the payment that kin are eligible to receive. Finally, it examines the opinions of frontline child welfare workers and administrators regarding how kin should be licensed and financially supported.

History of Financial Support for Kin

For the most part, federal financial support for the kin population stems from child welfare and income assistance policies. A 1950 Social Security Act amendment offered eligible relative caregivers financial assistance for children in their care through the Aid to Dependent Children (ADC) program. These families could apply to receive welfare benefits as a family unit if they themselves were poor, or they could apply and receive payment for only the related child, regardless of their income (a child-only grant). When the Aid to Families with Dependent Children (AFDC) program, the successor to ADC,[1] was replaced by the Temporary Assistance for Needy Families (TANF) program, states were given the option of continuing to provide child-only grants for non-needy relatives. All states except Wisconsin have continued this benefit.[2]

Most kin who acted as foster parents initially received financial assistance through AFDC. However, in 1979, the U.S. Supreme Court found in *Miller v. Youakim* that states must make the same foster care maintenance payments to kin caring for title IV-E–eligible children (those eligible for federal reimbursement under title IV-E of the Social Security Act) as they make to non-kin foster parents, provided that kin meet the state's foster care licensing standards. States were left to decide how to assist kin caring for children not eligible for IV-E and those who do not meet licensing requirements. While each state sets its own foster care licensing standards, the federal government provides financial reimbursement to states to cover certain costs associated with foster care placements. There are certain minimum procedural guidelines that states must meet to receive financial reimbursement. In 1997, Congress passed the Adoption and Safe Families Act (ASFA), which clarified the conditions under which the federal government would provide financial reimbursement. The act and the ASFA Final Rule of January 2000,[3] which documented how the U.S. Department of Health and Human Services (HHS) would implement the act, included a number of provisions that affected or clarified the federal reimbursement of foster care payments made to children placed with kin. Under the new law, states may not collect federal reimbursement for all kin caring for IV-E–eligible children. Instead, "relatives must meet the same licensing/approval standards as non-relative foster family homes." Waivers for certain licensing standards may only be issued on a case-by-case basis, not for kin as a group. No waivers can be granted for safety issues. In addition, the final rule prohibits states from claiming IV-E reimbursement for provisionally licensed or emergency placement kin homes.

While the federal government will not reimburse states for foster care payments made to kin who are not licensed according to the same standards as non-relative foster homes, neither ASFA nor the Final Rule prohibits states from assessing kin and non-kin differently. Some argue that kinship care is a unique situation and should not be held to the same standards as non-kin placements. Traditional foster care requirements, especially those not related to safety, may be irrelevant in a kinship care placement. The potential benefits of living with a family member or close family friend may outweigh the need for nonsafety requirements, such as space. However, safety is the most important concern to child welfare agencies, which may be reluctant to waive safety requirements or hold kin to less stringent safety standards than those non-kin foster parents must meet.

Licensing Standards

The licensing process kin must complete may or may not be the same as the process required of non-kin foster parents.[4] In addition, most states allow kin to care for children in state custody before they have completed all the requirements of licensure.

In 15 states, kin are required to meet the same standards as non-kin foster parents to care for a child in state custody. No standards are waived or modified for kin that cannot be waived or modified for non-kin foster parents in these states, and no separate approval process is offered. Furthermore, the number of states that require kin to meet the same standards as non-kin must meet has grown in the last few years. In 1997, 7 states required all kin to be fully licensed; by 1999, 10 states had this requirement.

Twenty-three other states apply non-kin foster care licensing standards to kin, but may waive or modify one or more standards that all non-kin foster parents are required to meet.[5] Sixteen states offered this assessment option to kin in 1999. Also in 1999, more than half of these 16 states waived requirements for kin as a group, not on a case-by-case basis. However, most likely due to the ASFA Final Rule, all of the states that currently waive requirements do so on a case-by-case basis, and therefore many kin in these states meet the full licensing requirements of non-kin.

The most commonly waived requirement for kin is space. Of the 23 states that offer a waived standard to kin, 12 waive or modify the space requirement. For example, Arkansas and Maine require a certain amount of square footage per occupant in non-kin foster homes, but may allow children to be placed in kin homes with less space. Other space-related requirements that may be waived include space between beds, number of children per room, and the length of time given to secure adequate beds.

Eleven states waive training requirements for kin. While most of these states will waive training entirely for kin, a few of them have made kin-specific modifications to the training program. For example, Connecticut requires a 27-hour foster parent training for non-kin, but offers an individualized training program for kin. Kentucky also offers an individualized training plan for kin, which is approved by the child welfare director, and Mississippi allows kin to watch a training-related videotape instead of attending classes.

States may also waive caregiver-specific requirements, such as age or income. Eight states waive age requirements, often lowering the non-kin requirement of 21 years of age to 18 years for kin. In Kentucky, non-kin must be under 65 years of age to care for a foster child, but the agency allows kin to be over age 65 if they can meet the needs of the child. Income requirements are waived for kin in five states.

A few other requirements may also be waived for kin, including transportation, marriage, and other nonsafety standards. For example, a foster family in Arkansas must have its own car, but kin may have this requirement waived. Kentucky requires non-kin foster parents to be married at least two years, but kin married less than a year can be approved if they meet the needs of the child. Finally, a general equivalency diploma (GED) or high school diploma is required of non-kin in New Hampshire, but both are waived for kinship caregivers.

In addition to a full or waived standard, states may also offer a separate approval process for kin. Twenty states offer this option to kinship caregivers, a drop from the 32 that offered it in 1999. Fifteen states have discontinued this option since 1999, and three states have begun offering it since then.

Almost all states offering a separate approval process to license kinship caregivers report that they consider the criteria used in this assessment process to be less stringent than those applied to non-kin foster parents. Only one state found the process to be equally as stringent, and none found it more stringent. All of the 20 states assess kin by a criminal background check and a child abuse and neglect registry check. More than half (13) of the states require a home study before kin are approved. A few (6) states conduct an income check of the kinship caregiver. In addition, more than half (13) of the states listed other requirements by which they assess kin, including court approval, training, a Department of Motor Vehicles (DMV) check, a physical and mental health check, references, an interview, and housing square footage.

Pre-Approval Placements

Unlike foster parents, kin are often unprepared when related children are placed with them. There is little time for them to buy new furniture, prepare mentally, or make other arrangements before the children appear. Therefore, there is ongoing debate about the safety of pre-approval placements. Due to the urgency of these placements, the kinship caregiver may not be assessed as thoroughly as a licensed foster parent. Kin are often unable to meet the full standards in the brief time that these placements must be made. In addition, state payments to kin are not federally reimbursed during this pre-approval period. However, agencies may see an advantage in being able to place children quickly with relatives and may be reluctant to move children again after the placement is stable.

Most states will place children with kin who are seeking to meet the assessment standards but have yet to do so, sometimes referred to as provisional licensing or approval. In 42 states, this option is available to kinship caregivers. Of the 15 states that require full licensure, 13 pre-approve for this option. Eleven of the 16 states that require the waived or modified standard pre-approve kin. Of the 13 states offering both full licensure and a separate process, all pre-approve for full licensure, and 8 do so for the separate process. Eight states pre-approve for both full licensure and the separate process. Finally, five of the seven states offering waived or modified and separate process pre-approve for the waived standard, and three do so for the separate process. Three states pre-approve for both the waived and separate process. In all, 11 states offer a pre-approval process for more than one standard, resulting in a total of 53 pre-approval possibilities. However, many of these states are clear that they do not issue a provisional license to kin, nor do they refer to the practice as provisional licensing; yet they may place with kin before complete approval.

Almost all of the states require a criminal background check and a child abuse and neglect registry check before a child can be placed with kin. Of the 53 pre-approval processes offered in 42 states, 48 require a criminal background check, and 47 require a child abuse and neglect registry check.

Payment Based on Licensing

Kinship caregivers may be eligible to receive financial assistance from a variety of sources, such as state- or federally funded foster care payments, TANF child-only grants, or Social Security benefits. As mentioned above, *Miller v. Youakim* required states to provide all kin caring for IV-E–eligible children with foster care payments so long as they meet licensing requirements. If kin are not licensed or are not IV-E eligible, the state can decide whether or not to provide financial assistance in another form. All kin who are related by blood, marriage, or adoption are eligible for a TANF child-only payment, which is usually much smaller than a foster care payment. In addition, child-only payments are prorated at a declining rate for each additional child and do not vary with the age of the child, as foster payments do.

Payment after kin are fully licensed or approved can vary across categories. This variation is partly due to regulations regarding the use of federal money to support kinship caregivers and state flexibility in using state funds to support this population. All states make state- or federally funded foster payments to kin who meet the full licensure standards, except for California and Oregon, which do not provide foster care payments to kin who do not care for IV-E–eligible children, regardless of how they are licensed. Instead, these kin are referred to welfare for assistance.

However, there are many kin caring for children in state custody who do not receive foster care payments. In 26 states, kin may be denied foster care funds for many reasons, and often there is more than one way to be denied funds in a given state. Several states do not provide foster care payments for children placed with kin assessed by a waived or modified standard. Two states, Georgia and Ohio, offer only TANF payments to kin assessed by the waived or modified standard, while two other states, Indiana and Rhode Island, deny kin foster care funds either if the child is not IV-E eligible or if kin meet only the waived or modified standard. In all four of these states, however, kin who meet the full licensure standard are eligible for federal or state foster care payments.

In addition, many states offering a separate approval process for kin do not pay foster care for this option. Of the 20 states offering this option, 14 do not pay foster care. Instead, kin may be referred to the TANF office, where they can receive assistance if they are eligible. Kin who are pre-approved may also be denied foster care funds during the pre-approval period. Nineteen states deny kin foster care funds while pre-approved. In 9 states, kin who are pre-approved for the full licensure process cannot receive foster care payments. Five states withhold foster care payments from kin who are pre-approved for the waived standard, and 10 do so for kin pre-approved for the separate approval process.

Voluntary Kinship Care Placements

Most states, under certain circumstances, will help arrange for a child who has not been adjudicated abused or neglected to live with a kinship care provider following an investigation. However, fewer states reported making such arrangements in 2001 than in 1999.[6] We found that 31 states may intervene for a limited amount of time to help arrange for a child to be placed with a kinship care provider in cases that have not been adjudicated. In many states, this type of arrangement is known as a "voluntary placement"—the birth parent(s) voluntarily place(s) the child with kin without much involvement by the child welfare agency. The agency's main responsibility in these cases is to ensure the ongoing safety of the child in this new home, but custody usually remains with the parent, guardian, or kinship caregiver.

Although agency involvement is limited in these situations, there are a number of standards kinship caregivers are required to meet before the child is placed. Kin are assessed by a criminal background check in 21 states, and a child abuse and neglect registry check in 22 states. Less frequently required are a home study (9 states) and an income check (2 states).

While state policies for licensing and payment of kin and the use of voluntary kinship care are well documented (as described above), relatively little is known about how these policies are interpreted and implemented by local child welfare offices and frontline staff. Some state policies are flexible, allowing local offices some discretion in implementation. Moreover, state policies often do not address all practice-related issues.

Thus, there are many reasons to expect that local licensing and payment practices may vary. In some states, under certain circumstances, kin caring for children in state custody may not be licensed. In every local site visited, kin may not be licensed at the point in time that they receive a child. In different localities, workers identified different licensing standards that kin may have difficulty meeting. In a number of locations, kin may receive a waiver from these standards, yet the process of receiving a waiver varies greatly. How localities financially support kin who are not licensed, not initially licensed, or who have certain standards waived also varies, even among localities within a state.

Placements with Unlicensed Kin

In all of the study locations, kin may be caring for a child before or without being licensed. In Alabama, most children are placed with kin voluntarily, and kin are generally not informed that becoming a foster parent is an option. Kin who are diverted from the system or caring for related children under a voluntary situation may still have to meet assessment standards, such as abuse and neglect checks, criminal history checks, and informal home studies. In the other counties studied, workers may place children with kin who are not yet licensed, but who have passed an initial background check. In some cases, the court may order a kinship care placement without requiring that kin become licensed.

Voluntary Placements

In Alabama, where the state rarely takes custody of a child if kin are available to act as caregivers, supervisors told us that the state will take custody only if the kinship caregiver has financial problems, and even then only in cases of severe financial distress.[7] If a kinship caregiver is in need, caseworkers will first look to other sources for financial support. If kin meet the criteria to receive a TANF child-only grant (related by blood, marriage, or adoption), workers may encourage kin to apply for this assistance. Workers also mentioned that food stamps or SSI payments serve as substitutes for child welfare agency assistance.

However, in a case where an Alabama kinship caregiver has exhausted all available resources to support the child and still needs financial assistance, the worker may suggest licensure as a foster parent. Workers said that they usually discuss licensing with kinship caregivers only if there is a financial problem, and kinship caregivers are generally unaware they can become licensed as a foster parent. Administrators reported that they discourage kin from being foster parents, citing the stigma associated with the child being in foster care. However, counties appear to vary widely in their willingness to take children into custody. Talladega, a rural county, was the Alabama site most likely to take custody of children in kinship care, followed by Mobile and Jefferson counties.

> "Grandparents can't afford it at times, so DHR [Department of Human Resources] takes custody and we license them as a foster home and give them a board payment. Birth parents can't care for them, so the children will remain there." (Alabama foster care worker)

> "We don't usually say, 'Would you like to be a licensed foster parent?'" (Alabama investigative worker)

> "If they don't meet the TANF definition of a relative, we would license them to get the board payment." (Alabama administrator)

> "You know, we do everything possible to try to keep them from trying to be a foster parent—but with a lot of relatives, it's because they want that board payment, because the board payment is more than the TANF payment. If you get a large sibling group, then with what you get from TANF, you can't afford to properly care for the child[ren]." (Alabama administrator)

> "I have had my kids all their life, and I have only been a foster parent for the last year and a half. I've had a good ride since foster care. Before that I was on TANF. Nobody ever said anything to me about being a foster parent. [DHR] never told me. The probation officer in family court told me about foster care." (Alabama kinship caregiver)

Caseworkers in several study sites noted that they might also take into account the length of the placement in advising kin to become licensed. They may encourage kin who are intended to be long-term caregivers to become licensed. However, if the child is being placed with kin in a temporary situation, with the intention of reunifying or finding another out-of-home placement, workers may be reluctant to suggest that kin become licensed as foster parents.

> "[Licensing] depends, too, on how long that child will be in care. If we're looking at 30 days and then this child is going to return home, don't go through licensing." (Indiana investigative worker)

Protection from birth parents is another reason that workers may suggest licensing as an option to kinship caregivers. Although the title of "foster parent" may only provide limited legal boundaries between the birth parents and the child and kinship caregiver, many kin feel more protected from possible birth parent aggression when their position as a caregiver is formally sanctioned by the child welfare agency. The agencies we visited recognize the benefits of licensing kin in this situation.

Placement before Licensure

In all of the study states except California, workers reported that they place children with kin before they are fully licensed or approved, usually pending future approval within a certain time frame. Many sites also provide financial assistance to kin during this pre-approval period. While Alabama provides kin who qualify with a provisional license until they are fully approved, the other three states have less-structured pre-approval processes.

Generally, the counties studied are willing to place children with kin before licensure if the kin caregiver presents a safe placement option. Although agencies will place children in shelter care or non-kin foster care while waiting for qualified kin, some staff commented that agencies are reluctant to do so if there are kin available who meet such basic requirements as a criminal background check, a child abuse and neglect check, and a home study. Respondents emphasized the need to minimize disruption in the lives of the children, a goal that is apparent in many agencies' practices.

In Alabama, where the vast majority of children are not in state custody, all counties will provisionally license qualified kin caring for children in state custody and provide them with foster care payments before they are fully licensed. This is a new policy and administrators estimated that only about 10 percent of kin receive this type of license. Expressing the strong belief that provisional licensing is often necessary to keep children with family, workers are reluctant to place a child in foster care while kin become licensed. Alabama requires that provisionally licensed kin be lifelong residents of the state. Alabama counties may also require foster parent training before kin can be pre-approved for placement or require a medical check within 10 days of placement. Mobile County workers also noted that a child must have been through some type of crisis or trauma for kin to obtain a provisional license. Alabama counties give kin six months to become fully licensed. The license cannot be extended or renewed after this time, and foster care payments are discontinued. However, some staff noted they stretch the time limit beyond six months for some kin or encourage them to take custody of the children themselves.

All three of the Connecticut counties place children with kin for a short time before licensure and provide foster care payments during this period. Connecticut supervisors estimated they place with kin before licensure in about 70 percent of cases. Connecticut counties may require that kin have a blood or marriage relationship to the child; other kin, such as neighbors or godparents, may not qualify for pre-approval placement in Connecticut. Kin must also pass emergency criminal and abuse and neglect history screens, which workers describe as minimal and intended to only screen out kin who are obviously inappropriate. Workers report that these screens can be completed quickly, and they can often place children in one day. Workers noted that there is some supervisor discretion as to what must be completed before placement. Workers in Hartford reported that the agency was becoming stricter, requiring kin to complete all required paperwork before placement, though this requirement still falls short of full licensure.

Connecticut counties allow kin 45 to 90 days to become licensed after a child is placed in their home. Workers report that most kin can make this deadline because the state does not require kin to complete training classes. Connecticut will "certify" relatives who do not complete the licensing process within 90 days.[8] Supervisors commented that relatives are often certified for six or seven months before they are licensed. Foster care payments to kin may stop during this period and workers may encourage kin to accept legal guardianship of children in their care rather than complete the foster care licensing process.

Indiana's counties do not provisionally license kin, although they will make emergency placements with kin before they are fully licensed. In addition, family court judges can and often do order children to remain with unlicensed kin. Under agency policies, workers are not supposed to recommend that a child be placed with unlicensed kin, but workers noted that they can make it clear to the judge that they would support that placement if ordered by the judge. A Lake County administrator observed, "The court order is our shield." At the same time, workers noted that sometimes judges will order a child to be placed with an unlicensed relative who may not meet the agency's standards. Before a child is placed with an unlicensed kin, workers are typically required to complete a home study.

Of the three Indiana study sites, only Marion County pays kin foster care during this pre-approval time, which is a major strain on the county budget since these payments are not federally or state reimbursable. Marion County also finds it difficult to encourage kin to complete the training classes required for full licensing since there is no financial incentive for them to take this extra step. This situation can prompt a struggle between workers and kin. Occasionally, workers face a decision about kin who refuse to meet licensing standards. If kin do not meet the appropriate requirements, workers might threaten them in three ways: no license, no payment, or removal of children from the home. Indiana calls kin who fail to meet standards "probationary" placements. Probationary status lasts for one year, after which time payment will stop, but children usually remain in the unlicensed home.

In practice, workers have a significant amount of discretion in making decisions about removing children from the home of a kinship caregiver. It is rare for a child to be removed from kin who do not complete the process or meet the standards required for full licensure. However, workers noted they use the court to intervene and order kin to meet standards. At the same time, some workers admitted that they tell the court that kin are "close to getting licensed" when this may not be true. Workers expressed frustration at the need to balance the child's needs with agency rules regarding licensure. Workers are reluctant to remove a child from a kin placement that they feel is in the best interests of the child.

California is the only state that does not permit emergency placements with kin, and therefore many children have to be placed with non-kin foster parents or in emergency shelters before kin are approved for placement. Data from the Child Welfare Research Center at the University of California, Berkeley,[9] show that of all the children who first entered foster care in California in 2000 and were still in care six months later, 44 percent of those who eventually entered kinship care were placed there directly, while the remaining 56 percent were placed in non-kin care first. While emergency placements with kin are not permitted, one of the study counties reported that workers will place a child with a kinship caregiver before the full criminal history check is processed. San

Diego workers noted that they can place a child with a kinship caregiver who has passed a local criminal history check while they await the results of a more extensive check, called "LifeScan," that may take a week or two to be completed. Workers in the other California study locations cited the LifeScan process as the reason why few children in their counties were initially placed with kin.

Barriers Kin Face in Meeting Standards

Workers in most of the study sites noted that kin often have difficulty meeting certain licensing standards, including criminal and child protective services (CPS) background checks; housing requirements, including those related to space and safety; and training requirements. Sometimes the licensing process itself is an impediment, making it difficult for kin to complete the process quickly. Workers also report that some kin simply refuse to cooperate with the licensing process.

The difficulty kin have in meeting requirements varies greatly among the states and counties studied. Relatively few workers in Indiana reported significant numbers of kin had difficulty, while in California, almost all workers reported difficulty for the majority of kin. While this could be due to differences in the stringency of the licensing process, California licensing standards appear to be no more exacting than those in Indiana. Thus, the variation in the difficulty that kin experience appears to reflect the different pools of kinship caregivers available in different localities.

Criminal Background and CPS Checks

Workers in California and Connecticut reported that most kin who are denied placement are denied because of child abuse or neglect substantiation or a criminal history. Workers in these sites noted that kin with even minor past criminal offenses might be denied a foster care license. In California, many workers said the criminal history check amounted to denying a license to "anyone with anything more than a traffic violation." Furthermore, several states require a background check for everyone in the household over age 18. This additional requirement can lengthen or complicate the process if a household member's background is not clear. Staff in several study locations mentioned cases where the histories of other adults living in the household prevented kin from being licensed.

When kin have a conviction in their background, states may still allow them to become licensed, but may assess them by more demanding standards than those applied to kin with clear backgrounds. In California, kin with a conviction may be required to go through the more stringent non-kin licensing process. In Connecticut, workers told us that, in the past, kin with drug charges could not be licensed but instead could become certified as a caregiver if the judge approved of the placement. However, the state is moving away from certification and is requiring all kin to become licensed.

"If they have had a drug history within the last five years, they have to be excluded. If they have ever had a [child abuse or neglect] substantiation with us, they are excluded. It actually acts as more of an impediment because, quite frankly, in the inner city, a good portion of the families have histories; a lot of them are generational, it is a real impediment in terms of family resources that are available." (Connecticut investigative supervisor)

In several sites, workers noted that criminal history and CPS checks can delay placement of a child with kin. The findings from criminal background checks often take a few days or weeks to be approved, a problem when workers are trying to place a child with kin quickly or in an emergency. California administrators called the criminal background check the most difficult part of the relative approval process. The overall process can be very slow, since the checks must be approved by the state rather than by the county.

Space

In all study locations, workers reported that kin often had difficulty meeting space requirements (e.g., enough bedrooms or square foot of space per child). Space requirements were particularly problematic in some California counties where housing is expensive and most middle-income residents live in small homes. Supervisors in Santa Clara County said that space is the most common reason that kin do not meet requirements. In some cases, the physical structure of a house may prevent kin from becoming caregivers if the house does not have such things as two exits from each room, fences around pools, screens on windows, locks on doors, and so forth.

Training

As noted earlier, many states do not require kin to complete the same training as non-kin foster parents. The four states in this study are at different stages in developing and conducting training programs for kinship caregivers. While California is not requiring they be trained, Connecticut is in the middle of developing a kin-specific training program. Alabama and Indiana require that relatives complete the same training as non-kin foster parents.

Indiana just recently started requiring kin to meet the same standards as non-kin, and administrators said they are "struggling to make it work." Kinship caregivers must complete 20 hours of training, the same amount required of non-kin foster parents. Kin attend an orientation session and seven training classes. Supervisors in Indiana are concerned with the amount of time it takes kin to finish the training classes. The agency's ideal time frame is two to three weeks, but this goal is rarely achieved. Workers estimated that at least 20 percent of kin do not complete the training requirements. Kin may delay the process because they do not want to attend or they may be unable to attend for various reasons. In LaPorte County, training is only offered three times a year, although county residents may go elsewhere to take it. Workers voiced frustration about the difficulty of "selling" the training classes. Many kin, particularly those who have been parents before, do not understand why they need training to care for a related child.

Kin in Alabama must complete a 10-week, 30-hour foster parent training (therapeutic foster care training involves an additional 10 hours). The program is offered two times a year, and kin have six months to complete the training. Alabama respondents voiced concern that kin are not able to finish the training within the six-month time frame.

Connecticut is in the process of adapting its foster parent training to fit the needs of relatives. At the time of our visits, child welfare officials were not yet requiring that kin complete the training, but were still developing a curriculum that addresses the issues that kin face. Once the training is in place, workers plan to require kin to begin the program within 90 days of a child's placement in their home.

California does not require training of kin related to the child within the fifth degree. Only kin related beyond the fifth degree have to meet the same standards as non-kin, which involves training. However, closely related kin may also have to go through training if they have a criminal conviction in their past.

Waivers

States may grant waivers or exceptions to standards for kin going through the assessment process. Seven of the local study sites grant waivers to kin infrequently, and the three Alabama counties report not granting any waivers, as state policy prohibits it. In counties that have waivers, respondents listed a number of requirements that may be waived for kin after checks are run, emphasizing that safety issues may not be waived. Instead, standards such as space, criminal history (when limited to minor crimes), child abuse and neglect (when reports are unsubstantiated), and non-safety physical checks were often mentioned. Space standards that may be waived include sleeping arrangements and the number of children in the room.

Of the kin populations receiving waivers, interviewees noted that non-related kin who are required to be licensed as non-kin foster parents may be receiving them most often. Respondents described a typical waiver situation as a teenager who runs away from home and lives with a friend and the friend's parent(s). In order for the child to stay in that home, some agencies will require that the parent(s) become licensed as non-related kin, but may waive standards to make the process faster and easier.

Waivers generally serve two purposes. If they are temporary, they may allow kin more time to meet a given standard. For example, workers mentioned that waivers could buy a family time to get a bed or make other necessary living arrangements. Under the conditions of a temporary waiver, kin are expected to fully comply with licensing requirements at a later time. States may also offer kin a permanent waiver or exception to certain licensing standards. In these cases, kin are not required to meet the full requirements later; they are simply exempt from those standards.

In Connecticut, supervisors reported that one-third of all kin placements necessitate some type of waiver, usually because of a criminal or child abuse and neglect history, before placement can occur. At the same time, workers in Connecticut report that they are granting far fewer waivers than in the past. Managers in Connecticut appear to differ greatly about when to pursue a waiver. Typically, a worker asks a supervisor for a waiver, who asks a local director, who, in turn, asks a regional director. The workers said they felt pressure from above not to request waivers as often, and they believe that waivers will not be approved.

In Indiana, workers said that they can seek waivers for kin by contacting the state child welfare agency, but not a single interviewed worker in Lake or LaPorte counties reported ever doing so. A few workers in Marion County suggested that they have some discretion in making exceptions, such as in cases where a potential kin caregiver does not have a phone in the home, has limited income, or has some minor criminal history. Indiana administrators noted that waivers are usually initiated by the court and that workers rarely request waivers without court intervention and support.

In California, there appears to be great variation in the process for granting waivers and in the extent to which waivers are granted. Workers and administrators in Los Angeles said that waivers require state approval and described the waiver process as cumbersome and lengthy. Workers noted that they are not permitted to ask for waivers; a judge must initiate requests. Los Angeles workers said they were reluctant to ask a judge to do so, fearing that if anything bad happened in such a placement they would be blamed. Workers in Santa Clara and Santa Cruz counties reported that they occasionally grant waivers and do not always seek state approval. These workers noted that there is considerable confusion over whether the county or state has the authority to issue waivers for different standards. Santa Cruz workers said they were reluctant to grant kin waivers because then kin would not meet the adoption standards. Of the locations studied, San Diego County appears to grant kin the most waivers. Local officials noted that they have authority to grant waivers without state approval.

Opinions about Licensing

Overwhelmingly, workers and administrators argued that kin should not be held to the same standards as non-kin foster parents. In particular, workers and administrators believed that kin should not have to abide by the same standards related to criminal and CPS history, space, minimum income, and required training. In many of the study locations, workers said that requiring kin to meet non-kin licensing standards would significantly limit the number of kin who could act as foster parents, making it difficult to find homes for foster children.

Many respondents argued that space and sleeping requirements should be less stringent for kinship caregivers. Some respondents also noted the need to be culturally sensitive when making decisions concerning sleeping arrangements.

> "I think that for some of our families who don't meet it [our requirements], some of it may be a cultural thing and maybe we need to think a little differently about how we handle different cultures, because I don't think we can do a 'one size fits all.' But I do think there's a standard that we can't compromise on. Safety of the child is something we can't compromise on. Especially with their arrest history. Sometimes it's pretty hard and fast, and I'm not sure if that's a good idea." (Connecticut administrator)

> "Even if kids have to sleep on the couch, who cares if it is your grandmother's house?" (Connecticut investigative worker)

> "If there is a relationship between that grandmother and a five-year-old child, then to remove that child because the bed of the child is in the same room as the grandmother, how would that be beneficial to that child?" (Connecticut investigative supervisor)

> "I really believe that the kids would prefer to be with grandma in one bedroom with all of their siblings, sleeping on the sofa, rather than with a stranger. I think that the relationship between the children and their family is more important than their space." (California ongoing supervisor)

> "But there are certain considerations that really have to do with what is an acceptable standard in the common community and what's a standard among people in my family. One difficulty I've had over the years [is] with Hispanic children going to middle-class foster homes and having to go back to a very poor family. I remember one family where we had three girls who went to three different middle-class homes, where they had their own bedrooms with a TV in the bedroom, as well as other accoutrements. They had to go back home to sharing the same bedroom, and mom

barely having enough money to put food on the table. It was a big crisis for them to go back to that home. Whereas if they had gone to the home of an aunt, who would have had similar circumstances, i.e., they would have had to share a bedroom, that move back home would not have been nearly as traumatic." (California investigative supervisor)

Criminal history and child abuse and neglect history are two other standards that many workers feel may be unreasonable for kin to meet. Workers want checks on criminal and child abuse and neglect history to be much less stringent. Workers maintained that not only are minorities overrepresented in the criminal justice system, but sometimes their history is not supported by much evidence or the charges may not be relevant to raising a child.

"I have some concerns about our policies regarding criminal records for relatives, particularly with certain minority groups who are more involved with the criminal justice system. We have to take into consideration what the offense was and how that offense relates to parenting, and where the person is at that point in their life. Our policies are not like that; they are pretty strict and rigid. If there is a criminal record, they are not eligible, and I think that has an adverse effect on our ability to place with relatives." (Connecticut investigative worker)

"I think it is unfair that we make a decision not to allow that person to be a [foster] parent based on a charge that was not connected to violence, not connected to risking injury to a minor, and we made the leap, the tremendous leap, that that person cannot now be a [foster] parent, despite serving his or her time." (Connecticut investigative worker)

"But there are a lot of histories that involve people getting slapped with an abuse or neglect charge with little evidence, if any. Sometimes just a child's word is enough. There might not be any physical evidence of abuse. So I think we need to look at each case and what is documented [evidence of abuse] before we exclude those with CPS histories from being a resource." (Connecticut investigative worker)

Respondents also commented on the type of training often required of kin. Many think that training of some type should be required of more kin, but should be modified to fit the specific needs of kin, which may be different than those of non-kin. Connecticut workers suggested that training be altered to address the goals of kinship caregivers. They commented that kin are often unprepared and overwhelmed when a related child is placed in their home, and asking them to attend training classes at the same time is impractical. Some caregivers also found that training can be inappropriate or unhelpful.

"For a lot of relatives, the kids are not there that long, so most times by the time training would begin, the kids go home." (Connecticut licensing worker)

"Relatives really need a good parenting class. They are not getting this. The relatives have the same skills as the parent we removed from." (California investigative supervisor)

"According to these parenting classes, they are teaching us how to raise kids, but we already raised our kids and have been successful at doing that." (Indiana unlicensed caregiver)

"[They have] been in our lives all of their lives. It would be different if the child were coming from somebody else's home. We are talking about children that have already been in our lives since the day they got there." (Indiana unlicensed caregiver)

A few respondents felt that kin should be held to the same standards as non-kin. Some workers commented that they might feel more confident about the safety of kin placements if the standards were stricter, or if kin were consistently required to meet foster parent standards.

"Standards should be the same for relatives and non-relatives. We won't settle for less. We won't put a child in a risky situation just because the caregiver is related. Safety is the first concern." (Alabama investigative worker)

"I liked the tightening of standards for relatives, because as a continuing worker, I had some placements which were not very good at all, and that's 10 years ago, and now I see a great improvement. . . .

Well, in the old days, the ER [emergency response unit] workers just used to find a relative and that's it. I don't think they did any checks. So you were placing a child in a home that was often not much better than the homes the children were removed from." (California supervisor)

"I think there need to be some pretty big changes in the standards. These days, the overriding rule is to place with relatives at all costs. The criteria for kin becoming caretakers in our system is that they have to be alive, they won't kill the child, and they will sign the forms—that's about it." (California ongoing supervisor)

Other respondents commented that they would like to see kin held to the same standards as non-kin, but that this was not realistic, given the need to rely on kin and the backgrounds of kin available.

"I think it's a good idea [to hold kin to non-kin standards], but I don't know if it's realistic. It'd be nice, because I feel bad when I leave kids and two babies have to share a bed or there aren't fire alarms, and I think, 'What if there's a fire tonight?' So that's my feeling. I'd like it if we could, but I don't think it's realistic." (California worker)

"Bottom line is that our foster care system is in such a horrendous state. We are removing far more children than we have in terms of our recruitment of foster parents. We are going to have to realistically look at what we expect people to do when they decide to take in these children, and I think we are going to have to relook at it. The bottom line is that we are picking from the bottom of the barrel at this point, we are placing kids in homes that aren't even licensed yet, because we are removing at such an alarming rate. We are going to have to kick up the support. I mean do whatever is necessary to salvage the placement . . . it would be different if we had an abundance of homes." (Connecticut investigative worker)

Many workers were concerned about the potential impact of making kin meet the same standards as non-kin foster parents. In addition to the impracticality of such a requirement, respondents also spoke of major problems securing caretakers that such a change might cause. Agencies frequently would not be able to use kin as resources, and they would need to separate siblings more often. These changes would greatly affect the current practices of many agencies.

> "Even if relatives could meet the licensing standards for one child, a lot of them don't have enough space to be licensed for all of the siblings—if that were the case, the siblings would have to be placed in different homes." (California ongoing worker)

> "We are dreading a change in policy that would make requirements more strict".... "It would shut us down".... "It would just cripple us. And our relatives wouldn't qualify to be licensed".... "Relatives don't want to be scrutinized; they'll just say forget it. It would be a relationship change between us and relatives." (California supervisors)

Many staff members also contended that existing standards are not a good basis for judging whether a person will be a good caretaker. They questioned whether the standards are really about safety and quality of care. Are workers really looking at whether or not the caregiver will provide a high level of care? Can safety actually be measured by examining the physical structure of the home?

> "We might, in the ideal world, want the perfect home for every child, [but] it's throwing the relationship into the assessment process [that] balances the scales between the stranger and the relative." (California administrator)

> "I don't feel that our assessment of foster care gets to the issue of what you really want to identify . . . somebody who is the best caretaker for a child. I think that's a whole other debate—about looking at physical plant—and that should be on the bottom five percent of priority. It's given way more weight in California. And there really has not been the funding that allows us to really do a thorough home study. Since we place a high value on the issue that they are related, there should be some connection that transcends the stranger." (California administrator)

> "Safety means something different to everyone. We all bring perspective, history to the agency. No two people are on the same page all the time." (Connecticut supervisor)

Another problem in applying licensing standards for kinship care-givers is the variation among supervisors in what is allowed or accepted. When it comes to waiving standards and allowing certain exceptions for kin, there is a good deal of difference in how policies are applied across states and counties.

> "There's policy and there's practice, and they're two totally different things. What it really means is, things are black and white in the policy manual, and when a situation comes up, you all sit around the table and argue about it, and whoever squawks the loudest walks out with a grin on their face. It's pretty disturbing." (Connecticut investigative worker)

> "One supervisor sees it in one way. Another in another way. I have had six supervisors in the last three years. I would like the department to be a little bit more realistic with relatives and understand that DCF [Department of Children and Families] foster homes are different and we cannot expect everything that we expect from relative foster homes." (Connecticut investigative worker)

Barriers Kin Face in Receiving Payment

In addition to not always being eligible for foster care payments, kin may face long delays in getting paid and may not receive supplemental payments for which they are eligible. Kin may also not complete the required steps to receive payment.

Kin often experience delays in receiving foster care payments because these payments can take several months to begin. Once kin in Indiana are licensed, the payment may not start for six months to a year. In California, kin typically wait three to five months. Even in Connecticut and Alabama, where payments can start almost immediately, workers note that all payments are made in the month following the month in which care is given, so that there is a built-in waiting period of at least a month. Some types of payment can begin more quickly, such as the clothing allowance that San Diego provides within a week of placement. Such quick payments can be very helpful to kin, who are often unprepared for the placement and need financial assistance right away.

Many kin do not receive a supplemental payment for a child with special needs, although they are eligible. While the amount of these payments varies greatly, they are often much higher than basic foster care rates. Kin may not receive these supplemental payments because they are unaware they are eligible for additional assistance and so do not press for them. Workers in several sites observed that they also do not offer special needs payments to kin.

> "If a relative is taking care of a medically complex child, we should give them that special rate as well. The workers don't offer it." (Connecticut licensing worker)

> "We give relatives a disadvantage sometimes when we place a special needs child in their home and [do] not give them the extra per diem. If they don't ask for it, we ain't giving it to them. We do some funny stuff." (Indiana continuing worker)

Kin may also not take the steps required to obtain financial assistance. Some kin assume the placement will be short term and that they can meet the child's needs without assistance. Some are intimidated by the process of getting assistance or are unable to produce the required documentation—a birth certificate, for example. Caregivers may even refuse assistance because of the burden it places on birth parents. In many states, birth parents are required to reimburse the state for all costs associated with a child's out-of-home placement. So a relative caregiver may feel guilty taking foster care payments, knowing that the birth parents will be responsible for paying the agency back.

> "Sometimes we have to convince relatives to take money. Try to tell them to just put it in a savings account if they feel they don't need it." (Indiana continuing supervisor)

> "The birth parent wages get garnished if they're working; if they're not, they'll just owe a lot of money. I have an uncle who's supporting his nephew. He can't afford it, but he feels so sympathetic toward his sister (the birth parent) 'cause she's got another child living with her." (California continuing worker)

All the respondents mentioned referring kin to the TANF agency if they are unable to receive a foster care payment. Some agencies assist kin with the process of seeking TANF. In San Diego, the TANF referral process is particularly easy; workers need only process an interagency program transfer, and kin do not have to come to the office again. Workers may also recommend that kin apply for Medicaid or food stamps. While they are helpful in referring families to other agencies for support, respondents expressed concern for families receiving TANF instead of a foster care payment. Particularly for families caring for several dependent children, TANF can be second-best help by a substantial margin. While the foster care rate doubles for two children and triples for three, TANF payments increase only a small amount for each additional child.

Opinions about Payment

The majority of respondents felt that kin who act as foster parents should receive the same financial support as non-kin foster parents. They noted the significant immediate needs faced by kin and the hardship they face due to delays in getting assistance. As described in chapter 5, workers noted that, unlike most non-kin foster parents, kin often have very limited incomes. On the other hand, some workers and administrators expressed concern about how foster care payments affect kin's motivation to care for a related child. In addition, many workers recommended that kin only receive foster care payments after they complete the licensing process so that they have an incentive to take the necessary steps to be licensed. Caseworkers said they sometimes search for kin who can support the child without help from the agency, and some respondents commented that kin who ask for financial support up front might not be the best caregivers down the road. In some cases, a request for financial support may reflect negatively on kin, causing workers to question their motives. Such bias may, in turn, cause kin to feel discriminated against.

> "Workers think that relative caregivers do not need a payment. They bring in their own bias and sometimes don't inform the caregivers enough about the ability to become a . . . foster parent." (Alabama supervisor)

> "Now, it's like the word is on the street . . . it's almost like the blue-light special because they tell each other, 'DCF's gonna come and ask you—if they took your daughter's kids—they are going to come and ask you to take care of them. You tell them you have to

have foster care, because now you're going to get $600.00 and they're going to buy the kid's clothes and the kid is going to get free lunch.'" (Connecticut ongoing supervisor)

"I'm straddling the fence here; relatives threaten to give kids up if they don't get a check. To me, then you are not totally committing to that child, and the child is going to eventually associate their care with money. . . . I might as well put them in a nontraditional foster home; if you are going to hang this over the child that when the paychecks stop, you're out." (Alabama foster care worker)

"It concerns me that I have to pay you to assist with your own grandchild. That tends to bother me a little bit. Something just doesn't sit right with me morally." (Alabama supervisor)

"With the federal government slowly easing out the welfare system and they're putting foster children in private contractors—it's not welfare anymore—they're being assigned to private agencies. And they aren't allowing the relatives to get assistance to help their own family members; they have to go in foster homes. So the only ones left to take care of our black children, to compensate for the relatives who can't, are white people getting these big lucrative checks. So I put it on record, there's something wrong behind it." (Indiana caregiver)

Several respondents mentioned local debates about paying kin to act as caregivers with some community members maintaining that kin should not need money to care for their own family. Workers also admitted to wondering how committed kin are to children when they threaten to give them up if they receive no payment. On the other hand, kinship caregivers remarked that they often feel penalized compared with foster parents and birth parents. They have trouble understanding why in some cases they do not receive the same services and financial assistance as non-kin foster parents.

"Some [relatives] ask for a stipend and then [DCF] takes the child away, because [DCF] feels that if they are asking for money, then they can't take care of the kid. That is a problem. I have seen children moved out of homes because people were asking for some financial assistance." (Connecticut licensing worker)

"Most relatives are not aware that they can receive a payment; taking care of children for a while can certainly deplete a family's resources, though. Many relatives sign on for temporary care, then start to need to make legal decisions, such as guardianship." (California administrator)

"A lot of them don't know the procedure they have to go through to get the per diem. They think that they just get the kids and it is given to them. We explain it to them. They want it right off the bat ... want it without going through that. Some of them go through the foster parent training and some of them won't." (Indiana assessment supervisor)

Summary and Discussion

Although states set kinship care licensing and payment standards, local practices can differ considerably. For example, states' use of voluntary kinship care varies greatly. Even in Alabama, a state that relies primarily on this type of arrangement for children placed with kin, we found significant variation in the willingness of local offices to take custody of a child placed with kin. While states may require that all kin who care for children in state custody be licensed, we found that family court judges may ignore this requirement and order child welfare agencies to place foster children with unlicensed kin. Three of the four study states allow children to be placed on an emergency basis with kin before they are licensed; however, the requirements that these kin must meet and the financial assistance they will be offered before they are licensed vary, not only among states but also within states. Likewise, three of the four study states have procedures in place that allow for waivers of certain licensing criteria, yet the processes for getting a waiver and the frequency with which workers pursue waivers differ greatly among the localities studied.

Decisions about how to license and financially assist kinship caregivers are difficult to make for counties, states, and the federal government. This situation is clear from the large number of states that have shifted their kinship care licensing and payment policies within the past few years—and not in consistent ways. Plainly, agencies regard kin as valuable resources for many reasons, yet they struggle to determine when to hold kin to the same standards as non-kin and when to make exceptions to take advantage of the potential benefits kin can offer to abused and neglected children. Moreover, the debate about how to financially compensate kin continues.

The debate over requiring kin to meet non-kin foster care licensing standards turns on the question of whether allowing kin to meet less stringent standards impairs the safety or well-being of children placed in kinship care. The vast majority of respondents felt that kin should not have to meet non-kin licensing standards; they contend many of the standards do not accurately measure the quality or safety of a placement. At the same time, when respondents were asked whether these standards should be eliminated for non-kin foster care as well, nearly all said no— existing standards should remain for non-kin caregivers.

The federal government has provided little assistance on this front and has left the definition of safety requirements up to the states. In a July 2001 information memorandum to the states from HHS's Administration for Children and Families, the federal government addressed the issue of licensing standards. The memo suggested that states that use broad language to define their licensing standards may allow agency workers to have more discretion in licensing caregivers, while still satisfying federal requirements.

Several states have applied broadly defined licensing standards. For example, California's kinship policy manual uses broad language in describing foster care standards. The placement is based on, but not limited to, a series of factors. One factor is "the willingness and ability of a relative to meet the child's needs, to facilitate family reunification, and provide the child's permanency alternative, if necessary." The phrase "meet the child's needs" is broad enough that it leaves some discretion to the worker while also helping to ensure a safe placement.

State child welfare agencies may have great difficulty modifying their licensing standards to incorporate such broad language. In many states, the licensing standards for foster homes are regulated by an outside agency, often a health agency. These regulatory agencies may be reluctant to set requirements that are difficult to interpret and enforce.

Determining what kin must do before a foster child can be placed with them on an emergency basis is also problematic. The less that is required of kin, the greater the risk to the child. The more that is required, the greater the likelihood is that the child will first have to be placed in shelter care or non-kin foster care before a kinship placement is approved. One could argue that the risk to a child during a short emergency placement is sufficiently small to warrant minimal requirements. At the same time, if little is required of kin before a child can be placed with them, then the risk is greater that the child will have to be removed when more information about the kin is discovered.

One can also question the extent to which existing foster care licensing standards actually prevent appropriate kin from caring for children, especially given the ability of judges to order placements with unlicensed kin and the waiver processes most states have. Many workers would probably argue that standards would not need to be lowered for kin if workers had greater flexibility in applying standards, or as HHS has suggested, states make licensing standards broader. The problem with providing greater flexibility is that it can lead to great differences in how the standards are applied.

The debate on how to compensate kinship foster parents turns on two very different questions: (1) What financial support are kinship foster parents "deserving of"? and (2) How does the financial support provided to kin affect the well-being and permanency of children placed in their care? Thus far, most of the debate has focused on the first question. While most respondents felt that kin should receive the same compensation as non-kin foster parents, many others expressed reservations about offering kinship caregivers the higher foster care rate. Some argue that it is kin's familial responsibility to care for related children and they should not be compensated. Others argue that providing assistance to kin creates an incentive for parents to turn their children over to kinship care. Moreover, if a voluntary situation allows kin to receive only a TANF payment, then kin may find an incentive in welcoming child welfare involvement, which could provide a higher foster care payment.

On the other hand, one could argue that kinship foster parents deserve at least to know what their rights are for receiving financial assistance. States may see a financial incentive to limit the number of children in the custody of the state, instead asking kin to provide voluntary placements. This may not be an incentive in Alabama, yet we found convincing evidence that kin were not being informed of their options. As documented above, many states have more than one assessment option for kin, and often these options provide different levels of financial support. It is unclear whether kin in these states are told that they can receive additional assistance by meeting a higher standard.

There is little information available to assess whether and how the level of financial assistance provided to kinship foster parents affects the well-being and permanency of the children in their care. Many workers who argued that all kin caring for foster children should receive foster care payments like non-kin pointed out that kinship caregivers are doing the same job. It is interesting that most of these workers focused on the financial needs of the kinship caregiver as opposed to the financial hardship's effect on the children.

When to begin providing kin with foster care payments is also problematic. Workers pointed out the immediate financial struggles kin often face when they agree to care for a child and argued that payments should begin immediately. At the same time, providing foster care payments as soon as care begins can reduce the incentive for kin to complete the requirements for licensing, as shown by the experience of Marion County, Indiana. Telling kin that a child in their care will be removed if they do not complete licensing is an empty threat, since both workers and kin know that the court is unlikely to upset a stable placement. By the same token, cutting financial assistance to the kinship caregiver may unintentionally harm the child.

Of course, states' decisions about how to support kinship foster parents are greatly affected by federal policies guiding reimbursement. It seems hypocritical of federal policy to allow states to place children with kin before they are licensed or with kin who meet standards different from those set for non-kin foster parents, but then refuse to reimburse states for costs associated with these placements on the grounds that they are unsafe. If the federal government believes such placements are unsafe, then it should not permit states to use these placements at all. The federal government has allowed each state to develop its own foster home licensing standards, which reflect local norms and values. As a result, licensing standards vary considerably across states. Thus, a kin foster parent meeting a relatively low standard in one state could still be satisfying a more stringent standard than one met by a non-kin foster parent in another state. Yet the federal government would consider the non-kin placement to be safe and the kin placement unsafe.

NOTES

1. The Aid to Dependent Children (ADC) program was renamed the Aid to Families with Dependent Children (AFDC) program in the 1960s.

2. In Wisconsin, the child must be at risk of harm if living with biological parents for the relative caregiver to be eligible for a TANF child-only payment.

3. ASFA Final Rule as published in the *Federal Register*, January 25, 2000, page 4033.

4. Data in this section based on the 2001 Urban Institute survey of state kinship care policies. See Jantz et al. (2002).

5. New Jersey and Ohio require full licensure of broadly defined kin but allow waivers for close relatives. These states are included in the waived category.

6. In the 1999 survey, 39 states reported that they help arrange kinship placements without seeking state custody. Fewer than half reported they conduct background checks on kin or perform a home study.

7. As described in more detail in chapter 7, other localities rely on voluntary kinship care, but to a lesser degree and only under certain circumstances.

8. At the time the study was being conducted, Connecticut was changing its policy to eliminate relative certification as an option.

9. Unpublished data provided by Barbara Needell.

4

Casework Practices with Kinship Foster Parents

Rob Geen and Karin Malm

Kinship foster parents are different from non-kin foster parents in a variety of ways, and these differences affect how child welfare caseworkers must work to most effectively use kin. Unlike traditional foster parents, kin are typically not prepared to act as foster parents when they take on the job. They have not been licensed as foster parents or attended training on what it means to be a foster parent. Unless they have been foster parents before, kin typically do not understand the child welfare system. They do not know what to expect from the child welfare caseworker, the courts, or other involved parties. Kin are also typically not physically prepared to take on parenting responsibilities. They may not have many things needed to care for children, including a crib or bed, car seat, and toys. Many kin are also not emotionally prepared for their new roles.

Kin are also different from non-kin foster parents in that most already have a relationship with the child in their care and the child's birth parents. In fact, kin may have already been caring for the child before child welfare authorities officially placed the child in their home. Thus, kin can ease the trauma children experience when they must be removed from their parents' homes. Moreover, kin can be a valuable resource for caseworkers in understanding the child's needs and the broader family circumstances.

While this prior relationship can be very beneficial and one of the reasons why child welfare agencies seek out and give preference to kin over other foster parents, the prior relationship may also present challenges for kin and the child welfare caseworkers. In addition to putting their lives "on hold" to assume new parenting responsibilities, many kin are grandparents and must acknowledge their own children's failure to effectively parent. Birth parents may pressure kinship caregivers to allow unscheduled or unsupervised visits with children. Kin, especially those who question the child welfare agency claims that birth parents have been abusive, may not comply with agency or court-ordered restrictions on parental visitation. Kin may also not inform caseworkers of problems that the birth parents are facing—for example, if parents show up for a visit while "high" or intoxicated—if they feel such information would hurt the birth parents' chances for reunification. On the other hand, kin who have seen the birth parents fail in the past may not be willing to give them another chance. Kin who have tired of seeing birth parents abuse or neglect their children may intentionally or unintentionally try to sabotage reunification efforts.

The unique circumstances of kinship foster parents point out the need for child welfare agencies to examine whether and how casework practices with kin should differ from practices with other foster parents. This process includes how caseworkers inform kin of their role and responsibilities and those of the child welfare agency and the court, develop a case plan for the child, supervise placements, and monitor birth parent visitation.

Given that kin typically have less experience than non-kin foster parents with the child welfare system, are often not required to complete foster parent training, and give caseworkers cause for concern about birth parents' inappropriate access to children, it might seem that child welfare agencies would spend additional time informing kin of their responsibilities, monitoring the well-being of children in kinship care, and supervising birth parent visitation more closely. However, past research has not found this to be true.

Most states' kinship foster care policies require caseworkers to provide the same level of supervision for children in kinship care as is provided for those placed in traditional foster care (Jantz et al. 2002). However, several studies show that child welfare workers tend to supervise kinship care families less than non-kin foster families (Beeman et al. 1996; Berrick et al. 1994; Brooks and Barth 1998; Chipungu et al. 1998; Dubowitz 1990; Gebel 1996; Iglehart 1994). For example, one study found that caseworkers conduct less frequent home visits and telephone kinship caregivers less often than they do non-kin foster parents (Gebel 1996). Another study found that more than one in four kinship caregivers went a year or more without having any contact with a caseworker (Dubowitz 1990). In addition, research has shown that caseworkers provide less information to kinship caregivers than to non-kin foster parents and are less likely to discuss the role of the child welfare agency with kinship caregivers (Chipungu and Everett 1994; Chipungu et al. 1998).

One explanation suggested for why workers may provide less information and supervision to kinship caregivers is that workers view kinship placements as separate from and possibly outside the child welfare system, or as fundamentally safer than placements with non-kin foster parents (Berrick et al. 1994). In addition, workers may not initiate or sustain regular contact with kinship caregivers, believing that kin prefer limited contact with the agency (Thornton 1991). Workers may also believe, based on their own experience, that kinship care placements are fundamentally safer than other placements and thus require less supervision (Berrick et al. 1994).

The limited supervision that kin receive raises concerns about the safety of kinship care placements, especially in light of past research showing that birth parents have much more frequent and unsupervised contact with children in kinship placements (Barth et al. 1994; Berrick et al. 1994; Chipungu et al. 1998). Child welfare workers report that they often have difficulty preventing unsupervised parental contact when children are placed with kin. Parents often make unscheduled visits with children in kinship care (Chipungu et al. 1998). Parents of children in kinship care are also much more likely to see their children in the foster home than are parents of children in non-kin foster care, who typically see their children at an agency office or visitation center (Chipungu et al. 1998). While these increased opportunities for visitation may have a positive effect on children, they also raise concern about how to prevent visits that may be harmful.

This chapter examines how local child welfare agencies inform, involve, and supervise kinship care providers throughout the case planning process. The information caseworkers provide to kin who agree to become foster parents for a related child is described, and kin foster parents' understanding of not only their role as foster parents but also the role of the child welfare agency and court is explained. We examine how and why caseworkers supervise kin and traditional foster parents differently. We also assess how caseworkers approach case planning with kin as compared with other foster parents and how engaged kin feel in the case planning process. Finally, we document how birth parent visitation differs when children are placed with kin instead of in traditional foster care.

Kin's Understanding of What Is Expected of Them

"I can tell you first hand that they [relatives] do not have a clue as to what's going on. I work with a relative support group and the first question is always, 'How long is the child going to be here? Why is the child removed from the mom?' Very little information is given by [investigative] workers. They have to work in such a rush; it's a short time period. Kin don't understand the underlying issues that brought child into care . . . whether there's domestic violence, substance abuse. They don't understand a lot about that. They don't understand the pull and dysfunction of substance abuse or a domestic violence situation. They don't understand the court system. They don't understand why the child has to visit [with his birth parents] or why the child can't go back home. The information that they [relatives] are getting is very little." (California foster care worker)

This quote illustrates how much caseworkers feel kin are uninformed or misinformed about what is expected of them as foster parents. Given that they are often thrown into their role unexpectedly, it is not surprising that kin typically do not understand what is expected of them when they agree to care for a child. They may not understand the needs of the child placed with them, agency rules and regulations, or the role of the child welfare agency and the court. Caseworkers often fail to provide kin with needed information and report difficulty communicating with kin. When kin do understand agency rules and regulations, they often do not accept, agree, or comply with these requirements. Generally, most kin expect and want the child welfare agency to be less involved than they are. However, in Alabama, where most kin are not caring for kids in state custody, kin expect the child welfare agencies to be more involved.

Kin may not understand how a child has been affected by abuse or neglect and may also not have realistic expectations for the child's behavior. Kin often hear conflicting stories from the agency and the birth parents as to why the child was removed, and consequently, kin do not always believe that a child has been abused. Because kin often are not trained, workers report that kin may not understand the special needs a child has and how these needs must be addressed. In addition, while most kinship caregivers are grandparents, many are aunts or other relatives who may not have prior parenting experience. As a result, kin may take it personally when a child acts out, blaming themselves for not doing a good job, rather than understanding that the behavior may be typical of abused children. At the same time, a few workers suggested that, compared with non-kin, kin have a better understanding of the children placed with them because they already know the child and the child's family. However, kin also report that they were often unprepared emotionally for how their relationship with the child would change—from being the grandmother or aunt to being the substitute parent.

> "I had an uncle say to me recently, 'I just wanted a good kid. I didn't realize he was going to be this way.' As if it was this kid that was the problem and creating all this chaos. When part of the problem was that their expectations of this child were so unrealistic that he couldn't possibly have met them ever, and the other problem was that their experience with children was very limited. They'd never had children, so it was a whole lifestyle change, included things like after-school care and games and things for him to partake in. They wanted this kid to come home and mind his own business and do his homework, and he's a kid that gets in trouble, he's a kid with a few behavior problems." (California foster care worker)

> "I'm finding relatives get involved and they don't realize the difficulty that it is to raise the population that we serve. Kids have a lot of separation and loss issues and attachment issues. They [the relatives] just figure if they raise this child like they raised their other children, everything will be fine. They are not very receptive to services and those problems." (Connecticut foster care worker)

Many workers noted that kin often do not understand or agree with the child welfare agency focus on reunification. Kin may feel like birth parents have had enough chances and should not have a right to visit their child. Other kin did not feel that birth parents should be given a year to "get their act together." At the same time, workers report that some kin react the opposite way. Some kin do not believe the birth parent was abusive and that the agency should limit visitation or they think that caseworkers should give the parent more time before pursuing termination of parental rights. Many kin noted that they understood what taking care of the child would mean, but did not understand how involved the birth parents would continue to be. Many kin also were overwhelmed by the reaction of other relatives; some blamed kin for taking the child away from the birth parents and ostracized the kin.

> "You don't get kids in a vacuum; you get mom, the dad, the other relatives. You get the visitation, the social worker, the court. All of the problems don't just magically disappear. Mom's not dead, she's out there and she's gonna be buggin'." (California investigative supervisor)

> "I didn't want to deal with the mother, because she was a drug addict . . . real negative. I didn't want to deal with her. I did not want to do it—it was really frustrating. I'm doing all this work, now he is going home. She still has no job, no place to stay; they're living in a hotel room. Now they are going to give back all five of these children. I just don't understand it. I feel like it is a waste of my time. I feel like I am putting all this time and energy into molding him into a good person, and now he is going right back to this ghetto life. One little room with five kids and no transportation, and I feel like he is going to go back to the same way." (California kin caregiver)

> "I think a lot of times with the kin they have this glowing vision— 'I'm going to save family'—and they don't really realize what they are getting into . . . that they're going to be dealing with the court system, with us, with the animosity of the family." (Indiana investigative worker)

Kin typically are unaware of or disagree with many agency rules and regulations. Workers readily admitted that the agency is very intrusive and limits the decisionmaking authority that foster parents have. Non-kin foster parents may be prepared for this, but kin may not expect it and therefore react negatively. One of the regulations that kin often fight is the prohibition on the use of physical discipline. This is especially true when kin have cared for the children in the past, spanked them, and are now being told that spanking is wrong. Kin also question why they can spank their own kids but not the related children they are caring for. Workers note that kin often do not realize that they must ask permission for a variety of activities, such as allowing children to travel out of the state, even for a school field trip. Kin also do not ask the agency for consent when a child wants to stay overnight at a friend's house, though permission is required. In one county we visited, the agency requires foster parents to seek permission before a child can have his hair cut.

Workers acknowledge that it is easy for kin to be confused. On the one hand, kin foster parents are told to treat the child like their own, but on the other, regulations force parents to constantly check in. Kin are often hostile with agency workers because they feel they are doing the agency a favor and that the agency should step back and let them care for the child.

Finally, many kin find the licensing process intrusive and demeaning. They ask why they have to be fingerprinted to care for their own grandchild.

"They always say, 'Why can't I spank them? I was raised that way.'" (California foster care worker)

"We have this uncle that is saying 'Why do you have to know what color my underwear are?'" (Connecticut foster care supervisor)

"Non-relatives, they expect their lives will be looked into more, because they are not a relative and they are responsible for providing care for some other children, but relatives may feel that 'This is my family, why are you probing into my life? I'm just here to help this child.'" (Indiana foster care worker)

Because kin typically have not been foster parents before, they often have a very limited understanding of the child welfare system and what to expect from the agency and the court. They do not understand how involved the agency will be—that workers will be conducting home visits and checking up on children. Kin are often resentful of agency workers telling them how to raise a child, especially when young social workers without children of their own are the ones coming to their home. Kin are surprised by the number of different workers who may be involved. Kin often do not understand the timing of events in the system. They do not understand how long the child will be in their care: Some think it will be forever, when actually reunification is planned; others think it will be short term, when in reality reunification is unlikely. Workers noted that many kin think they have custody of the child when they do not. By contrast, Alabama workers, who typically make voluntary placements of children with kin, said that kin often mistakenly think the agency has custody.

> "We are very intrusive, and I don't think they know how intrusive we will be when the child is placed there. Because let's say the aunt gets a boyfriend and the boyfriend moves in, we have to get the date of birth, check DCF [Department of Children and Families], check criminal records. I don't think they [relatives] understand how intrusive they [Child Protective Services (CPS)] will be, because maybe they would think twice or three times if they did know." (Connecticut investigative worker)

> "Another thing the relative really fails to understand and accept is that we advocate for them to get custody of children so that we can get out of the picture as fast as possible. A lot of them don't want us out of the picture, which can create a lot of problems. They think we can finance them forever, when we cannot." (Alabama foster care worker)

> "A lot of their role is passive; they find they are not as empowered as they think they might be. Ultimately, the decisions are made by the court and the social worker. We like to get information from them, and we don't share perhaps as often as we should or involve them in the decisionmaking as much as possible. That is oftentimes a complaint on their part that no one is listening to them, that it isn't in the best interests of the child, and they find that it isn't up to them. Their role is to be the surrogate parent with little input. Courts follow the social worker's recommendations. We can't afford extensive contact with the family, and our system isn't designed to mediate with them as much as we would like." (California investigative supervisor)

> "They [kin caregivers] come in with a good heart and wanting to care for the children. They have a true concern for the kids but don't understand the legality—that we are legally responsible. A

lot of the time they feel, 'I'm his relative, I make those decisions.' They don't understand that they have to report to us and that we are the ones that make the ultimate decisions. There's a lot of stuff where, I don't know if they're not told when they become a foster parent or if they just don't understand it, or what." (Connecticut foster care worker)

Finally, kin often do not understand how big a burden caring for a related child will be on them, both financially and emotionally. They tend to focus initially on what it takes to simply meet the basic needs of food and shelter and less on the long-term impact. Many kin have difficulty accepting the uncertainty about the long-range plans.

"They say 'It's gonna be easy, it's not going to be a problem.' This is one thing I've heard over the years—that it's not a problem. That's what scares me about relatives—that it's not a problem—it *is* a problem and how you deal with it is the key. Here we always talk about 'three hots and a cot,' as if with a kid all you have to do is feed them and give 'em a place to sleep. And I think that our people sometimes get into that modality. All we need to do is feed 'em, give 'em clothes, get them to school, and they'll be fine." (California investigative supervisor)

"I think they go in wanting to help their family, but they are thinking short-term. I think they're thinking, 'Okay, I'll help them for three months and then they'll be back in the home.' And even though it's explained to them that this may be a six-month process, in the back of their minds they're still thinking he'll be back in the home in three months. And I think that's where the stressors come in, when they're dealing with little Johnny one-on-one and they're thinking, 'Oh, what did I get myself into? I don't think I can deal with this for another three months.'" (Indiana investigative worker)

What Workers Tell Kin Foster Parents

The information that child welfare workers provide to kin varies greatly. Often they fail to provide needed information, and sometimes they provide incorrect or misleading information. There are many reasons why kin are not well informed. Some have to do with the relatives themselves, some with worker knowledge or motivation, and some with difficulties in communication between workers and relatives.

The amount of information kin receive varies greatly, depending upon the workers involved in the case. Foster care workers note that one problem they face is that they do not know what investigative workers have told kin. While foster care workers feel that the investigative workers should provide kin with certain information, investigative workers reported that they have so little time to spend with kin that they often provide little or no information. In Indiana and Connecticut, licensing workers (who become involved following investigation and placement) have greater contact with kin but report that they leave it up to the investigative and foster care workers to inform kin of agency policies. Agency policies about what information should be provided are vague, according to workers, and add to the variability in what workers tell kin. Many workers noted the need for better guidelines about how to work with kin to inform them of agency rules and regulations.

> "We have a lot of word of mouth—a lot of problems, since there is no set policy on how we pay things. We pay a lot of stuff for families to keep them stable. If they go to another worker, they may have a lot of restrictions from their supervisor, and payment—it is based on what the supervisor feels they should have. They want those services and they feel like they need unlimited resources. They know what you've given someone else, and they expect the same thing." (Alabama foster care worker)

> "I also believe it's the worker's approach. It's the worker who has the time and the energy, the sensitivity to be able to communicate to that relative caretaker that these are the expectations. This is what we look for, this is how it's done, and this is what will happen next. It depends on how many referrals I have to go to after I do this particular one. The majority of our emergency response referrals happen after 3 p.m., so my workers are out in the community placing or at least assessing referrals at 8, 9, 10 o'clock at night every day. If I have three or four referrals under my belt, and I've got to place this particular child, how much time can I really spend with you to discuss the expectations when I've got referrals I've got

to see and it's already 8 p.m.? This happens every day." (California investigative supervisor)

"It's dependent upon how the child came into custody. If they came in through the command post (after hours), they [after-hours workers] don't do a real good job of informing them [relatives]. ER [emergency response unit] workers don't always have time to give relatives a lot of information about their expectations. Some relatives know the score—if this is the seventh baby they have gotten from the parent, they know what's going on. It's difficult to really have the time to explain the process." (California foster care supervisor)

"A lot of the time we are not the social worker that did the initial placement into the relative's home. We get a case and it [placement] has already been done. You don't know where the relative is as far as different things [information received]. Every social worker is different in what they tell the relative. That is why uniform training would help, so you know what the relatives were taught up front." (Connecticut foster care worker)

"Part of it depends on who does placement (emergency services or a case manager). If [emergency services] does the placement, the relative doesn't know what the expectations are, and it requires follow-through from the case manager with the relative agreement and everything." (Indiana foster care worker)

Some workers feel they do enough and that kin do not understand because they choose not to. However, the majority of workers and administrators admit that they do not do a good job of informing kin. Kin are typically given written information and asked to sign forms, but workers do not often sit down and explain what is in these materials. Many kin felt like the agency kept secrets from them. They claimed that the agency told them their responsibilities—what they had to do and what they couldn't do—but nobody told them what their rights were, what they could expect in terms of help from the agency.

"My perspective is that we've always known that we probably have not done as good a job as we could have with relative caregivers—even though we think we give them a lot of information." (California administrator)

"They think it's ridiculous. Most, because we don't explain it well, they don't understand and see it as bureaucracy. I think some of it is ridiculous. It's not family friendly. It probably doesn't make sense to use policy and procedure in some areas with relatives. We don't sit down with relatives or foster parents and talk with them about what the agency does. There may be an expectation that we do this, but there is no time to do this." (California administrator)

"They fill out some forms and get very little information about what is available. They get a telephone number to call with questions." (California foster care worker)

"It varies on how much information they got at the beginning of the case and who their social worker is, because some feel absolutely clueless. I've gone to some meetings through the kinship center with some of their representatives and they've said they've been very frustrated that there's not a system set up to transfer information to them like there is to foster parents, that there's not a licensing process that they go through where they're handed a handbook that says this is what you can and can't do. So what happens, they're never told sometimes—if their social worker doesn't inform them—that they can't leave the state if they want to without getting permission from the court, and that kind of thing. There is a relative handbook, but most don't know about it and most haven't received the information verbally either, so it varies." (California family unity worker)

"Our relative caregivers get nothing other than what the social workers and placement specialists tell them. It is a very small piece of what licensed foster parents get." (California placement specialists)

"CPS is working on an emergency basis, and they're not spending the time necessary for the relatives to understand. It's not just child care; they're expected to show up for case conferences, sign off on things, have input, [and] must attend court, counseling. We're trying to salvage placements. We spend a lot of time in children's services going over things, and the relatives say, 'They never told me' and then we're trying to salvage placements, so we don't have to find foster care placements, especially for troubled kids." (Indiana foster care worker)

Some workers acknowledged that kin often receive misinformation from the agency. Sometimes this is because workers themselves do not know agency policies. In addition, since there may not be set agency policies, workers promise assistance they later discover they cannot deliver. A few workers also suggested that their agency might intentionally mislead kin to get them to care for a child. Workers in Alabama and Connecticut noted that when they arrange a voluntary placement, they might have the birth parents sign a relative agreement that gives kin temporary custody. These agreements are sometimes intentionally vague, so birth parents think that they are under agency order and must comply, when, in fact, this is a voluntary placement.

> "The CPS had a case transferred to me. The family was promised all these things—it is taking me half the time I am spending on the case to straighten out the myths that CPS put there. That just needs to be cleaned prior to the transfer. That's the biggest problem I have. And then the children end up suffering, because the families then say that they can't have them there and that was the only reason they accepted the children, and the children end up going to new places. I really hate it, but I know that they would not be there if they [the relatives] had been told the truth at first." (Alabama foster care worker)

> "We don't tell people the whole truth, because we don't want them to run away, we want to keep them. We hope they'll just 'get it' when the child is placed, but it doesn't always work." (Connecticut foster care supervisor)

Workers noted that they often have difficulty communicating with relatives. Kin typically receive children without notice and are emotional, almost in shock, and may not hear what workers are trying to tell them. Many kin also start out with misinformation about what child welfare is, and these myths must be identified and overcome before these caregivers can learn agency policies. Kin often do not read the materials that workers give them, sometimes due to language or literacy barriers. Workers also noted how complicated the system is and how much they are asking kin to absorb. In addition, relatives may have their own dysfunction that does not become apparent right away. Some kin simply do not believe what workers are telling them. They think they know the child and the parents better. Many are in denial, especially about the length of time the child may stay with them. Some kin are depressed or face other mental health challenges. At the same time, workers noted that some kin have already been foster parents, having cared for another child of the birth parent or the child of another relative.

"The family is in the middle of a crisis. It's just like any other crisis—you don't think. You're not thinking at that time. Someone's sticking something in your face and saying 'sign this' and 'read this.' They're talking and you're not hearing those words. In a crisis, you're not hearing those words." (California administrator)

"It takes us [caseworkers] more than two years to learn everything, and we expect these people to just know all of it. I didn't believe that it would take me that long to learn everything, but I am still learning. And we expect these well-intentioned people to pick it up in no time." (Connecticut foster care worker)

Involving Kin in Case Planning

Workers acknowledged that kin can be a valuable resource in developing a case plan and in the broader case planning process. Moreover, respondents in each site noted that local policy and guidance is consistent with state policies, which call for equal involvement of kin and non-kin in case planning. In practice, kin sometimes have greater involvement in case planning than do other foster parents, but often they have less input. Workers described ways in which they approach case planning differently with kin.

In every site we visited, administrators, supervisors, workers, and court personnel agreed that the case planning process is no different for children placed in kin versus non-kin foster care. Workers are required to invite both kin and non-kin foster parents to conferences in which case plans are developed or updated. Both types of foster parents are invited to attend court hearings and may be asked to provide input into court reports or at the hearings.

Several workers noted that, because of kin caregivers' prior history with the child and typically with the birth parent, they may have valuable input during case planning, and seeking out their assistance is good social work practice. In addition, workers suggested reasons why kin were sometimes *more* involved in case planning. Workers pointed out that kin are more invested emotionally with the child and are more apt to advocate that the agency meet the child's needs. In addition, workers suggested that kin were more motivated than non-kin to ensure that the needs of birth parents were being met.

"It's good social work practice to include them [kin caregivers] in planning for the child." (Connecticut foster care worker)

"The perspective of the relative is different from the foster parent on what kids need. Foster parents expect you to tell them what the child needs and what you are going to do to meet it. Relatives have a different perspective or way to meet the need than what DHR [Department of Human Resources] can do. They are more active in telling us what the child needs, they see the whole family process, dealing more with the family dynamics. The foster parents focus more on basic needs, such as clothing and food." (Alabama foster care worker)

"Relatives are more in touch with the child's needs, because they have such a history with them. The foster parent does not have such a history with them and looks to us for more guidance." (Alabama foster care worker)

"They [kin caregivers] have insights that others might not because of their role in the family." (Connecticut foster care worker)

"Relatives will tell you when other family members are not willing to help. Relatives are more readily willing to call and tell you what is going on overall." (California foster care worker)

"Sometimes the relative caregivers know a little bit more about the family or will tell us a little bit more." (California foster care worker)

"The relative works as an informant to the worker—crucial information can be provided by them—because the relative knows the mom." (California foster care worker)

Many workers noted reasons or circumstances under which kin are not much engaged in the case planning process and may be less involved than non-kin foster parents. Workers in several locations noted that kin are not always invited to administrative case reviews (ACRs), even though policy requires it. Workers in Bridgeport and Hartford counties in Connecticut and Marion County in Indiana specifically mentioned that, historically, kin were often neglected in the case planning process and cited recent changes to ensure their involvement. Workers in several sites noted that both kin and non-kin foster parents may have little involvement in case planning until reunification has been ruled out and the agency is seeking an alternative permanency option.

In addition, several workers noted that ACRs and court hearings are held during the day, and many kin have difficulty attending because they work. The most cited reason for kin not participating fully in the case planning process was their lack of knowledge or understanding of the process. Workers noted that kin did not understand the purpose of case plan review meetings. Other kin, workers suggest, believe the planning process is a formality and that they do not have any real input. Many workers understood this reaction, noting that the courts set the official case plan, but that kin do have greater input in the broader case planning process. Finally, workers noted that children are sometimes placed with non-kin first, and that a case plan has already been developed when kin begin caring for the children and thus they do not have input until the case plan is reviewed.

"Relatives are not invited to that [case review]. They should be, but they are not. There was a big thing where relatives were supposed to be invited to the case review at their leisure; if they [relatives] needed to do it in the evening, then arrangements would be made to do so. This is not happening. They want the relative foster parents to come to these things, but the people who do them [case reviews] are not willing to do them after hours." (Connecticut licensing workers)

"We haven't always included relatives in the case plan conference. Now they are invited." (Indiana administrator)

"I think that it is the exception to the rule if you do have a relative included. Usually it's the parent and the social worker that sit down and come up with what needs to happen.... It's changing, though; it's supposed to be changing, according to the way we're supposed to do the ACRs now ... you will be working with caretakers more." (Connecticut foster care supervisor)

"A lot of relatives just think that this is all a formality, it's you all's job, it has nothing to do with them, they're just caring for the kids. It's an inconvenience to be at court hearings, and they really don't think they have any major input, because you've already made the decisions up front." (Indiana foster care worker)

"[Relatives will say to workers] 'The court's just going to do what you say anyway, so what's the point?'" (Indiana foster care worker)

"The case plan is based on the court orders, and there is not room for innovation." (California foster care supervisor)

Workers suggested that beyond more or less involvement in case planning, they might involve kin in a different way than non-kin foster parents are involved. In all of our study states, workers noted that when children are placed with kin, case workers discuss permanency options with kin earlier in the placement. Workers do not want to get non-kin foster parents' hopes up about the possibility of adoption, but they frequently ask kin about their willingness to care for a child permanently early on in the process. Some workers suggested that kin's willingness to permanently care for a child was a factor in deciding whether to place a child with kin. Some workers also suggested that they were more willing to discuss the specific challenges faced by birth parents with kin and to seek their assistance in working with the birth parents. Case planning is completely different in Alabama, however, because most children placed with kin are not taken into state custody. Workers in Alabama treat kin placements as in-home service cases rather than foster care. In these cases, kin are treated more like birth parents than foster parents in the case planning process.

"I think they're probably more involved. I think the workers probably feel freer to discuss the case—there's a different comfort level around how much can be shared or how much can the relatives be involved than there is with foster parents." (California administrator)

Many child welfare agencies around the nation, including those in four of the study sites (Los Angeles, San Diego, and Santa Clara counties in California and Marion County in Indiana), have adopted specialized case planning models to involve kin more. These models, often called family group decisionmaking, family group conferencing, or family unity meetings, seek to involve the entire extended family in developing the case plan in child protection cases. Family members structure and direct case planning meetings, assisted by a trained facilitator. The meetings are designed to identify how family strengths and resources can address the needs of the child and birth parent under protective supervision and determine the best placement options for the child. Workers in sites that have tried such models believed they were having impressive results.

> "Social workers have changed their positions about the case as a result of these meetings. When they said, 'Oh, wait a minute, this family is pretty functional,' they've come up with ideas that I didn't even think about, and I'm willing to change my recommendations." (California family group decisionmaking worker)

Worker Supervision of Children

When it comes to supervision of foster care placements, just as with case planning, respondents in each site noted that local policy and guidance is consistent with their state policies, which call for equal supervision of kin and non-kin placements. However, workers stressed that the amount of supervision they provide depends upon the circumstances of a particular case. Thus, to the extent that kin care for different types of children, there may be differences in the level of supervision they receive. In practice, many workers noted that they provide less supervision of kin placements, and some workers commented that kin were more difficult to supervise than were other foster placements.

In each of the study sites, minimum requirements for contact for both kin and non-kin placements were similar, although the frequency of contact required in each state varied widely. For example, in terms of child monitoring, caseworkers are required to make face-to-face contact with children in kin and traditional foster care every three months in Mobile, Alabama, every two months in all three Indiana localities, but monthly in most other locations. Workers explained that contact minimums for visiting caregivers do not always mirror child visitation minimums, since visits with the children often take place in settings outside the home, including schools, day care, and so on. For example, in Marion County, Indiana, where a child is monitored at least once every two months, there is no standard at all for visiting caregivers.

Many localities, however, employ telephone contact to supplement face-to-face contact.

In practice, workers suggested several reasons why they often have less contact with kin than with other foster parents. Some workers suggested that kin placements are seen as safer, since kin have a greater emotional investment in the children they care for. Many workers noted that they often pay closer attention to cases in which foster parents are contacting them—"the squeaky wheel get the grease"—and kin appear much less likely to contact workers for assistance (see chapter 5). Workers argue that kin want less contact. Workers also noted that they provide minimal supervision of children in long-term foster care, and children in kinship care are more likely than children in traditional foster care to have this permanency goal. In California, few kin foster children but many non-kin foster children are placed with private family foster care agencies, which provide greater supervision than the public agency workers can provide.

> "It's a big difference, I'm going to be honest. I think the workers have less contact with relatives. We are mandated to have contact with them monthly. But I think when we know we have a situation that is going well, we tend to have less contact, because they're handling it. If she [the caregiver] needs me, she has my phone number and can contact me. We just kind of move on, since that's going well." (Alabama foster care supervisor)

> "Workers feel more secure knowing their children are with relatives. You don't worry about that case as much. They just feel that the family member is going to do whatever needs to be done, and generally that's the case. Usually they handle it." (Alabama foster care supervisor)

> "I am more apt to leave them [the relatives] alone and be less of an aggravation to them." (Connecticut ongoing worker)

> "Sometimes it's a little more natural to become more lax with a relative. I don't think you see it the same sometimes . . . because they are with family." (Connecticut supervisor)

> "I have a whole lot of relative placements, and they just do whatever they think is appropriate—they might call me, they may not. And basically, I do not monitor every decision they make—

whereas [with] a regular foster parent, I would." (Alabama foster care worker)

"If the child is with a relative, most of the time they are perceived as better off than they would be with a foster parent. When I was taught—the rule is that you always have to check up on the foster parent." (California foster care supervisor)

"They [CPS workers] also, possibly, have the tendency to feel that the relative home is safer than the parents' home . . . or the foster home, because it is a relative, and we know relatives are going to take good care of their kin." (Connecticut foster care supervisor)

"If it's a relative we trust . . . I don't think we monitor at the same level." (Indiana court contact)

Some workers suggested that kin may be more difficult to supervise and should receive greater supervision than non-kin foster parent receive. While non-kin foster parents expect that case workers will be conducting home visits and meeting with children in school or elsewhere, kin may see this as a lack of trust and an intrusion into their private lives. Workers said it is often hard to assess the motivation of kin, their relationship with the birth parents, and how the family dynamics may impact the safety of a child. Workers also noted that kin often do not follow agency rules and regulations. Kin may not see themselves as foster parents and feel that they do not have to follow agency rules. They also may simply be unaware of agency regulations, since they typically do not attend foster parent training.

"We might need to be creative with relative care at times. Because the relatives are going to have a lot more influence from the biological family that we are not going to be aware of. Sometimes that influence is going to be negative. We may need workers to go to some homes once a week instead of once a month." (Alabama foster care worker)

Supervising Visitation

In general, child welfare agencies expect more of kin with regard to supervising the visits that birth parents have with their children. Both kin and non-kin foster parents may supervise such visits, but workers in each of the study sites stressed that they much more often rely on kin to supervise visits. This is largely due to the willingness of kin to supervise and the usual unwillingness of non-kin foster parents to have such contact with birth parents.

While kin typically supervise parent-child visits, there are times when they are not expected to do so. Some agency respondents reported holding parent-child visits in the office rather than in the relative's home at the start of a placement. Others mentioned certain case circumstances that would result in the agency supervising visitation.

"What we try to do is to have the visits start in the office, so it's set up more like a foster parent basis. And then when things improve, schedule visits at home with the relative. This way it's easier for them [the relatives] to take on the role of a foster parent as opposed to grandparent or aunt. It seems to help; [it] gives them [the birth parent] a message." (Connecticut foster care supervisor)

"Depends upon what you're dealing with. I have a relative case where they [the relatives] are cooperative, but I don't let mom visit with the child alone, because it's a drug case. Most of them [drug cases] are supervised to start with." (Alabama foster care worker)

"Usually visitation is monitored at first. If relatives get along, I allow discretion and don't put any restrictions on it, and [they] can do it at their convenience. With relatives it does not need to be structured as long as the visits are monitored [by the relative]." (California foster care worker)

"A lot of time when a child is placed with an aunt or uncle, I will encourage that we [the agency] do the visitation, because I think sometimes the relative who is doing the foster parenting gets caught in the social problems that the mother or father has, and that's only going to add more to the stress on the relative, and they're more likely to come to us and say, 'I can't do this, take the child back.' I think sometimes up front it's better for a third party to do this [visitation]." (Connecticut administrator)

When a child is living with kin, parent-child visitation is far less structured than when a child is placed with a traditional foster parent. Agency respondents noted that non-kin foster parents are usually not willing to give up their weekends for parent-child visits. In addition, non-kin are often caring for children from different families and have to adhere to visitation plans for each child, necessitating scheduled visitation. States vary in terms of how structured parent-child visitation is when the child is living with kin. In Alabama, unlike the other three states, the degree of formality depends in large part on whether the agency has custody of the child. If the agency does not have custody and safety is not an issue, then the agency may not address visitation with the family.

In one local office in Indiana, respondents noted that both kin and non-kin foster parents can receive a slight increase in the board payment if they supervise visitation. In a local office in Connecticut, investigative workers noted that recent regulations call for non-kin foster parents to have birth parent visits in their homes as well, without the agency's supervision unless there are clear reasons for it. Not all workers agreed that this regulation was realistic.

"I disagree with that. I think it's unrealistic for us to expect foster parents to have crack-addicted criminals in their home. It is altruistic at the highest level to be a foster parent. . . . To expect that DCF [is] going to have good recruitment [of foster parents] and demand that [birth] parents come to these people's homes is unrealistic. Strategically ridiculous." (Connecticut investigative worker)

Many respondents noted the benefit of having kin schedule and supervise visits, as it translates into less legwork for the worker. The typical foster care worker has a caseload of 20 or more families, which may mean 50 or more children. Making logistical arrangements to ensure that all of the birth parents have an opportunity to visit with their children (who are often in multiple foster homes) places a large burden on a caseworker's time. When kin can make such arrangements and supervise visits, workers have more time for other important duties.

"Life is good with grandma and she's a big help with visitation. [The relatives have] done all the visitation, they supervise visits, they do all the transportation for dad and the kid, a big strain off of me." (California foster care worker)

"We have a shortage of visitation supervisors. We'd have to go to our resources here, so if relatives will do it [supervise visitation], it makes it a lot easier on the whole system." (California foster care worker)

"I'm always glad when we can place with a relative. Sometimes they monitor visitation. You don't have to worry about transporting to visits, relatives will do that." (California supervisor)

"I usually try to solicit their help [to have visitation in their homes]. One less thing for us to do. If they have a good relationship with the parent, we ask them about how they would feel about handling the visit, are they afraid or worried, would they feel comfortable." (Connecticut foster care worker)

Birth parent visitation is an essential component of all case plans in which the goal for the child is reunification. A judge is unlikely to agree to reunify a child with his or her parent unless the parent has shown commitment to the child and improved parenting skills, as demonstrated by frequent and successful visitation. Moreover, such visits give birth parents an opportunity to reconnect and to develop a healthy relationship with their child. Respondents noted that children who live with relatives visit with their birth parents more frequently and for longer periods of time.

"That's the chance we take when we place [the child] with a relative. Relative care gives them the best chance of seeing their parents. Who's to say that that is bad or good." (Alabama foster care worker)

"But when it comes to reunification, I always feel better when [a child is] with a relative, because they can give more access to the parent, because they know the parent. The visitation aspect usually is not an issue. I know that they are going to be visiting a lot." (California continuing worker)

"The child gets a chance to see the parent more often when they are with a relative. Because mom can drop by any day, any time, and most of the times, the relatives will allow them to visit unplanned. With foster care you have to call and arrange the date and time. And if the mom, for one reason or another, does not show up, she has to wait another two weeks or a month before she can make another appointment to see her child." (Alabama foster care supervisor)

"Family will allow family to stay all day. Sit at the table and eat, be comfortable. A lot of time foster parents, because it [visitation] is here in the office or at an assigned meeting place, they only have an hour. Also, most foster parents have more than one child and they may have other things going on." (Alabama foster care supervisor)

"I have a couple cases in my unit where the child is placed with the grandparents and the grandparents have an open-door policy for their son or daughter to come in. The child is maintaining almost constant contact with the parents." (Alabama foster care supervisor)

"Any time you have greater contact, yes, you have those problems of the family politics, but there is also a higher likelihood of communication." (California foster care supervisor)

"Sometimes the hope is that visits are one hour weekly. With relatives sometimes we allow them to extend it [the visit] as long as the relatives supervise carefully. Sometimes relatives are more willing to allow frequent phone contact. It's harder with foster parents as they have their own schedule, managing several children. That's a plus I've enjoyed with relatives." (California foster care supervisor)

Caseworkers Receive Less Feedback from Kin-Supervised Visitation

While visitation is important for birth parents to achieve reunification, visits are also an opportunity to assess how birth parents are doing generally, and especially how well they are interacting with their children. If caseworkers supervise visits, they can assess for themselves the progress parents are making, though one can wonder if the structure and artificial nature of these visits undermines the validity of those observations. If someone else is supervising the visit, the caseworker must rely on that person to provide such feedback. Though respondents acknowledged the assistance that relatives provide in supervising birth parent visitation, they noted that relative supervision of parent-child visitation often means less feedback on how well the visits are going. Visits not supervised by the caseworker that involve children living with non-kin foster parents are less of a problem, since the children see their birth parents at a visitation center or at the agency's office where documentation of the visit is provided to the worker.

"The big difference is when we call for supervised visitation. If [the] child is with a foster parent, the supervised visitation would always occur at a visitation center and an official report would be made. No official report [would be made] when a relative is supervising a visit." (California continuing worker)

"[We] hold relatives to a lower standard for this [supervising visitation]. Foster parents can also choose to supervise visits in their own home, but they have to fill out the paperwork, and with relatives, we just let them do it and we don't know what's going on." (Indiana continuing worker)

"We'll allow the relative to supervise visits in their own home. Lots more flexible but open to a lot more potential for [the] relative not reporting back to you." (Indiana continuing worker)

"She [the birth parent] might come drunk or high to the visit, and because it's a relative supervising, you don't know that. At a visitation site, you'd get a note back saying the parent came intoxicated." (Indiana continuing worker)

"They [relatives] are more likely to hide things from you, like when mom comes [to visit] under the influence. Well, they might not want to tell the worker, because that means she [the mother] might not get her kids back." (California investigative supervisor)

"In one of my cases the only thing I can really do is ask that the maternal aunt let me know whenever the mother comes for a visit. The mother comes over to visit quite often, and sometimes the aunt remembers to tell me and sometimes she doesn't; sometimes she remembers what happened during the visit, sometimes she doesn't. It's a family environment and it is natural." (California continuing worker)

"I try to use them [relatives], but sporadically have them [the birth parents] go to the [visitation] center so that I get a report as to how the visit went—an objective view." (California continuing worker)

While agency respondents noted that visits that occur in a visitation center or at the agency allow for better documentation and feedback, caregivers had another view of visitation centers. Kin often did not feel that these centers did a good job of either supervising birth parents or providing feedback.

"Mine [my visits] were poorly supervised. She'd [the birth mother] go to the phone instead of visiting with her kids. The person that was supposed to be supervising would be called to do something, so they [the visits] were poorly supervised. They'd use my notes for court . . . the number of visits, how many times they came." (Indiana relative caregiver)

It was clear to many respondents that relatives need training on how to supervise visits, and there was concern that relatives were not skilled in monitoring parent-child interactions, particularly with regard to healthy parent-child behaviors. Kin may feel they want to give the parent and child privacy. Workers noted that kin do not understand that supervision of a visit requires them to be in the same room, listening and watching the interactions.

"I treat it [visitation] differently [with kin] in the sense that I have to explain what a monitored visit is, and I have to go into detail with the relative about how they need to protect the child and watch them. With foster parents I don't have to do this." (California foster care worker)

"Relatives don't know what to look for either. The parents could be on time [for the visit] and not on drugs or anything, but also not even touch the child." (Indiana continuing worker)

"Relatives are not trained on how to supervise visits. They don't understand what to look for. As well, the information we receive [from relatives] is biased." (California continuing worker)

"No one explained what supervised visits means. We thought it meant that we had to be in the house, not in the same room." (California relative caregiver)

Relatives may also allow inappropriate birth parent visits. Administrators noted situations in which relatives think the birth parent is doing better, so they allow more visits without consulting the worker. In addition, staff members expressed concern that children are not adequately protected when visits occur frequently and are not supervised by the agency. Many respondents mentioned that relatives have difficulty understanding the need to protect the child from a family member and may feel pressure from other family members to allow parents to visit.

"They think they know their relative better than you do and think the agency is just being way too protective and think there's no reason why the birth mom can't take the children for the afternoon. And then the worker goes out and finds out that every Sunday mom's been taking the kids because the aunt thinks mom is doing much better now." (Connecticut administrator)

"That's funny, because when I was a worker that was always the question I would ask relatives: 'What are you going to do on a nice Sunday afternoon when mom says she just wants to take her kids to McDonald's?' It puts the relative in a tough situation, and I think it's the ongoing worker's responsibility to get the relative to understand this balance. It's not always an easy task." (Connecticut administrator)

"The level of protection is my biggest concern with relative placements with young children. I have a lot of drug babies on my caseload and a lot of grandparent placements. I have three or four right now that are real shaky and I question whether or not the grandparent can protect the child from the parent . . . they [birth mothers] explain away these babies' symptoms to grandma, because she hasn't had experience caring for a drug-addicted baby." (California foster care worker)

"Some of the concerns I have with kinship placement is one, the protection. Are they [the relative] going to keep the child away from the alleged perpetrator, whether they be mom, dad, or whoever? I know it's up to the ongoing worker to keep an eye on that. I think they [the relatives] need as much support, if not more, initially than the foster parents do. Intensive services in the home, the counseling. Sometimes they are a little resistant to going to that. They think the kids are fine. But I think they need to work on it as a family." (Indiana investigative worker)

"I have the same issue with failing to protect child from birth parent . . . mom, who's not supposed to be in the home, answers the phone. I can't camp outside the house to make sure that doesn't happen." (California ongoing worker)

"Relatives are torn between [their] children and grandchildren, to make the right decision for their grandchildren when they know their children are not doing the right thing. Some become fearful of their kids, some are afraid of what they [the birth parents] may do if they do not allow them to come to the house anymore." (Connecticut foster care worker)

"[I had a] case recently . . . grandmother gave back grandson, because her son can't come over. He was getting irate with her. Emotionally it was too much. It's a very touchy aspect of relative placement." (Connecticut licensing worker)

"I had a case where the son was violent and on drugs and the grandmother could not say 'no' to him coming over. Ultimately it came down to 'You either stand up for yourself and do not let him into this house or we are going to have to take the child.'" (Connecticut foster care worker)

Agency respondents spoke of recent cases in which they struggled to get the relative to understand the agency's intent and case plan. Workers pointed to the need to be clear about boundaries when children are placed with relatives. They also discussed their views on why this difficulty exists with relative placements. Some relative caregivers understood what was expected of them, but were quite blunt about having a view of parent-child visitation different from the agency's view.

"We had a case in which the father severely abused the infant and the child almost died. The investigative worker placed the baby with the maternal grandparents and I wondered about it at the time: 'Does the grandmother get it [that the father is not to have contact with the baby]?' The grandmother is asking why we're doing this, because her son-in-law's a regular guy. Here we've [the agency] put her in the position of not just caring for the child— clearly she and her husband are providing wonderful care to the child—but was this a good idea to place the baby with them, since no one in the family is 'on board' with the fact that this man should never be a part of this baby's life?" (California foster care worker)

"We need to be very clear about the boundaries. That the kid is in our care. I know it is your sister or I know it is your brother, but the kids can't be alone with them, and if we find out that they are, we will have to remove them. I have a sheet of paper that is a list of basic expectations about who they [the children] can talk to on the phone, what to do if you want to go out of the state, emergency phone numbers, what to do in case of injury, things they would have learned in regular foster care cases. They don't know any of that." (Connecticut foster care worker)

"With non-kin foster parents, the boundaries are real clear. Maybe they get this in their training, maybe [it's] just that they don't usually have a relationship with the parents to begin with. Relatives, it's different. Their understanding of the boundaries is not very clear. They may think they know the boundaries, but not when you consider it in the framework of the system." (California investigative worker)

"Even if they [relatives] know there's court-ordered supervised visitation, they won't always listen. They say it hurts them too bad to do what the court order said." (Alabama foster care worker)

"I just don't think it comes naturally for a relative to 'get it' that they need to protect the child from the offender, a family member." (Connecticut foster care supervisor)

"It's human nature to allow parents to see their kids. They'll say, 'I don't care what the judge says.' It's a cultural thing to let the parents see them. It's the American way of life." (Alabama foster care worker)

"My sister sees her kids whenever she wants to with no problem. They [the child welfare agency] said that they [the birth parents] are not allowed to see them [the children] . . . set up a visitation, but that's my sister, these are her kids, we're family, and she can see them whenever she wants to." (Indiana kin caregiver)

Kin May Prevent Parents' Access

For the most part, children living with kin visit frequently with their parents; however, many relatives do not approve of parent-child visitation. In each of the study states, some relatives who participated in our focus groups had negative reactions to parent-child visitation.[1] Relatives noted that children are often uncomfortable with visits and that visits may be good for parents but not for the children. Relatives spoke of parents who disappoint their children by coming late to visits or not showing up at all. Other relatives spoke of the disruption in children's behavior and children feeling responsible for the parent's circumstances.

> "Originally, we had contact with the [birth] mother because I knew her. It just didn't work. It was disrupting the child's behavior because she was telling him [lies]. I was trying to make him stable and she was making him unstable." (Connecticut kin caregiver)

> "The six-year-old has visits every month with his mom. He used to come back crying and all upset that he was going home for Christmas and that she [his mother] was halfway better. He was coming home all confused, and I have to try to mold him back, help him and console him, and you just can't do that every week." (Connecticut kin caregiver)

> "My kids have no contact. If she calls my house and she [the child] hears her mother's voice, the next week every day her teacher is calling me. So we have no contact. I had to cut if off completely. I had to put her in therapy." (Alabama kin caregiver)

> "This to me is the hardest part about kinship care . . . you not only have your daughter or your brother, it's a whole big family thing, and everyone has an opinion, and you want to create family harmony. What gets lost is what's best for the child, and that constant 'You have to see your dad once a week,' everything you've been working for, then it's gone, it is so traumatic, it's good for the parents but not good for the child." (California kin caregiver)

Another agency concern was that when children are placed with one set of relatives, either maternal or paternal, there could be problems in allowing the "other" birth parent to visit. Other concerns mentioned were related to when parents and related caregivers do not get along with each other.

> "In-laws can really be a problem if the kids are with mom's family and they don't want to engage fathers." (California continuing supervisor)

"Sometimes it [relative placement] makes visitation a lot easier. If it's the mother caring for her daughter's children, it is normally an easy visitation to arrange. But if [the] child is placed with paternal relatives, [they] may not like mom, sometimes for good reasons. But sometimes they will put up a lot of obstacles." (California continuing supervisor)

"[I have] one case where the mother and grandmother don't get along and the grandmother doesn't want to bring the children to the agency, so the children don't visit with the mother." (Alabama foster care worker)

"Relatives sometimes take into account how much contact they have to have with the [birth] parent. Sometimes they're estranged, or they just don't have a close relationship, or they've got a 'drudge' sister and they don't want her around. We have to let them know they need to cooperate with visitation. Even though we can offer visitation centers where the contact is limited, there still has to be phone contact." (California investigative supervisor)

"I have one relative care case that the mother can come visit any time she wants to, but the relative caregivers don't want the daddy in the house." (Alabama foster care worker)

Summary and Discussion

This study confirmed prior research that found that child welfare workers have different casework practices with kin and non-kin foster parents. Despite the fact that kin are typically unprepared for their role as foster parent, caseworkers often fail to provide kin with needed information, may provide misleading information, and report difficulties communicating with kin. Workers recognize the potential benefits of involving kin in case planning, given their prior knowledge of the child in care, yet report that kin often are not involved and in any event may be less involved than non-kin foster parents. Similarly, workers report that kin may require greater supervision, as they are more likely not to follow agency rules and procedures. Yet workers often provide less supervision of kinship placements. Workers rely much more on kin than non-kin foster parents to supervise visits that children in their care have with their birth parents. Children in kinship care appear to enjoy more frequent and informal contact with their birth parents than children in traditional foster care, but workers raised concerns about the ability of kin caregivers to effectively supervise visits.

Child welfare agencies need to develop strategies to better inform kinship caregivers of what is expected of them as foster parents and what they can expect from the agency and the courts. Because kin typically step in to help during a crisis, it is unlikely that kin will be well informed at first. Thus, agencies must work intensively with kin during the early stages of a placement to get them "up to speed." Simply referring kin to foster parent training is unlikely to help, since workers found that kin were unlikely to attend such training. Moreover, kin may not respond well to offers of training but may be interested in orientation meetings or support group meetings during which they can receive needed information.

Kin particularly need information and guidance in how to monitor birth parent visitation, including following court orders, what to look for in the interaction between birth parents and children, and how to provide feedback to caseworkers. Some locations pay kin to supervise visitation, and kin may be more open to receive training when they are paid and see supervision as an additional responsibility.

Child welfare agencies may want to consider training workers in how best to communicate with kin and use kin in the case planning process. Based on the results of this study, it appears that workers clearly understand the unique circumstances of kinship care placements and acknowledge the benefits that kin can offer in case planning. Yet workers also acknowledge having difficulty establishing and maintaining effective working relationships with kin. Agencies may need to be more flexible in their approach to working with kin. Workers in some agencies noted that they were able to get kin participating in case planning by holding meetings in the evening or on weekends and at locations more convenient to kin, such as local community agencies or churches. In some study sites, workers noted that court reports include a section for kinship caregivers to provide feedback and request assistance, and this ability has helped kin feel part of the decisionmaking process. By all accounts, family group decisionmaking–type models appear to be effective in empowering family members to identify problems, needs, and solutions.

By involving kin in the case planning process, workers should have a much better sense of kin's ability to ensure the safety of children in their care and the level of supervision workers must provide. Because of the family dynamics of kinship care placements, agencies may want to consider whether workers need to have greater face-to-face contact with kinship caregivers than they are expected to have with other foster parents. In addition, workers may need to supervise some visits between kin foster children and their birth parents in order to personally assess their interaction.

Critics of kinship care have raised concern about the safety of these placements, many citing the adage "the apple does not fall far from the tree," meaning that kin who raised abusive parents may be abusive themselves. While there is no research to support the claim that kin are more likely than non-kin foster parents to abuse children in their care, workers were concerned that kin may allow birth parents to have inappropriate access to their children, placing these children at risk. To ensure the safety of children, workers must do a better job of informing, involving, and supervising kinship foster parents.

NOTE

1. Relative caregivers who participated in our focus groups were generally relatives who had been taking care of the children for a number of years. While some of the children were likely to be reunified with the parent, for the most part, relative respondents did not appear confident that reunification would occur. Thus, it is not surprising we heard negative reactions to parent-child visitation.

5

Providing Services to Kinship Foster Care Families

Rob Geen

Child welfare agencies are responsible for ensuring that the children they place in foster care are cared for appropriately. Agencies may provide or refer children for a variety of services to meet their needs, including services that address issues arising from the abuse or neglect they suffered. Agencies also provide a variety of supports to foster parents in their effort to care for children. Kinship foster parents are different from non-kin foster parents in several ways and these differences may influence the services they, and the children they care for, need from child welfare agencies.

By definition, kin foster parents are related to the child they are caring for and typically have a relationship with the child and the child's parents. While experts argue that kinship caregivers are thus likely to have a special interest in the well-being of the child in their care, kin must often deal with a variety of family dynamics that non-kin foster parents do not face.

Kin are often not prepared to care for children. Unlike traditional foster parents, kin typically have not been licensed as foster parents or attended training on the roles and responsibilities of foster parents. Kin are also usually not physically prepared to take on parenting responsibilities. They may not have many things needed to care for children, including a crib or bed, a car seat, and toys. Moreover, their homes may not be "child proofed." Many kin are also not emotionally prepared for their new role. Since most kin are grandparents, they must, in addition to assuming new parenting responsibilities, also acknowledge the shortcomings of their own children as parents.

Kin characteristically have no experience with child welfare agencies. Unless they have been foster parents before, kin usually do not understand the child welfare system. They do not know what to expect from the child welfare caseworker, the courts, or other involved parties. Indeed, they may mistrust or fear the child welfare system.

As discussed in chapter 1, kin themselves are likely to face many challenges that most traditional foster parents avoid. Research has consistently shown that kinship foster parents are more likely to be single, poorer, older, and have less formal education than other foster parents. While the evidence is mixed, some studies have found that kin are more likely than other foster parents to be working. Kinship foster parents also more often report being in poor health. In addition, the children placed with kin may be different from those placed with non-kin foster parents. For example, research has shown that children in kinship foster care are younger than children in non-kin foster care. Children in kinship foster care are also more likely to have been removed from their parents' home due to neglect and to have been born to parents who were young, never married, and had a substance abuse problem.

This chapter examines how local child welfare agencies serve kinship foster care families and non-kin foster families differently. It examines how the needs of the two types of foster families differ, why caseworkers may offer fewer services to kin, why kin may request fewer services, and barriers that kin may experience in accessing services.

Needs of Kin versus Non-Kin Foster Parents

In all of our 13 study sites, workers, administrators, and kinship foster parents commented that kinship care families often have needs that differ from those of traditional foster families. Their different needs stem from the fact that, compared with non-kin foster parents, kin are more likely to be poor, working outside the home, older, less educated, unprepared for their new caregiving role, and isolated from others in the community. Workers also noted that since many kin try to take care of things without child welfare assistance, when they finally do ask for help, they are often in a crisis. Thus their needs are more immediate and intense. At the same time, workers pointed out that kin are quite a heterogeneous group and have varying needs, depending upon individual circumstances.

According to workers, the starkest difference between kin and non-kin foster parents is the level of financial assistance required. Few non-kin foster parents are poor. In most states, having sufficient income is a foster care licensing criterion.[1] However, kin are often in financial distress or are just getting by—even before they take on the responsibility of caring for a child.

> "It's more of a financial need with relatives; many are one step away from poverty. And you're not dealing with the regular foster parents who are poor, because they couldn't get licensed." (Connecticut foster care supervisor)

> "Finances play a big role with relatives. A lot of grandparents, their income is limited. Enter a sibling group of two or three and they have no transportation . . . even though DCF [Department of Children and Families] sends money to cover expenses, you see how limited they are to go to [the] grocery store or do activities. This is where we need to modify and add support to these families . . . maybe transportation by the state to assist these families." (Connecticut licensing worker)

> "When you fill out the application to be a foster parent, they won't really take you if you don't make a certain income. So really poor people aren't foster parents, but there are poor people who want to take care of their relative children, and poor people can be relative foster parents." (Alabama foster care worker)

> "The relative caretakers need more money. Foster parents automatically get paid by the agency, but with relatives it is pending whether or not they are going to get some kind of income. It takes three months before they get paid, and they don't get reimbursed for the money spent." (California investigative worker)

> "They [relatives] have financial needs. There is a big push to give the children to kin, no matter what the hardship on the kin is." (Alabama foster care worker)

In addition to needing financial help, workers noted that kin are more likely than other foster parents to need child care assistance. Workers found that non-kin foster parents are more likely to be married and often at least one parent is not working full-time outside the home. Thus, traditional foster parents often have less need for child care assistance.[2] Most kin are single (many are widows or widowers) and work outside the home. Given their already tenuous financial situation, kin have great difficulty locating child care they can afford. In several locations we visited, workers noted that they would open or keep open a child welfare case mainly as a way to secure child care assistance for kin.

Child care is also a bigger issue for kin because they typically take on the care of a child without advance warning and thus cannot secure child care beforehand. Kin reported great difficulty locating child care, even when they can afford it. Especially for younger children, there are often long waiting lists for affordable, center-based care. Many kin reported that they had to quit their jobs to take care of related children because they could not find child care assistance quickly.

Besides child care, kin face other challenges because they are not prepared for their new caregiving role. Kin often do not have furniture, toys, or other child-related items. Many do not have adequate space in their homes, especially when they agree to take in several siblings. In some states, kin may not be allowed to care for one or more children unless they have adequate space, and in other states, lack of space means they cannot be licensed and thus cannot receive a higher level of assistance.

"In some cases they [relatives] are accepting this child into their home and they don't even have the proper provisions—for example, car seats, cribs. They don't already have a license, they are not expecting the child, so they are not prepared. I came to a grandmother with two babies one night. She had nothing, because she didn't expect them, but she was running around caring for them. So I told her it was okay to put them in her bed for the night, and I would come back in the morning and help her get what she needed." (Connecticut investigative worker)

"A foster home is geared to accept a certain amount of children. If they take in three of our kids, they're not going to have to move out; babysitting is already set up. They know who to call if they need something. Their daily lives don't change, because they know what to expect. In a relative home, from today to tomorrow they now live a completely different way." (California investigative worker)

Another key difference between kin and non-kin foster parents is their relationship with the children's birth parents. Kin caregivers often need counseling services to help them deal with birth parents, their own feelings about parenting again, and their new relationship with their related children.

"They all need counseling, because they have to deal with the family of origin. Because if they are good and they have cut off all ties, we are bringing them back into the dysfunctional family and making them have contact. We need to help them deal with that." (California administrator)

"A big issue grandparents are talking about is parenting the second time around. Moving from grandparent to parent roles . . . turning on the mother [role]. They need layers and layers of support, and if we can give them what they need, we might be able to preserve even more homes. It takes more time." (Connecticut administrator)

"Relatives have different service issues: denial, loss have a big impact on how they see the case and move forward." (California administrator)

"I think they need help in setting boundaries with the [birth] parents." (California ongoing supervisor)

Because kin are often older and not well educated, workers and kin noted that they need more support in meeting children's educational needs and providing recreational opportunities. Several kin mentioned how hard it was for them to assist children with their homework and wanted to get tutoring help. Other kin questioned whether they were doing a good job as a foster parent, because their age limited the physical activities they could do with their children. And because of age and lack of transportation, workers noted that kin are often isolated from others in the community. While non-kin often interact with other foster parents through foster parent associations, kin rarely participate in such groups.

Most workers believe that these circumstances also mean that kin have greater needs, but a few argued that traditional foster parents have equal or greater needs. These workers said that having known the child before, kin are a step ahead of other foster parents.

"Regular foster parents are more needy because I think the commitment of the relative is a greater one and they are more tolerant of certain behaviors of the kid. We also have increased transcultural situations, where the foster parent is of a completely different race or culture from the child, and that is a brand new scenario that we haven't as an agency started to provide much more increased information or support for." (Connecticut investigative supervisor)

"Non-kin need more services than kin because they are not familiar with the child and there is no prior relationship." (Alabama administrator)

Fewer Services Offered to Kin Foster Families

In each of the sites we visited, caseworkers, supervisors, and administrators acknowledged that kinship foster parents were typically offered fewer services than traditional foster parents. While many provided some explanation of when and why certain kin receive fewer services, several workers noted that this was "just the way it is" and believed that all kin probably receive fewer services. Similarly, many kinship caregivers felt that the availability of services was hidden from them.

"It is more of a situation where you find a relative, put the kid in there, and see if the relative sinks or swims, and whatever happens, happens—as opposed to putting the child in there, build[ing] an alliance with the relative, and then [providing] appropriate referrals. That piece is missing." (Connecticut foster care worker)

"I doubt if workers are going down the list of services that can be offered to a relative, because unless you know they need it, you are not even going to mention what's out there." (Alabama foster care supervisor)

"What do relatives need? We don't have time to find out beyond complaints they have." (California foster care supervisor)

"I get the impression that the social worker is told to give out the least amount [of services] possible." (Alabama licensed kinship foster parent)

Many workers noted that they offered few services to kin *or* non-kin foster parents unless there was an obvious need. If foster parents did not ask for help, many workers assumed that they were doing fine. Many workers noted that they spend most of their time handling crises and thus have little time to assist foster parents who do not complain or seek out assistance.

> "I've had that experience as well. 'Amen' to what she said about fires getting all the attention and the quiet families getting ignored. I find that the quiet caretakers are usually the best . . . kids are doing fine. They are providing a higher level of care than the ones who are calling you and nickel and diming you to death about everything the child needs." (Alabama foster care supervisor)

> "Everyone breathes a sigh of relief when there's relatives available, but they don't get enough attention. They're a little lower on the list, because their case is more stable. Relatives don't call us and complain, because they want to keep the kid and they're committed." (California supervisor)

> "Historically, we haven't provided the same services to relatives. They want support. Historically, we have thought they are with a family and just kind of forget about them. We focus more on [non-kin] foster care kids." (Connecticut licensing worker)

> "If you don't know and you don't ask questions, you will never know. Come and get an application, because they are not going to give it to you. You have to do it yourself. . . . I have been thinking that they were doing that. I noticed it is the squeaky wheel that gets the oil." (Indiana licensed kin foster parent)

Other workers commented that they tended to have higher expectations for kinship foster parents. Because relatives knew and had a strong emotional bond with the child in their care, workers sometimes assumed that the kin would take good care of the child and did not need agency assistance. In many ways, workers noted, kin's commitment to caring for children worked against them. Workers knew that even if they did not pay very close attention to them, kin would continue caring for children, and thus workers felt less obligated to assist kin.

"You have higher expectations of relatives, you just look at it like. . . . Oh, well, that is the aunt or that's the grandparents. Whereas with the foster parents you are offering so much—'Let me know if you need school supplies.' And when school starts, you get on into the school year before you realize that you never called the aunt to offer her services and vouchers. And you forget you even have those cases. You do your monthly visit and you don't put as much into 'What can I do to support you?' I'm guilty of it as a worker and I think a lot of us are. You get a break and think, 'That's family, they'll be fine. Let's deal with this one that isn't family.' " (Alabama foster care supervisor)

"We as workers expect more from related foster parents than non-kin. Because a regular foster parent, they can call us to take the child to the doctor, get medical help, they expect us to do all that. Whereas, we don't give that service to kin caregivers—not to say that we won't—but we expect that if a child is placed with a relative, they will do all of those things. Which is not fair. Some of them even get to the point that even if they need help, they feel like they can't call us 'cause we expect them to do it. Some don't expect us to respond to them. Up front, we make it appear that they'll have to do it all . . . even though the child is in state custody. We have to jump when non-kin says jump, because foster care parents volunteer their services and they are really not obligated to do those things." (Alabama foster care supervisor)

"Foster parents today somehow have risen to the level of the Greek gods. I mean really, honestly. I think it's a wonderful thing that you do, so I won't minimize that. But I think a lot of times . . . that I bend over backwards for them, because if not for people like them, we have no place to place the children." (Indiana investigative worker)

Several workers noted concerns about kinship foster parents becoming dependent upon public agency services and support. These workers argued that their job was to help the kinship caregivers become self-sufficient, so that they could care for children without agency support. Some workers felt that kin tried to exploit or game the system to get additional support.

"They become dependent upon these services, so then they don't want to terminate their relationship with the agency because then they will lose these services." (California foster care supervisor)

"We also have an obligation to try and show them how to have their own abilities to take care of those children and not depend on the agency to just provide financial services for the next 18 to 20 years." (Alabama investigative worker)

"The trend has been that the relative caretakers, especially the African-American caretakers, have become married to the system. They come to expect this level of income or this and that, and they begin to understand how they can exploit the system to get more. And they will threaten, saying 'This child will come into [traditional foster] care if I don't get my gas bill paid,' or whatever. Where in other races, money is not the issue. It's a catch-22. You want to put the child with relative caretakers, but you also want the relative caretaker to understand, after a while, after we get you adjusted and get the child into your home, we want to pull out. We are not there forever." (Alabama foster care worker)

"They are so needy of support, they want you to do it for them. They need hand holding, but when a worker tries to empower them, they want solutions *now*. They want you to help them by doing it for them. Their needs are so great that it takes a while for them to actually assimilate what they need to do." (Connecticut licensing worker)

Kin may also be offered fewer services than are offered to non-kin foster parents because kin are rarely recruited by private foster care agencies. In many states, child welfare agencies contract with private family foster care agencies (FFAs) to recruit, license, monitor, and support foster parents. Of the states included in this study, California relied most heavily on FFAs. Many workers in California noted that FFAs provide greater support than the public agency can—financial support as well as services. Moreover, workers said that very few kin were part of FFAs. Many of the services that kin report having difficulty accessing from community providers are provided to non-kin foster parents directly through FFAs.

While the overwhelming majority of interviewees for this study concurred that kin are offered fewer services, a few pointed out instances in which kin may be offered and receive more services than other foster parents receive. Workers who said they offered greater services to kin also noted their greater needs.

> "For me, more attention is given to relatives for things like referrals and assistance, as opposed to non-kin foster homes, where there is more consistency. So you kind of help the relative more, and find more services geared to help the relative provider and not just the child." (Connecticut foster care worker)

> "At times we've had to give them [relatives] some[thing] extra. Foster parents and relatives are supposed to be able to financially manage their own situations, but we've bought beds to make it work. We wouldn't probably buy a bed for a foster home, but we would for a relative home." (Indiana investigative worker)

> "With foster parents, I leave it on them to ask for services, but with kinship, I'm much more likely to call them and ask, 'How are things going? . . . Are there needs that aren't being met (clothing, counseling, more visits)?' I'll call in the beginning for foster parents to see how they're doing, but don't offer a whole lot to foster parents. I leave that on them." (Indiana foster care worker)

Fewer Services Requested by Kin Foster Families

While child welfare workers and administrators agreed that the agency typically offered fewer services to kin, they also agreed that kin generally requested fewer services than did traditional foster parents. Workers suggested that kin tend not to request many services because they are unaware of what is available, they fear the agency, and they do not need or want agency assistance.

Many workers reported that kin were often not open to agency assistance, because they either did not feel services were needed or simply had a "take care of my own" attitude. Other workers noted that kin's pride stood in the way of their requesting help from the agency. Kin may be reluctant to admit to themselves that they need assistance.

"Relatives are more open to services now. In the past and in certain cultures, you did not bring up the subject of counseling to anybody, because relatives felt the issue would be dealt with within the family, community, or church. They didn't feel it was appropriate to go to counseling." (Connecticut licensing worker)

"I think, too, grandparents are family members that are taking over that role [kinship caregiver]. They, in fact, have a difficult time wanting to get involved in services. There must be a belief somewhere along the line that 'these are family members and I should be able to take care of the needs and issues within the family.' I think they might feel as if there is a social stigma attached to going to a social service organization. So the needs are clearly there, but they also might be needs that are different and need to be identified in a separate way at times, because they may not want you to help." (Connecticut private agency provider)

"Sometimes they think they know best, because they are relatives. 'Don't tell me what I need. I know what I need. This is my family.' So they don't seek it, because they think they know what to do." (California administrator)

"As we engage families, we get to know them better. They are more willing to talk with us. Then we may get at some of the underlying needs. Sometimes it's hard to convince caregivers they need help or should get help from us. Many see this as a short-term thing at first and are not invested in long-term solutions." (Alabama foster care supervisor)

"Sometimes relatives feel like they can do it on their own. I think that sometimes the higher functioning the relative is and the less familiar they are with dealing with systems, the less likely they are to ask us for help. They feel like they should be able to care for these kids." (California investigative worker)

Many workers commented that kin often do not understand what they are getting themselves into. They think they will be caring for a child for a short period of time and that they can handle it. They do not always focus on the needs of the child and the costs associated with caring for the child, especially if the child is not returned home quickly.

"I think that in the beginning they have misconceptions about what they are able to do. Then when the bills start piling up, it's a problem." (Alabama foster care supervisor)

Moreover, because kin lack experience with the child welfare system, they are often not aware of services that may be available and are thus less likely to request these services. Unlike other foster parents, kin rarely are part of foster parent associations, a key source of information about what services may be available to foster parents.

"Relatives need to be aware that the same services available for regular foster parents are also available to them. I do support groups for foster parents (relatives and regular), and the relatives are complaining that they never knew that certain services were out there. Relatives are feeling that the treatment worker thinks that since it is a relative, they should be able to take care of the child and not need the services." (Connecticut licensing worker)

"They [foster parents] call to ask about stuff they know they are entitled to. I think it is important to remind them [relative care-givers] that they are entitled to a break also. Regular foster parents know they're entitled to respite, and we forget to tell relatives that they are entitled to 14 days off." (Connecticut ongoing workers)

"But they [relatives] don't ask, because they don't know (i.e., extended day, respite). Sometimes [relatives] ask for less, because they are not aware of what is available." (Connecticut licensing worker)

"What the relatives get is what we give them; they're not always savvy about what's available to them." (California investigative supervisor)

"I think another reason is because they don't know what is available. I think if they knew, they would be asking for more. Relatives don't have that networking like foster parents." (Alabama foster care supervisors)

"Relatives don't know as much as foster parents, because they didn't receive training. It puts a damper on what services they will ask for. If the worker doesn't offer, they [relatives] will be waiting a long time before they receive any type of service." (California ongoing worker)

Workers report that kin also request fewer services because they may be seeking to avoid agency contact. Some kin intentionally hide information from workers because they fear the agency will not reunify a child with his or her birth parents if he or she is not doing well. Other kin hide information from caseworkers because they do not want the intrusion of the agency, preferring to handle the situation privately.

"Foster parents tell you up front what's going on, what they need; the relatives hide stuff from you. You don't really know what other stuff they need until it's ready to blow. You don't know if a kid's been putting holes in the wall the whole time he's been there, and now they want you to get the kid out. The kid might have needed a psych[ological] evaluation or anger management skills. They don't call you, you're spinning your wheels trying to find out what they need, and they're ducking and dodging or not being forthright about what they need." (Indiana foster care worker)

"But a lot of relatives don't want other services in the home, don't want the intrusiveness." (Indiana foster care worker)

"Maybe there are different service desires. Relatives tend to want less services, because they don't want DHR [Department of Human Resources] involvement. Foster parents can be much more demanding. Kin request services less frequently." (Alabama foster care supervisor)

"They [relatives] see us as invading and controlling. They don't see us as trying to protect the child and give them services to make the situation easier. They only see negative aspects. They are in a tough situation, so it is understandable, but it makes our job harder." (California ongoing worker)

Workers also report that many kin are afraid to ask for assistance, believing that if they do, the agency will conclude that they are not capable of caring for the child. Kin also may not be very assertive in asking for assistance because they fear the agency will view them as difficult.

"Sometimes they [the relatives] don't know if it's okay to ask. Sometimes they are scared, because they think we'll think they can't do it." (Indiana investigative worker)

"A certain percent of relatives are afraid that if they tell us that the child is misbehaving . . . we'll just come in and remove the child. . . . They save all of this until it's so chaotic and they've just lost it and don't know we can put more services in the home instead of removal." (Indiana ongoing worker)

"It's also a cultural issue on both sides, African Americans and Latinos. Very often they may feel that if they push and ask for something, we may not let them have the child. They don't know what to push and ask for. Maybe because some communities are on top of it all, or they have attorneys, they're more affluent, they pick up the phone and tell us what they want. Then you have this other poor, maybe rural family and they're busy saying 'We'll just have to take care of our family.' They don't feel they're entitled to anything, and they don't ask for it." (California administrator)

"A lot of times they may not ask because we sometimes will say 'You are taking this child, so you are assuming the responsibility of this child,' which will kind of give an individual the clue not to ask for anything, even though they may need something. Sometimes I think that is why they are so apprehensive about asking for help. They just don't want to rock the boat. They don't want us to think they can't handle it. They need to know that we want to help them keep that child in their house. We don't want to take that child into foster care. They need a better understanding of the agency." (Alabama foster care supervisors)

"If relatives have needs, they come with their hat in their hands. If foster parents need something special, they will call and we will write POs [purchase orders] and they will get what they need. Kin come to us and feel like they are begging. We give them the impression that they are supposed to be responsible. It feels like welfare that they are not comfortable with. Consequently, they let things go until they are a disaster before they ask for help, and then you have a crisis on your hands." (Alabama foster care worker)

"Many times our older relatives are not as assertive or aware as younger relatives, so there is also a sense of compliance. You know, 'I called and the worker wasn't there.' There's a lack of awareness or assertiveness. Many times kids go without, because [relatives] did not push the issue, did not push for services." (California administrator)

Barriers Kin Face in Accessing Services

Even when kin request services or workers seek to offer services, kin may have difficulty accessing the ones they need. Kin are not eligible for various services and may have difficulty completing applications for assistance. They also often find it difficult to locate services available from community agencies. Workers who want to help kin obtain support often report having difficulty doing so. Workers note that kin often have to wait for a long time to obtain the supports they need.

Because kin do not always complete the same licensing process as non-kin foster parents, kin may not receive or even be eligible for a variety of services. In addition to a monthly foster care payment, foster parents may automatically be provided a variety of services, including health insurance for the children they care for; payment for health-related services not covered under insurance; vouchers for clothing, school supplies, or other specific needs; and child care and respite care assistance.

In many states, kin who are not licensed as foster parents are denied foster care payments and instead may be referred to the welfare office for financial support. Not only are welfare payments significantly less than foster care payments, but many kin are ineligible for or have difficulty obtaining such payments. However, kin who are poor enough to meet eligibility guidelines themselves may receive welfare benefits for themselves as well as the children they care for (a family grant). Kin who are not poor may receive payments for only the related children they are caring for (a child-only grant). Many older kin have little or no income but are ineligible for a family grant due to assets they own. Several older kin asked why they had to sell their homes, for which they had worked their entire lives to afford, to care for a related child.

Kin may be denied child-only grants for a variety of reasons. Child-only grants are available to relative caregivers, but a kin caregiver may instead be a godparent, neighbor, or close family friend (or too distant a relative to be eligible). Even if caregivers are related, they may have a problem proving their relationship to a child. Workers reported that many kin did not have children's birth certificates, which are needed to obtain welfare benefits. In addition, if a kin caregiver is a paternal relative, he may not be able to prove he is related unless paternity has been legally established. Moreover, even if kin meet eligibility requirements and have all required documentation, welfare workers may mistakenly deny them benefits because of a lack of understanding of welfare eligibility rules for relative caregivers.

In addition to welfare payments, kin may not be eligible for other services or supports available to other foster parents, depending upon the local child welfare agency. For example, in Alabama, workers noted that kin receive Medicaid for foster children, but this is a limited blessing because Medicaid does not cover many things children need, including certain prescriptions. The child welfare agency will pay for these expenses when children are in non-kin foster care, but not if they are placed with kin. In one local office in California, administrators noted that respite care services are available to non-kin but not kin foster parents, and in another California office, workers reported that obtaining day care for children in kinship care was problematic.

Because they are often denied services, kin are often resentful of the child welfare agency. Whether the differences they see in the services they are given compared with other foster parents are real or simply perceived, kin often feel they are being taken advantage of. While kin in many sites expressed their resentment, those in California and Alabama, where many do not receive foster care payments, were most outspoken.

> "Why do strangers get money to raise your grandkids, but we don't get anything?" (California kinship caregiver)

> "We love them naturally, because they are our blood. And it's not that we're trying to be greedy or anything, it's just that we feel like we want them to treat us like they would treat strangers taking care of your children. Because they're still not our children." (California kinship caregiver)

One of the main barriers to kin accessing services is knowledge. Because most kin lack experience with the child welfare system, they do not know where to look for or how to access community resources. Workers in several states noted that a key problem for many kin foster parents is finding doctors who accept Medicaid. In local offices in Connecticut, workers specifically noted the difficulty in finding dentists who take Medicaid. While non-kin foster parents face the same problem to some extent, many have developed relationships with doctors who accept Medicaid since they have cared for other foster children previously. In one California local office, both kin and non-kin receive health insurance for their foster children, but kin who do not receive foster care payments receive health insurance through a managed care organization, which makes it harder to access services.

> "The kids in foster care probably get better care because their providers are more accustomed to accessing services, versus relatives, who are less sophisticated. Services coming from our agency are the enabled services. There can be tons of complications, but those established caretakers are more likely to be able to navigate. Relatives are really handicapped. The worker can't be advocating for them all the time." (California ongoing worker)

> "In dealing with MediCal, there are very few doctors who are willing to accept patients. Foster parents can talk doctors into taking the new child, since they know them and have a prior relationship." (California ongoing worker)

> "Foster parents already have structure set up: medical, dental, clothes. Relatives don't." (California investigative supervisor)

> "Foster parents already have supports set up before they go into fostering; that's why they get into foster care. Relatives, like most of our clients, don't have many of the same supports because of money, or whatever." (Indiana ongoing worker)

> "Foster care is utilizing services in the community. Grandparents are not used to knowing about community centers or counseling services. They have been out of the loop for so long because they haven't had the need to know. Finding community resources is a real problem for them." (Connecticut licensing worker)

Even when workers try to help kin obtain services, kin may not be as successful as other foster parents. From the information collected from workers in many sites, it appears obvious (and many workers admitted) that many workers do not understand the eligibility requirements for services provided by other agencies. Some workers believed that kin would not be eligible for Medicaid or Temporary Assistance for Needy Families (TANF) for their related children if the kin had too much income. Many workers expressed frustration that they themselves did not know the services available to foster children. They noted that in some cases experienced foster parents know more than they do.

"When the reliance is on the social worker, it's hit or miss. Tenure of the worker will affect their knowledge of the system. Kinship services, they are all changing. I feel like I don't know everything that is happening with it. We don't even have a good handle on it." (California ongoing supervisor)

Another major barrier for kin in accessing services is time. Workers and kin report that the wait for services can be long and place a considerable burden on kin during the waiting period. This is particularly true for services that are linked to licensing. Unlike non-kin foster parents, kin are typically not licensed when they begin caring for a child, and the licensing process can take two months to a year or even longer.

"With [licensed] foster parents, we place the child and have them sign the paperwork and the services start immediately. With relatives, we have them evaluated for [eligibility for foster care payments], which takes 30, 40, 60 days. Then we tell them to go out and apply for aid, and they may not get assistance. They're doing us a favor and then they have to go out and fight the system." (California investigative supervisor)

"It's not that you don't get services, it's the way they give them to you. It takes forever. Some services you don't hear about until [they're] not needed any more." (Alabama licensed kinship foster parent)

"While waiting for TANF, [a] relative will call us. 'What am I supposed to do while I wait?' They'll say, 'I have to buy them Pampers, I have to buy them food, what can you at the agency do to help me while I wait?' They will say, 'I love my grandbaby but I can't afford to keep the child.'" (Indiana ongoing supervisor)

Kin may also have personal issues that prevent them from securing services. Many kin who are not eligible for a foster care payment do not want to apply for welfare benefits because of the stigma associated with welfare. Others are scared away by work requirements, even though the requirements do not apply to kin who only receive child-only payments. In local offices in Connecticut and California, workers noted that many kinship caregivers were Spanish speaking and faced language barriers working with many community providers and the child welfare agency. In addition, some kin are undocumented immigrants and nervous about being involved with a public agency.

"The relative caregivers I have on my caseload, most of them are Spanish speaking and undocumented. They don't want to take the children they are caring for to therapy because they are afraid of deportation. I have one that won't leave the house. I have to arrange for a case aide to pick them up and take them everywhere they need to go because of that fear." (California ongoing worker)

While the overwhelming majority of persons we spoke to agreed that kin receive fewer services, a few workers pointed out services that kin receive that are not offered to other foster parents. In some localities, child welfare agencies provide transportation assistance (e.g., bus passes or tokens), support groups, or other services only to kinship caregivers. As described below, several child welfare agencies have concluded that kinship caregivers often require different and greater support than traditional foster parents require and have developed special kinship care programs to address these needs. While most workers and administrators noted that kin had long been underserved and welcomed the new programs, a few noted that the agency was now providing more support to kin than non-kin foster parents.

Programs Targeted to Kin

In several of the locations we visited, child welfare agencies are making efforts to improve service delivery for kin. Many child welfare agencies have developed or provided financial assistance for relative support groups that are similar to those organized by foster parent associations. Other child welfare agencies have contracted with private providers to offer a range of services and supports to kinship foster parents. While certainly not the only programs developed to support kin, the two programs we visited seek to provide additional support to low-income kinship caregivers.

Alabama Low-Income Kinship Programs

Mobile is the pilot site for what Alabama hopes will be a statewide program supporting low-income kinship care families. The program, created with federal TANF funds, serves kin caring for children who have been abused and neglected and placed by child welfare but do not receive foster care payments. The program also serves kin caring for children without child welfare involvement if these kin receive a family or child-only grant and are having difficulty caring for related children. The program provides eligible caregivers with the following:

- child care
- respite care
- a special-needs payment of $500 annually per child
- emergency expenses of up to $500 annually
- assistance in meeting court costs associated with obtaining custody or guardianship
- counseling
- job support services, such as transportation assistance, general equivalency diploma (GED) test fees, books and supplies, and work clothes

Caregivers may be referred to the program by child welfare or welfare workers. Caregivers who go on their own are first screened by child welfare intake workers, who can refer them to the kinship program or attempt to meet the kin's immediate needs themselves through information and referral. Most caregivers are referred to the program for the special needs payment or child care. In addition to the services listed above, kinship program workers provide ongoing case management, which includes helping the family access services available in the community by making referrals to service providers or by helping to schedule appointments. Before providing any service directly, program workers must document that there are not services available in the community.

San Diego Kinship Support Services Program (KSSP)

Beginning in 1998, San Diego's child welfare agency contracted with community agencies in each of the county's regions to provide a wide range of supportive services to low-income kinship caregivers.[3] The stated goals of the program are to reduce the number of kinship placement disruptions and to improve the outcomes of kinship families in health, education, and family functioning. Each community agency began with a list of welfare families headed by relative caregivers as well as kin foster parents. The community agencies contacted each of these families and informed them of the new program. The agencies accept referrals from any community provider as well as self-referrals. KSSP services for children include the following:

- assessment of needs
- mentoring
- tutoring and after-school care
- information and referral
- case management
- recreation
- transportation to activities

In addition, for relative caregivers, services include the following:

- assessment of needs
- support groups
- parenting education
- respite care
- school advocacy training
- emergency assistance for food, clothing, transportation, and other needs
- adoption services
- homemaking skills
- recreational activities
- information and referral for other services

Many of the caregivers come to the KSSP providers for the support groups and then are linked to the other services. While the concrete services, such as financial assistance and respite care, are much needed, workers and kin both noted that the support groups were most appreciated.

"I heard about [KSSP] because [another kin caregiver] told me about it. She kept telling me it was a great group and that I had to come. And I was very leery of the system, but she kept telling me it was a really good group. Finally, I was so tired one night I couldn't deal with it anymore. So I said, 'Fine, I'm going.' It was a godsend to sit there and hear everybody else talking about what they were dealing with and going, 'Oh my gosh, that's what I'm going through.' It has been so helpful. My grandsons both have ADHD [attention deficit/hyperactivity disorder] and when I had to go to school for them, a worker said, 'We will go with you,' and it was like I finally had somebody at my back."

"I was afraid to go out in public, because I was ashamed. I didn't want anyone to know, almost like I was guilty. So I 'hermitted' myself. It was so nice to come to [KSSP]. When I came, I just cried. I mean I just let it all out. It was nice to know that other people were going through the same thing."

Summary and Discussion

We found almost unanimous consensus (from administrators, supervisors, workers, judges, and kin) that kinship foster parents are receiving fewer services than their non-kin counterparts, despite having greater service needs. While there are a number of subtle differences across states and localities as far as why kin receive fewer services, for the most part, the sites we visited exhibited several common characteristics:

- *Workers offer fewer services to kin than they offer to non-kin foster parents.* Some workers acknowledge that they have higher expectations of kin or that they do not want kin to become dependent upon the public agency. However, most workers acknowledged that, for a variety of reasons, the agency was simply failing to adequately meet the needs of kin.
- *Kin request fewer services of caseworkers than do non-kin foster parents.* Kin do not know what to ask for, are afraid to ask out of fear of appearing unable to care for a child, or may simply want to avoid public agency intrusion.
- *Kin face barriers to accessing services.* Kin are often unable to obtain support when they seek it due to eligibility constraints, lack of familiarity with community resources, or waiting lists for services.

Due to the unique circumstances of kin, many have service needs that are different from or greater than most other foster parents. These needs include financial assistance, child and respite care, counseling and support groups, and transportation. A number of child welfare agencies have acknowledged these unique needs and are carrying out programs to provide greater support to kin.

The findings from this study suggest that both caseworkers and kinship caregivers could benefit from additional training. Caseworkers acknowledged that working with kin was in many ways different from working with non-kin foster parents, yet few had received any information or training on how to approach kinship caregivers differently. Workers also admitted to having limited knowledge of community resources and often relying on non-kin foster parents for information they then used to advise kinship caregivers. Moreover, many workers appeared confused about the eligibility criteria and the application process for a variety of public services for which kin are eligible.

Unlike their conditions for non-kin, many child welfare agencies do not require kinship caregivers to complete any formal training to be a foster parent. Since kin are caring for a specific child they already know, kin may not need precisely the same training that non-kin foster parents complete. However, it seems obvious that kin could use training in a variety of areas related to service delivery, including what services are available from the child welfare agency, other public services kin may be eligible for and application procedures for these services, and services offered by community agencies.

Child welfare agencies may also want to examine whether their policies inadvertently deny kin services they may need to care for a child. When support is linked to licensing, many kin will fail to receive support because many are not licensed, and those that are seeking licensure may find it takes a long time to obtain. Workers also identified a need for greater clarity in child welfare agency policies about the services that may be available for kin.

Child welfare agencies should also experiment with new approaches to engage kinship care families. Family group conferencing programs (also called family group decisionmaking) that bring the entire family network together to plan for the care of a child appear to be a promising approach, one that many agencies have already instituted. Agencies may also want to explore ways to bring kinship foster parents together more. In many localities, experienced foster parents are recruited to mentor new non-kin foster parents. This approach may also work well with kinship foster parents. In addition, non-kin foster parents benefit greatly from participation in foster parent associations. Increasingly, child welfare agencies are helping to develop kinship caregiver support groups. Support groups can not only provide an opportunity for kin to share experiences with one another, but they also can be an effective way to educate kin about the child welfare system and services available to kinship caregivers.

Foster children can benefit from the love and commitment of kinship caregivers and from a sense of belonging and permanency. However, these children still experience the trauma of being separated from their parents. Whether they are placed with kin or non-kin foster parents, foster children require considerable support. Child welfare agencies need to reflect on the uniqueness of kinship care arrangements and develop strategies to ensure that kinship caregivers have the necessary knowledge and resources to care for children entrusted to them.

NOTES

1. In five states that have a minimum income requirement, kin who seek to be licensed as foster parents can have this requirement waived. In many other states, kin can choose to care for a child without being licensed.

2. More non-kin foster parents have child care needs than in years past; it appears that there are more non-kin foster families with two working foster parents.

3. This kinship care model is being implemented in many counties in California.

6

Permanency Planning with Kinship Foster Parents

Rob Geen

One of the primary goals of our nation's child welfare system is to ensure that children who have been removed from their parents' homes are reunified or placed in another permanent placement (adoption or legal guardianship) in a timely manner. Prior research has documented that the permanency outcomes for children placed with kin appear to differ from those for children placed with non-kin. Research has shown that children placed with foster parents who are related to them tend to remain in foster care significantly longer than children placed in non-kin foster care (Cook and Ciarico 1998; Courtney 1994). Compared with children placed in non-kin foster care, children placed with kin are less likely to be reunified with their parents (AFCARS 1998; Berrick et al. 1995; Testa 1997) and are less likely to be adopted (Berrick et al. 1995; Berrick and Needell 1999).

Some research has found that kinship foster parents are reluctant or unwilling to adopt children in their care (Gleeson 1999; Thornton 1991). However, other studies show that if properly informed, most kin are willing to consider adoption (Beeman et al. 1996; Testa and Slack 2002; Testa et al. 1996; Zimmerman et al. 1998). Several studies have documented that child welfare agencies and workers approach permanency planning with kin in a different way than they approach non-kin foster parents. Other studies have found that workers believe that kin see adoption as unnecessary, and even when kin may be willing to adopt, caseworkers often fail to speak to them about this option (Beeman et al. 1996; Beeman and Boisen 1999; Berrick, Needell et al. 1999; Chipungu et al. 1998; Thornton 1991).

Because kin are already related to the children in their care, experts have questioned whether pushing kin foster parents to adopt is either appropriate or necessary. In recent years, many states have begun subsidized guardianship programs, giving kin an alternative to adoption that provides ongoing financial assistance similar to the subsidies offered to adults who adopt special needs children from foster care. Although many kinship caregivers choose to adopt children in their care, others feel that legal guardianship is a more appropriate permanency option. Unlike adoption, termination of birth parent rights is not required for legal guardianship. While kin who take guardianship agree to permanently care for a child, birth parents retain certain rights and responsibilities, including the right to safe visitation, the right to consent to the child's adoption at some later date, and the responsibility to pay child support. A 2001 Urban Institute survey found that 35 states had begun subsidized guardianship programs (Jantz et al. 2002).

In 1997, concerned about the length of time children spent in foster care, Congress passed the Adoption and Safe Families Act (ASFA). While promoting more timely permanency for all children, the act acknowledges the unique circumstances of kinship care and permits states to treat kinship care children differently from other foster children. ASFA requires states to seek termination of parental rights (TPR) after a child has been in foster care for 15 of 22 consecutive months. However, ASFA allows states to extend this time frame if "at the option of the state, the child is being cared for by a relative." This is not intended as a blanket exemption, but rather an option to be addressed on a case-by-case basis and an exemption that must be revisited periodically. The U.S. Department of Health and Human Services (HHS)'s guidance on implementing ASFA requires that "a state must continue to develop and reevaluate a child's case plan goal and conduct permanency hearings if the State decides not to file a petition for TPR because the child is placed with a relative."

ASFA is also the first federal legislation to address kinship care as a potential permanent placement. The act specifies that acceptable permanency options include reunification, adoption, legal guardianship, or permanent placement with a "fit and willing relative" and that states must have a "compelling reason" if they select any other type of permanent placement. HHS guidance notes that "the term [compelling reason] was adopted because far too many children are given the permanency goal of long-term foster care, which is not a permanent living situation for a child." While advocates of kinship care may applaud ASFA's acknowledgment of the unique circumstances of kinship care, opponents could claim that the act allows kinship care children to be placed in what amounts to long-term foster care without a compelling reason.

Research has demonstrated that states have taken the flexibility afforded under ASFA to treat kin and non-kin differently with regard to permanency planning. The 2001 Urban Institute survey (Jantz et al. 2002) found that many states are routinely not terminating parental rights. In 10 of 36 states that provided an estimate, officials reported that they did not terminate parental rights in more than half of the cases in which children were living with kin. In addition, 43 states reported that they allow children to remain in long-term foster care with kin.

This chapter examines how local child welfare agencies approach permanency planning for children living with kin and non-kin foster parents. The chapter assesses how and why caseworkers approach permanency planning differently when children are placed with kin as well as how ASFA has affected permanency-planning practices with kin. The chapter also examines how strongly agencies push kin to adopt children who cannot remain with their parents, how often kin foster parents are willing to adopt, and the reasons why some kin are not willing to adopt. Finally, the chapter suggests reasons why the permanency outcomes for foster children placed with kin are different from those for children placed with non-kin.

Kinship Care and Permanency Planning

Administrators and workers reported that permanency planning is different when children are placed with kin. When children are placed with non-kin and reunification is ruled out, workers seek termination of parental rights and then adoption. When children are placed with kin, TPR is often seen as less necessary and adoption is not viewed as the only acceptable permanency option. In some of the sites, child welfare agencies often help to arrange a voluntary transfer of custody from the birth parent to the kinship caregiver and consider this a permanent outcome. Allowing children to remain in long-term foster care is generally prohibited when children are placed in non-kin foster care. Long-term foster care is discouraged for children in kinship foster care as well, and

ASFA has made this option less acceptable. However, in practice, administrators and workers report that long-term foster care remains a common permanency outcome when children are placed with kin, for reasons that will be explained later. In addition, in all of the sites we visited, kin may become the legal guardians instead of the adoptive parents of their foster children. At the same time, the extent to which agencies push kin to adopt instead of take guardianship varies greatly among the sites visited.

Long-Term Foster Care

While adoption is the primary permanency plan for those children in non-kin foster care who cannot be reunified with their parents, workers in all the sites visited noted that they are less concerned about TPR, adoption, or closing a case when a child is in kinship care. In Alabama, administrators and workers confirmed that state policy prohibits TPR if a relative is willing and able to take a child. In Connecticut, many workers noted that transfer of guardianship was more common than TPR.

> "[Children in kinship care] have a much greater tendency to be in long-term foster care than to go on to guardianship or adoption." (California administrator)

> "Even if [children] are under age 2 and adoptable, relatives can take on long-term foster care." (California foster care supervisor)

> "But we can't TPR if there is a viable relative available; the agency can't do it. The relative could file for TPR. They won't get the adoption assistance payment." (Alabama administrator)

> "Another thing the relatives really fail to understand and accept is that we advocate for them to get custody of children so that we can get out of the picture as fast as possible. I have no intent to TPR anybody, why should I? They have commitment to their relatives. I have no reason to disrupt their lives." (Alabama foster care worker)

> "Usually if a child is placed with a relative, we don't terminate parental rights because it's usually going for a guardianship. On rare occasions, [we would terminate]." (Connecticut foster care supervisor)

"I think we are not filing as many TPRs for relatives. It's not as automatic as for children placed in foster care." (Connecticut foster care supervisor)

"I tell them [the birth parents] 'You can weigh the difference; it is either TPR or transfer of guardianship. So you decide. And if we TPR, there is a chance that the child might not remain with their grandmother.'" (Connecticut foster care worker)

In all the sites visited, administrators and workers noted that long-term foster care is discouraged, even for children in kinship foster care. Workers agreed that long-term foster care does not provide a child with permanency. In addition, ASFA has increased the pressure on agencies to avoid leaving children in long-term foster care.

"My guess would be, if we look at the data, we are going to see decreased relative placements because of ASFA, and I think also because agencies are ignoring the long-term foster care part of ASFA as being acceptable and have focused more on the adoption aspect of ASFA." (Connecticut foster care worker)

"I'm wondering if now we're not as committed to relative long-term placements, where in the past, we were okay with that. Now [following ASFA], we're pursuing more formal non-relative placements because of the goal to achieve more adoptions. This is a legitimate issue with the National Association of Black Social Workers, where they were very comfortable with the prevailing kinship practice, and now we are seeing a shift. And we don't know if it is beneficial." (Connecticut investigative worker)

"Only in the past couple of years have we had to file these motions for review, so that has opened the gate for us to have to explore all the family options before we say long-term foster care or adoption. It's very recent, with ASFA." (Connecticut foster care supervisor)

"I think that's going to be harder now because of the legislation [ASFA]. They don't want us to consider long-term foster care as a permanency plan." (Connecticut foster care worker)

Indiana policy prohibits child welfare workers from making a recommendation of long-term foster care to the court, although the court can and often does order that the agency leave a child in long-term foster care. While long-term foster care is discouraged in Alabama, California, and Connecticut, administrators, workers, and judges report that this is a common permanency option for children in kinship foster care. Long-term foster care is more common for older children, especially if they say they are not interested in being adopted. Workers also noted that long-term foster care is sometimes used when kinship caregivers need the greater support offered to families that remain in the system. However, if other relatives (and sometimes non-kin) are available and willing to make a permanent commitment, long-term foster care may be ruled out in favor of adoption or guardianship.

> "They do that [leave children in long-term foster care] if the relative needs extra support. Don't like to do that, but they will." (Connecticut foster care worker)

> "If we had concerns—not concerns about the care, but concerns because the child had some special need—certainly I don't think we'd be going ahead with a subsidized guardianship . . . not that we'd move the child, just that we'd leave the case open. They need the additional support the agency can provide." (Connecticut administrator)

> "When I look at relatives I really look to see whether I feel DCF [Department of Children and Families] case management services are needed. If they're not, I see subsidized guardianship as for the 'cream of the crop'—for those caretakers that can do this without us. So I tend to look for long-term foster care if they can do it [caretaking] well as long as we're involved. If they really need a case manager, I really look carefully at this before making a decision." (Connecticut foster care supervisor)

> "If the connection is there, if the child is doing well, chances are that we allow the child to remain there in what we call long-term foster care. It depends on the age of the child and the child's circumstances." (Connecticut foster care supervisor)

> "Long-term foster care is acceptable if there is no clear, convincing evidence that the child is adoptable, and we can't TPR. Legal guardianship is an option. If the child is in the relative's home for years and the relative won't do guardianship or adopt, I will accept

long-term foster care. It is detrimental to the child to be removed." (California judge)

"Permanent foster care is not a statutory option, but they do use it. When you terminate parental rights, the child loses all connections." (Indiana judicial administrator)

"[Long-term foster care is acceptable] if a kid's in kinship care and kin do not want guardianship, like for the financial reasons. Or if kids do not want to be adopted. It's pretty hard to tell a child who understands what is going on that he needs to be adopted." (California judge)

"If the child is very young and the family doesn't want to adopt but other, non-relatives do, we have to assess the situation. Long-term foster care is not unusual, but the department questions all long-term placements under the age of 12." (Connecticut administrator)

Adoption versus Guardianship

While ASFA has increased the focus on adoption, and some workers raised concerns that ASFA may be forcing kin to adopt, guardianship is still more common than adoption in almost all of the sites we visited. The extent to which agencies encourage adoption varies greatly, depending upon the local office as well as the specific child. Agency workers push most for the adoption of younger children. Most workers agreed that it is rare that removal is threatened if kin will not adopt; however, many kin say that they felt pressured to adopt. Workers reported that often it is assumed that kin will not be interested in adoption and thus it is not even discussed. Workers, administrators, judges, and kinship caregivers all noted that child welfare agency staff members do a poor job of explaining adoption and how it differs from guardianship.

"Relatives, typically, don't need to adopt. I think ASFA has generated a cultural change in practice and I'm not so sure everyone is going by the other various options it has. I know there has been a huge emphasis on the formal adoption part of ASFA, especially within this agency." (Connecticut investigative worker)

"We're in a shift [since ASFA]. Five years ago the issue was relatives becoming adoptive parents—it was kind of a shock for us. I've seen us make that transition. Now the mindset is to begin early on with relatives. Not so with foster parents as with the relatives. But if we place with relatives, we're [immediately] looking at permanency, at adoption." (California administrator)

In Alabama, the vast majority of children in kinship care are placed voluntarily, and temporary custody with the kinship caregiver is considered permanency for them. For the few that are in state custody, transfer of custody or guardianship is considered the first option.

"I would prefer temporary custody to adoption, because adoption is the only time they TPR. Temporary custody is not as much of an ordeal. We don't push relatives into adoption, although it is an option they have." (Alabama administrator)

"We lean more towards custody. Relatives are more comfortable with custody rather than adoption, because [adoption] terminates all the rights. It cleans the slate. With custody, you can always reverse that back. When you talk about adoption, it is a permanent situation. From my perspective, I don't think you're talking about adoption with relatives, I think you're talking about custody." (Alabama foster care supervisor)

In each of the Connecticut sites, workers emphasized guardianship more than adoption and this was the most common permanency outcome for children in kinship care.

"Relatives, typically, don't need to adopt. We have subsidized guardianship for them." (Connecticut foster care worker)

"Guardianship is the most frequent permanency placement. Subsidized guardianship is only about two years old. Most of our relatives are doing straight guardianship, with no payment. If they need services after, then we need to reopen the case." (Connecticut licensing supervisor)

"Not much adopting with relatives, they just assume guardianship. I think it depends on the age of the child. If it is an infant, we would most likely be talking about adoption instead of guardianship." (Connecticut licensing worker)

"Adoption is encouraged, but guardianship is fine if the relative is willing to make the commitment. The agency will not push relatives to adoption or guardianship if relative is not willing. The agency will allow the child to age out of the system as a foster child." (Connecticut foster care supervisor)

Workers in California mentioned a recent push for adoption, though they felt guardianship was still considered the preferred and most common outcome. Workers in Los Angeles and Santa Clara noted greater pressure to get kin to adopt. In San Diego and Santa Cruz, workers said that they are placing more emphasis on informing kin of the adoption option, but they are not pushing it.

"It is fairly recent, but we really sit and talk with the relative [about adoption]." (California administrator)

"The first adoption worker said if I didn't adopt them, they were going to be orphans. It was sort of a pressure tactic. They never said anything about the options . . . with adoption this is what happens, with guardianship this is what happens." (California caregiver)

"Many relatives want legal guardianship because it's more politically correct with their family [and] because it's reversible. I'm not sure that I would say there is pressure on relatives to adopt, but I know that people are asking them. The department and the court would like adoption, but I am not so sure that there is pressure on the relatives. But they certainly hear it from us an awful lot." (California foster care supervisor)

"Relatives feel pressure to adopt. The department will tell them to adopt or the child will be moved." (California judge)

"During the last three years we've discouraged guardianships and are moving for adoption instead, even if it's an older teen. If relatives don't want to adopt, we must do extra justification to show why it's an acceptable placement." (California intake supervisor)

"There has been a shift over the past few years from guardianship to adoption. The process has changed; we give more information about adoption to relatives now. We're assigning adoption workers to review all children every six months. Adoption workers contact relatives to discuss potential adoption." (California administrator)

"We fudge our findings, say [the] child is not adoptable because we don't want to break up a relative and child." (California judge)

Of the sites we visited, Indiana appears to place the greatest emphasis on adoption, especially for younger children. Workers in Indiana noted that they had to clearly explain why adoption was not possible or in the best interest of a child before supervisors and sometimes the court would allow another permanency option. However, even in Indiana, it appears that guardianship is still the most common outcome. Some workers were concerned that they were pushing unwilling kin to adopt.

"We try to push for adoption if at all possible so that we can close the case and provide permanency for the child. Relatives usually just want legal guardianship; they don't want to adopt. We push for adoption, but relatives usually push for legal guardianship. The court pushes legal guardianship." (Indiana administrator)

"Most kin are willing to adopt. Some that apply for the guardianship program only do so because that is what they have been told is available. Court people speak with the families and often find out that the agency worker has never even discussed adoption with them. So guardianship is pursued infrequently. If there is a case where grandma just cannot emotionally cut the ties to mom but will keep [her] kids permanently, then guardianship is considered. But there is a push for adoption." (Indiana court official)

"I think we force them to adopt, I really do. We force them and we bribe them with the per diem. Or we threaten them with removal, which is the truth of the matter, but it's very threatening. We do push them into it—both foster parents and relatives—push them into adopting on our time frames or the court's time frames. Sometimes they don't want to [adopt], because they really think it's drastic. It's their daughter [the birth mother] and maybe she'll get it together in a couple years. Their focus on permanency and their belief is not what we think. Our concept of permanency is different than theirs." (Indiana foster care workers)

Identification of Relatives Late in the Case Process

Many administrators, workers, and judges noted the problem of relatives who are identified late in the process, after a child has bonded with a non-kin foster parent who is willing to adopt. ASFA's focus on permanency has made agencies seek out kin more diligently earlier in the process and judges are pressuring agencies to identify relatives. However, it is still common for relatives to be identified late.

Judges have different perspectives on whether to give preference to these relatives. Most argue that relatives should not be punished due to the failure of the agency to identify them earlier and will still give them preference. Others question why the relatives were unaware of the child's situation. Workers expressed similar concerns about the intentions of relatives who show up late in the process. Some questioned whether the relatives would simply give the children back to the birth parents.

Overall, workers and administrators noted that this is an area where specific policies are lacking, prompting constant, case-by-case fights. In Indiana, foster parents gain "standing" after caring for a child for 12 months and get to petition the court for adoption. Foster parents with standing are typically given preference, though the court may still allow a relative to adopt if the judge believes it is in the best interest of the child.

"Because we have to work more quickly with ASFA, there's more of a recognition to identify family up front to keep the child within the extended family. Because even if their bio[logical] family isn't going to get it together in a year, it's better to involve the extended family sooner, up front, than a year or two down the line when you're really looking to make a permanent plan for the child." (Connecticut administrator)

"The relatives may not have thought that TPR would really happen. Then the relatives may show up, but it may be the relative's agenda to return the child to the birth parent. You have to determine what's best for the kids." (California foster care supervisor)

"Then you have the situation where the bio[logical] parents don't want to give you any information and they don't want the kids staying with relatives. And they are fighting everywhere to not get the kids to go with the relatives. And then you have other situations where the relatives won't come forward because they hear DCF and they don't want anything to do with DCF, until they find out that the child is going to be terminated [parental rights terminated] and they all come forward." (Connecticut foster care worker)

"I think that happens more frequently, where relatives come in late rather than earlier. Parents will say, 'They [relatives] are not a resource, they are not a good option,' until their rights are going to get terminated and then they'll say, 'They're not that bad.'" (Connecticut foster care supervisor)

"We have a graph in our head when we are making the decision. At the beginning, relatives are our first choice, but as time passes, the relatives' right to get the child decreases as long as the child is in a stable placement." (California foster care supervisor]

"We say that everyone has the right to be considered [for an adoptive placement] but when it comes down to it, it is almost always the relative given precedence." (Indiana foster care worker)

"If relatives show up late in the process, they are very seriously considered. This is a problem for kids who have been in foster care for years and the foster parents want to adopt. Legally, the court still has to look at relatives and will give them preference." (Indiana court official)

"Judges are happy to see relatives show up, even months or years later." (Alabama foster care supervisors)

Kinship Care and Permanency Outcomes

For a variety of reasons, children are apparently less likely to be reunified with their parents or adopted when placed with relatives. Birth parents are typically less motivated to complete case plan requirements for reunification when their children are with kin. While many kin foster parents do not want to adopt children in their care, it appears they are more willing than has been previously believed. As discussed earlier, kin often have good reasons for not wanting to adopt. Child welfare agencies have inadvertently created significant disincentives for many kin to adopt. Although they lacked hard evidence, many administrators and workers raised concerns about the long-term stability of guardianship arrangements. Several workers also pointed out that even after adoption or guardianship, children placed with kin may have an ongoing, and not necessarily healthy, relationship with their birth parents.

Birth Parent Motivation

We found overwhelming agreement among administrators, workers, and kinship caregivers in every county we visited that birth parents are less motivated to meet case plan goals when children are in kinship care. Many reasons were offered for birth parents' lack of motivation. When children are with kin, birth parents tend to have much greater access to their children. Typically, they can visit or call their children frequently—when they want (as opposed to a scheduled time) and where they want (as opposed to the child welfare office or a visitation center). Many kinship caregivers observed that birth parents are happy to have their freedom back and to pass along the responsibilities of parenthood. This is particularly true of substance-abusing parents, who can continue their addiction without concern about how it affects their children. Many caregivers also commented that birth parents do not feel shame when their children are placed with kin. Many children are raised by relatives in the community and this situation has less of a stigma associated with it than having children raised by foster parents. Birth parents are typically less likely to fight a transfer of custody or even TPR when children are with kin. In fact, workers suggest that birth parents may welcome TPR and a permanency arrangement, because it puts the agency out of the picture. Several kinship caregivers commented that they refused or considered refusing to take a related child because they did not want birth parents to lose the motivation to change.[1]

> "I think sometimes bio[logical] parents are not pushing for reunification as strongly because the child's with family. They think, 'I can see the child whenever I want, I know the child's taken care of when they're with grandma.' And it almost gives them permission to go and continue their behavior and not straighten out what created the problem to begin with because they know the child's with family and they're perfectly content with that and comfortable. I've seen that, especially with substance-abusing parents. . . . There's no reason, no motivation to change." (Connecticut administrator)

> "The mother is my niece and she is young, and I think she enjoys the fact that she doesn't have her kids and she can live her life and do what she pleases. And she knows that the kids are all okay. So she will see them when she wants to; otherwise, she really doesn't bother. I think my niece doesn't have an interest, not that she

doesn't love her kids, but as long as she knows that her kids are in houses where there is family taking care of them and providing for them, 'Why should I give up my life [niece's viewpoint]? I will go see the kids when I want to.' That is because they can go out and do what they want to do." (Connecticut caregiver)

"When they [the children] are in non-relative homes some [birth parents] tend to do a lot more than if they're with relatives. [In that case] they just lean back, you know, it's like, 'Okay, they're with family. I'll have access to them, I can see them,' but they continue on with their same path. I see it as negative. Positive for the child, because the child's with relatives, but negative in regards to it's going to be harder for the mom to rehabilitate." (Connecticut foster care worker)

"Some relatives won't take the child because they don't want the birth parents to get lazy. Relatives feel like if they took them [the children], the parent wouldn't do anything else, they wouldn't work towards their goals, they would get comfortable." (Alabama foster care worker)

"I was concerned. I thought I was helping out the parents. I thought it would be short term. The mother would go to a program and get her life together, and I'd get to be the grandmother. She just made lots of excuses, but my son was determined to stay with her. I made it a point for the kids to see the parents once a week. I tried to encourage bonding with the kids, hoping this would give them [the parents] some incentive to do whatever. But they decided, 'Mom's taking good care of the kids, so we'll continue doing what we're doing.'" (California caregiver)

"One thing I've found is that when a child's in a relative placement and if the birth parent is real comfortable with the situation, they have no motivation to complete services. They can see the children whenever they want, whereas if they're placed in a totally different placement, they tend to be a lot more motivated to complete their services and what they're required to do because they don't have free access to the children." (Indiana foster care worker)

"Removing the child from a parent and placing him or her in foster care has a punitive aspect to it, and the parent recognizes that 'I either have to get it together or give it up.' But when you place a child with a relative, the punitive aspect is really reduced. There's not a whole lot of incentive to get involved in drug treatment or become more responsible. Really and truly, what you do is give them an opportunity to be less responsible and not lose touch with their child, and there's a real problem with that when we're talking about time frames. What incentive is there to get their life together or get their child back when all they have to do is visit their mother to see their child? They're happy to play parents. They're content; don't have to have us hounding them. They're not in the system; foster care is an ugly word. Relative placement, they've no shame about. Because a parent can place a child legally with anyone they want. So it's almost like this is their decision. It's not like DHR [Department of Human Resources] stepped in and said they were bad parents." (Alabama foster care worker)

"What I've noticed is when kids are placed with relatives, they don't reunify. It's really convenient because they get to see the kids at family functions or they visit or go by. I think also the parents know that the kids are being taken care of by family and they get to see them, they know where they're at, and they don't reunify. I think there's a comfort level there. . . . 'They're going to be okay, if I get my act together, great, but if I don't, I still get to see my child.' I think a lot of that is knowing where the child is. When the kids are in foster care, they're in a confidential location, the mom may see them for a two-hour visit and that's it." (California foster care worker)

A few workers also suggested that they might neglect birth parents and make less effort at reunification when children are placed with kin. Workers noted that they feel better when children are with loving relatives and may simply pay less attention to these cases.

"If they are with a relative, I would say that most case workers would feel like the case is . . . that closure has happened. Would we neglect a birth parent by doing so? Good question. If they're with a relative from the beginning, you would probably neglect the birth parent." (Alabama foster care worker)

Willingness to Adopt

More relatives are willing to adopt than is usually believed. Workers reported that aunts and uncles are much more likely than grandparents to adopt and that all relatives are more likely to adopt younger children. Many grandparents, however, feel it's unnatural to become a child's legal parent when they are already the grandparent. Some older grandparents are reluctant to adopt because they do not know what will happen to their health as the children get older. Workers and kinship caregivers agreed that child welfare agency staff members do not do a good job of explaining the differences between adoption, guardianship, and long-term foster care. Many kin do not see guardianship as different from adoption.

Many kin do not want to adopt for a variety of reasons. Some feel that adoption punishes the parent too much. Many kin hold out hope that parents will eventually get better. Some kin said that they see taking guardianship as a challenge to parents, hoping it will convince the parents to take steps to get their children back. According to workers, many grandparents do not want to admit to themselves that they have failed as parents. Other kin fear that adoption will push birth parents who are already having trouble over the edge. In addition, if kin have a good relationship with birth parents, many will do anything not to upset this relationship, including refusing to adopt. Workers report that birth parents fight guardianship less than TPR and adoption. Many kin fear that adoption will not only upset the birth parent, but will also cause a rift among the larger, extended family. On the other hand, workers found that some kin are afraid of the birth parents and want to adopt, terminate parental rights, and cut off all contact.

"It'd be next to impossible for a parent, a grandparent, to say that their child is never going to succeed enough to get their child back. First of all, 'What does that say about me as their parent, what did I not do correctly for it to come to this?' If they say, 'No, they're a lost cause, they'll never change,' it says a lot about their relationship with the child [birth parent]. It's asking a lot of them to get to the point where they'll say, 'It's going to be forever.' I think they [relatives] may feel that way but aren't able to express it. And I don't think we should expect them to do that." (Connecticut administrator)

"Within the first two years they [agency workers] were really trying to push guardianship on me. And I kept saying, 'No, my job is to keep my nieces and nephews together until their mother is ready to take them back. . . . I don't need any kids; if I wanted them, mine would already be grown. I don't mind stepping up when I had to, to help out, but me going into this was with the understanding that eventually they were going back with their mother." (Connecticut caregiver)

"I think it's so contingent upon the relationship with the birth parent. If there's a relationship there and they can sort of work through their differences, I think they [the relatives] are going to be less likely to say, 'Go ahead and terminate [parental rights],' the goal being adoption." (Connecticut foster care supervisor)

"But honestly, I want to take DCFS [Department of Children and Family Services] out of my way already. They get too much into your business, into your personal life. Pretty soon I will have them out of my life, because I'm adopting her in December. 'Cause with them, you don't have a life." (Connecticut caregiver)

"I think a lot of relatives are more willing to do a transfer of guardianship than adoption because that causes a lot of conflict in the family. So, it's obviously a lot quicker to do a transfer of guardianship than to do a termination and then an adoption. That's one of the reasons I think kids move out of the system quicker with relatives." (Connecticut foster care worker)

"I had one grandparent say to me, 'As a woman, I know that my daughter is never going to get her act together, but as a mother, I still have hope.' Grandparents hold on the tightest in terms of holding out hope for the parents of the children. The aunts and uncles are able to detach themselves a little more." (California foster care worker)

"It's a cultural issue. In some cultures, it's an insult to put a child up for adoption, for a grandmother to adopt that grandchild and the mother is still alive. It's a real hot topic. For some of them, they feel like they're giving up on their child [the birth parent] . . . 'They'll never do right again.'" (California administrator)

"Most kin are willing to adopt. Some that apply for the guardianship program only do so because that is what they have been told is available. Court people speak with the families and often find out that the agency worker has never even discussed adoption with them. So guardianship is pursued infrequently. If there's a case where grandma just cannot emotionally cut the ties to mom but will keep [the] kids permanently, then guardianship's considered. The agency doesn't do a good job of explaining the difference." (Indiana court official)

"With adoption, we have to tell relatives that there is no guarantee that they will get the child. We cannot tell them yes, though under the table we know they probably will. They feel threatened, but we try to give them confidence. We cannot tell them until after the termination of rights where the child is going to go. This is policy with kin and non-kin." (Alabama foster care worker)

"Me, too. I will not adopt my own grandchildren. I will not do that. I don't want to be their mother. I want to be what I am." (California caregiver)

"When you use relatives and then seek out adoption, how does this impact families? It can be a source of conflict. Mother and child become legal siblings. It puts grandparents at odds with [the] rest of [the] family." (California judge)

Workers and kinship caregivers noted that one major incentive to pursuing guardianship is that the process is much quicker than TPR and adoption. At the same time, while many kin want the child welfare agency out of their lives, many others want the agency to stay involved. Kin may be concerned about the long-term needs of the children in their care and about gaining access to needed services following adoption. Some kin said they wanted the court to remain involved so that the child welfare agency would continue to help them. Some kin expressed fear of being legally responsible for the actions of children with severe behavioral problems, such as being held liable if a child vandalized a neighbor's house.

"They [relatives] become dependent upon these services, so then they don't want to terminate their relationship with the agency because then they will lose these services. The relatives like to have the court involved because they have the support of the court to protect them from the parents." (California foster care worker)

"Relatives want to keep the child care, but also with a drug baby, as the baby gets older, relatives want that ongoing support because they know that the child is going to need services for a very long time." (California foster care worker)

"A lot of relatives will say they want to adopt the child, but then the child becomes free and they don't know what they want to do. They are afraid they won't get help." (California administrator)

"[Kin are reluctant to take permanent custody because they] know we're not going to be there to buffer. They're willing to care for the child forever, but still want us involved so they don't have to deal with parents. I think that's a big part of it. They want someone else to play the heavy, instead of them. They use us to deal with parents, denying parents access to kids so they do not feel as guilty. It takes the responsibility off of them." (Alabama foster care worker)

"Lots of families remain in long-term foster care rather than do guardianship or adoption. With a social worker present, it would be easier for the relative to access services. Many elect for long-term foster care because they can continue with the social worker and the agency, though some guardianship cases also ask to continue contact with [the] worker. They can often choose to have their case closed but it's amazing how many elect to keep the case open in foster care." (California foster care worker)

"They're afraid that once they get guardianship, they won't get any assistance from us." (California foster care worker)

Financial Deterrents to Adoption

Depending upon the state and the specific child's (and family's) circumstances, kin may face a variety of financial disincentives to adopting or taking guardianship. Some kin are not eligible for subsidized adoption or guardianship. In addition, kin often receive greater support if they choose long-term foster care or guardianship instead of adoption.

Some kin who can pass the licensing requirements to receive foster care payments cannot pass the requirements for subsidized guardianship or adoption or do not meet eligibility requirements. For example, in Connecticut, there is no drug screening for kin to become foster parents, but there is for subsidized guardianship and adoption. Interestingly, kin are still permitted to take guardianship or adopt if they fail a drug screen, but are not eligible to receive a subsidy. Workers in California commented that the criteria for adoption are more stringent than the foster parent licensing standards and thus kin who are licensed foster parents may not be able to receive adoption subsidies. In both Indiana and Connecticut, only blood-related kin can receive a guardianship subsidy. Moreover, in Indiana and California, kin may only receive guardianship subsidies if they care for older children or a sibling group. In Alabama, kin are generally prohibited from receiving an adoption subsidy and the state has no subsidized guardianship program.

> "They're the same [subsidized guardianship requirements and licensing requirements] except for the substance abuse. Licensing doesn't have substance abuse requirements. We did find out that in some cases, some of the things we've waived under licensing requirements . . . kin could not meet the subsidized guardianship requirements." (Connecticut foster care worker)

> "They must be eligible, too [for subsidized guardianship]. There is a higher standard for subsidized guardianship [than for guardianship]." (Connecticut licensing supervisor)

> "Again, that's why we have more subsidized guardianships than adoptions [because children don't have to fit any categories for subsidized guardianships, unlike for subsidized adoption]. This is stupid; it's better financially to do the subsidized guardianship." (Connecticut foster care worker)

> "We had a relative foster parent who had a sibling group of five and [the parents'] rights were being terminated, and normally the state will not give a subsidy to relatives who want to adopt. But with this we kind of went in through the back door and did a foster parent adoption so she was able to adopt the five children, get the state subsidy, and get out of child welfare." (Alabama administrator)

> "When a relative barely passes initial checks, you worry about them passing the checks later for adoption." (California foster care supervisor)

"Even with the director's exception, we have to make sure they'll clear the adoption test later, which is a higher standard. Otherwise, it's not a concurrent planning home. The relatives are upset because I told them, 'First, this is what you need for a director's exception. Now adoptions has some more concerns, so they want another assessment.' So it's a reasonable request, but the family's seeing it as, 'See, this is how you people are. First you tell us you need this. Then we do that, then you add something else we have to do.'" (California intake worker)

In addition to the barriers to accessing an ongoing monthly subsidy, kin in Alabama, California, and Connecticut may also lose access to other financial supports and services if they adopt or take guardianship. For example, these kin may not receive clothing allowances, school supplies, free summer camp, or other miscellaneous supports the agency provides for children in foster care. In Connecticut, foster children receive free college tuition. Kin who take guardianship receive similar tuition assistance for the children in their care but are not eligible if they adopt the children. Workers in Connecticut also pointed out that kin caregivers' income is not considered for Supplemental Security Income (SSI) benefits for a child if kin take guardianship, but their income is considered if they adopt, making them less likely to be eligible. SSI benefits are considerably more than basic foster care or adoption assistance subsidies.

Similarly, workers in California pointed out that kin who become guardians of foster children are eligible for a basic foster care rate, but not a specialized rate. Many kin care for foster care children with special needs and receive specialized foster care payments that may be two or three times the basic foster care rate. Workers in California also noted that kin receive child care assistance as long as the agency maintains an open case, but if kin adopt or take guardianship and a case is closed, they are no longer eligible.

"The clothing allowance [does not continue]. Certainly, with our flexible funding accounts, we can provide some additional supports, like summer camps, to our open cases that we couldn't provide to the subsidized guardianship cases. Once the subsidy happens, it's [the case is] over." (Connecticut foster care worker)

"I have a case with relatives who only want to be foster parents so the child can go to college. They are very honest about it and know that if they deal with CPS [Child Protective Services] for five more years, CPS will pay for college." (Connecticut foster care supervisor)

"DCFS needs more information for caregivers about differences between guardianship, adoption, and other options. If you have a difficult child and take adoption, a lot of services stop. Money follows, but they [DCFS] have to tell caregivers the difference . . . what it does and does not mean." (California caregiver)

"Initially when they [relative caregivers] are under us, they receive child care. So if you have a relative who is still working and they are receiving day care, day care is one of the most expensive bills a family can have. You know they need it because they can't leave the child alone. That stops when we close the case." (California administrator)

"We are running into problems with the new program Kin-GAP [subsidized guardianship] because the relatives will not sign off and allow the case to be closed. A lot of relatives are saying that they don't want the case closed because they want the social worker involved or they want the clothing allowance of $148 per year. Caregivers don't believe that they will still get services if they agree to close the case." (California foster care supervisor)

"Some don't want guardianship because they won't get services as they would if they stayed in long-term foster care, which is true. Those with older kids don't want to do it because of money and the money for college [which they would lose if they chose guardianship]." (California foster care worker)

"If relatives adopt, they often lose money. So there is a disincentive to what would otherwise would be the best result." (California judge)

"A lot of times, day care is the only reason we keep a case open." (Alabama foster care supervisor)

"Although I still have relatives who are electing to keep their cases open for other reasons. They say finances aren't the reason. I don't think they trust the system." (California foster care workers)

Long-Term Permanency?

Workers questioned how kinship care affects the long-term stability of permanency outcomes. While adoption is considered the most permanent and binding option, workers noted that birth parents are often very involved with their children even after adoption has occurred. Some relatives adopt or take guardianship of a child, but then allow birth parents to rear the child again if the relative believes that the birth parents have addressed the problems that prevented them from parenting appropriately. Workers noted that just as youth who age out of foster care often seek out the birth parents who abused them, children in kinship care who have been adopted still seek out their birth parents. Unlike some foster youth aging out of the system, children in kinship care have, by definition, retained contact with at least a portion of their extended family. As a result, children in kinship care are far more likely to have ongoing contact with birth parents post-permanency, such as at holiday celebrations or family events.

> "Relative guardians give kids back [to the parents] all the time. All of a sudden they think the parent's okay or . . . gets out of jail and they just give the child back. For the most part, we don't know about them unless there's another report. I think it probably happens more often than not." (Connecticut administrator)

> "With a relative, sometimes they [adopt] the child because the child is family, [but] they are often not really committed to that specific child. They often take the child thinking that they will reunify the child with the parents." (California foster care supervisor)

Three of the four states in the study have undertaken subsidized guardianship programs, and all states allow kin to seek guardianship (with or without money) as a permanency outcome. Workers and administrators acknowledged that they had no information to support their concerns, but many were worried about the long-term stability of guardianships. Based on our conversations, it was unclear if these concerns were based on anecdotal experiences in which guardianships disrupted placements or on the perception that guardianships by nature are fundamentally less stable. Many workers noted that adoptions, including those involving children adopted by non-kin, often disrupt.

"It's almost a vicious cycle. You get the children and you make permanency plans for them so they are in subsidized guardianship, which is transferring guardianship to a relative. So they're not really in foster care per se—but then, later on, as they get older—depending on what they were removed for—those issues might start coming out. So then they call us and say 'You've got to remove them, I can't take it anymore,' but based on this child, this is typical behavior." (Connecticut foster care worker)

"I don't think they really looked at the long-term effects of Kin-GAP. I don't think they put enough research into it. They put a Band-Aid on it. They didn't think about the long-term effects. What's happening now is that, before you can terminate [the case] in the court system, it's ending up back in the system. Relatives are dying and giving guardianship to other people who have [committed abuse/neglect] crimes against their sons and daughters." (California administrator)

"We need another category, not adoption and not called legal guardianship, but more permanent than guardianship. Legal guardianship is for the convenience of the adults. And adoption is for the permanency of the child. It should be packaged in a different way, but not any less permanent than adoption." (California administrator)

"What we're told is that guardianship isn't permanent because it can be set aside at any point and the kid comes back in the system. With adoption it is harder to set aside [the responsibility]. What are the real differences in the longer term? Do more children that end up in guardianship come back to us versus adoption? The belief here is that adoption papers equal more commitment."(California administrator)

Summary and Discussion

Kinship care has a far-reaching impact on child welfare agencies' permanency-planning efforts and the permanency outcomes of foster children. While long-term foster care is discouraged, workers feel much less urgency to terminate parental rights, close a case, or push for adoption when children are with kin. Birth parents may also feel less urgency to take the necessary steps for reunification when their children are placed with kin.

Kinship foster children are also less likely to be adopted. Many agencies do not encourage kin to adopt, and others do a poor job of explaining the need for adoption or how adoption differs from other permanency options. While we found that kin may be less opposed to adoption than was previously thought, they may have legitimate reasons and financial incentives for not wanting to adopt.

ASFA has affected how child welfare agencies approach permanency planning for children in kinship care. Agencies and the courts are stressing the importance of permanency and are, at least rhetorically, displaying less tolerance of long-term foster care. ASFA has also increased the pressure on workers to identify relatives early and to discuss their commitment to permanency should birth parents not be able to reunify with their children.

While most people interviewed acknowledge that adoption is more permanent than guardianship or long-term foster care, few sites were making a strong push to get kin to adopt. Many workers do not think adoption is necessary for children cared for by relatives, while others do not think many kin will consider adoption. If all things were equal, workers generally agreed that most kin would consider adoption. However, things are typically not equal. Workers acknowledged that kin were very concerned about how adoption would affect not only their relationship with the birth parents, but also with the child's larger family. Moreover, many kin would lose considerable financial or other supports if they chose to adopt.

Permanency may be conceptually appealing to plan and strive for, but it is very difficult to measure. Although we can assess how stable arrangements are, a child's perception of permanency is also critical. Do children in kinship care feel that their living arrangement is less permanent if their caregiver does not adopt them? Do kin feel a greater sense of commitment to children if they adopt? Research is severely limited on how the stability of children in long-term foster care and guardianship differs from those who have been adopted.

There is no rational justification for denying ongoing financial assistance to relatives who cannot meet adoption or guardianship requirements while allowing these same kin to care for children permanently. How can a kin caregiver be an acceptable adoptive parent, but not be an acceptable subsidized adoptive parent? If not being able to meet requirements means that kin are somehow not acceptable caretakers, then they should not be permitted to have permanent custody. If they are acceptable caretakers, then they should not be denied ongoing financial support—such denial only serves to punish the children.

This discrepancy points to the larger issue of the inconsistencies in requirements and support provided by different permanency options available to kinship caregivers. Child welfare agencies need to rethink how they approach permanency planning for children in kinship care. Agencies may want to experiment with methods to better assess kinship caregivers' commitment as well as how children in kinship care feel about the permanency of their living arrangement, rather than focusing solely on legal permanence. Both the adoption and the guardianship processes are difficult for kin (not to mention workers) to understand, and kin may simply get hung up on the word *adoption*. Agencies need to do a better job of articulating how a legal change in permanency affects the responsibilities of the kinship caregiver and the rights of the birth parents. Agencies may want to work with their state courts to design a permanency option that is culturally sensitive to concerns of kinship caregivers but allows for greater stability than guardianship is at least perceived to have. In addition, greater commitment, regardless of how it is measured, should not be rewarded with less assistance.

Finally, child welfare agencies need to acknowledge that birth parents will continue to be involved in their children's lives when kin either adopt or take guardianship. Agencies need to prepare both kin and the children to manage this ongoing relationship. Agencies may also want to consider providing some limited but ongoing supervision of these children post-permanency.

NOTE

1. One could argue that if birth parents require the punitive aspect of foster care to motivate themselves, they are very likely to relapse and cause the child to experience even greater instability. Substance-abusing parents who are not self-motivated may comply with case plan requirements but may be unlikely to make the changes needed to be effective parents in the long term.

7

Voluntary Placement or Foster Care Diversion?

Karin Malm and Rob Geen

There are times when child welfare agency staff may help arrange for a child to live with a kinship caregiver, but do not ask the court to adjudicate the child so the state can take custody. For example, during or after a child protective services investigation, a caseworker may advise a parent to let a relative care for a child. Both the parent and the relative are likely to know that if the parent refuses, the agency may petition the court to obtain custody. Nonetheless, we refer to such arrangements as "voluntary" kinship care placements. Many child welfare experts have argued that voluntary kinship care placements are common; the 1997 National Survey of America's Families (NSAF) estimated that close to 300,000 children were in such care.

There are many circumstances under which child welfare agencies may help arrange for a child to live with kin without seeking custody. In many cases, the level of risk to the child is not sufficient to meet agency standards for an official case opening, court involvement, and formal removal of the child from the home. However, caseworkers may still have concerns about safety if the child remains with the birth parent. In other situations, there is no parent with whom the child can remain. Agencies described cases in which a parent enters inpatient treatment or begins a jail sentence. In these cases, child welfare is often notified by the treatment facility or law enforcement agency. States' practices vary on the use of voluntary placement arrangements.

Most states acknowledge the use of voluntary placements. Based on a recent Urban Institute survey, 31 states (including Alabama, California, and Indiana, which participated in this study) have policies that allow caseworkers to arrange for a child to be placed with a relative following a child abuse and neglect investigation without seeking adjudication (Jantz et al. 2002). In 17 of the 31 states, custody remains with the parent, in 5 states the kinship caregiver is awarded custody, and 9 states reported that custody depends on case circumstances, most frequently going to the parent or relative.

These voluntary placements are treated differently by child welfare agencies than foster care placements throughout the case process—caregiver assessment, worker supervision, and services and payment determination. We know from the results of our policy survey that states conduct various kinds of assessments of the relatives in these situations. Twenty-two of the 31 states with policies that allow voluntary placements conduct a child abuse and neglect registry check on relatives, while 21 states conduct a criminal background check. Less frequently required is a home study or income check (nine and two states, respectively). Survey results indicate that the level of supervision of these cases varies widely, with 14 states (of 31) not requiring workers to provide any supervision to these arrangements. Overall, states note the amount of supervision is decided on a case-by-case basis and varies depending upon need and risk factors (Jantz et al. 2002). Services available to kinship caregivers in these arrangements are minimal, and since the children they care for are not in the custody of the state, their caregivers are also unable to receive foster care payments. However, these caregivers can obtain Temporary Assistance for Needy Families (TANF) child-only grants as well as some guardianship assistance payments.

Alabama is one of several states that appear to view voluntary placement as the best option whenever possible. Of all children placed in out-of-home care in Alabama, 60 percent are placed voluntarily with kin. In addition to Alabama, six other states[1] rely on voluntary arrangements for a majority of the children they place with kin. Other states rely on voluntary placements under more limited circumstances.

Most children who live with kin are doing so privately; a child welfare agency was in no way responsible for arranging their placement. Many private kinship caregivers seek assistance from these agencies in caring for a related child, and agency responses vary. The Urban Institute survey asked states to document policies for assisting these private kinship caregivers. For example, a child welfare agency may be aware of kin if an investigation of abuse or neglect was conducted in the past and kin previously accepted responsibility for a child without child welfare assistance. Twenty-six states report that they would offer some type of assistance to kin in this situation, ranging from opening a case to community referrals. When kin claim to be caring for a child who was abused or neglected, but no investigation occurred, 24 states report providing assistance, which may often include initiating an investigation of abuse or neglect. Finally, if a relative reports no abuse or neglect but says he or she is unwilling to continue caring for the child without assistance, 35 states report they would provide some type of help.

Although not taken into state custody, children in voluntary and private kinship care are vulnerable. A study by Ehrle, Geen, and Clark (2001) shows that many of these children face various socioeconomic risks to their healthy development. Almost one-third (31 percent) of children in voluntary kinship care and 43 percent of children in private kinship care live in families with incomes below the federal poverty level. Many of these children live with a caretaker without a high school diploma (55 percent of children in voluntary care and 33 percent of those in private kinship care). In addition, more than half of these children live with a caregiver who does not have a spouse (53 percent of children in voluntary care and 55 percent of children in private kinship care). And almost one-third (32 percent) of children in voluntary kinship care and 15 percent of children in private kinship care live with four or more other children.

Of even greater concern, 30 percent of children in voluntary kinship care and 20 percent of children in private kinship care face three or more of these socioeconomic risks simultaneously. The level of risk faced by children in voluntary and private kinship care is significantly higher than children nationally and is comparable with the level of risk faced by children in kinship foster care.

This chapter examines when and how child welfare agencies rely on kin to care for children who are not taken into state custody. Because so little is known about voluntary placements in terms of actual practices, this study was designed to be exploratory in nature, documenting written and unwritten agency guidance for placing children with kin voluntarily and how workers and supervisors translate agency policy and guidance into daily practice. Below we discuss the factors that affect whether and when agencies arrange voluntary placements; how agencies assess, monitor, and sometimes support these placements; how agencies approach permanency planning with children in voluntary placements; and how agencies respond when private kin seek assistance.

When Voluntary Placements May Occur

Child welfare agencies and workers use many terms to refer to placements in which they are somehow involved in arranging for a child to live with kin but in which the state does not take custody of the child. Some refer to this practice as *diversion*, since these children are diverted from the foster care system. Others refer to this practice as an *informal placement*, an *informal arrangement*, an *informal adjustment*, or an *informal* or *relative agreement*. Many workers (except in Alabama) were quick to point out that these situations should not be called placements, since the child welfare agency is not responsible for these children. While child welfare staff may suggest placing a child voluntarily with kin and may even assess the kinship caregiver, the arrangement occurs as an agreement between the birth parent and the kin.

> "The term 'voluntary placement' is really a misnomer. Legally [at this stage] an agency can only release a child to a parent. Thus, in a 'voluntary placement' situation, the agency is technically releasing the child to the parent, who is voluntarily placing their child with a relative." (California intake supervisor)

> "We [Department of Children and Families (DCF)] do not arrange it [voluntary placement]. You tell the family they need to do it. If you are arranging it, it gets sticky, because the relatives can argue that it's a DCF placement." (Connecticut investigative worker)

Despite the differences in terminology used across states and among workers, for the purposes of this chapter, we refer to all such arrangements as voluntary placements.

There appear to be both agency-related issues that affect whether agencies utilize voluntary placements as well as more case-specific issues that influence this practice. Agency issues that affect whether and when agencies utilize voluntary arrangements include the level of risk necessary for legally intervening and removing a child from the home, a "less is more" philosophy among agency administrators and workers, and resource availability. In addition, caseworkers identified numerous examples of case-specific criteria that would affect whether they would seek custody of a child or encourage a voluntary placement.

Agency Issues and Voluntary Placement

With the exception of Alabama, respondents in our study states noted that the level of risk necessary for legal intervention is central to the use of voluntary placement arrangements. Voluntary placements occur when there is insufficient evidence for legal removal of the child yet the agency still has concerns about the situation.

> "The first issue is safety; [we] have to take the child if there's any risk. [In one case] I've done recently, the mom is using [drugs] and she admits she's using, she goes into detox [substance abuse treatment] and detox knows she has kids, so they call it in to us. We go there and ask, 'Who is taking care of your kids?' The mom put the kids with grandmother and has no prior history with the department. We can take the kids into custody for neglect, but what's that going to do? She [the mother] is in treatment already and the kids are safe." (Connecticut investigative worker)

> "If a child claims he was abused but there was nothing going on, we offer voluntary services to avoid bringing them into court when abuse is questionable. We'll place with a relative until we can check it out further." (California intake worker)

> "Voluntary family maintenance units do it [voluntary placements with relatives], but it's a very specific agreement. For a voluntary agreement, the risk must be low, since the case is not going to court. It doesn't happen often. More often we would leave the child in the home and revisit the home involving family preservation workers." (California administrator)

> "Sometimes parents are isolated from relatives, and we'll ask if the parent has sought help from relatives. Try to get parents to think about other ways to deal with [the] problem. That's provided we're dealing only with a supervision issue and not something more serious." (California investigative supervisor)

"I hate to say we are arranging this [informal arrangement]. What we're [doing], as the initial response worker, we're very strongly encouraging this and inviting them to accept that this could become an 'either-or' situation. You [the birth parent] either agree that grandma takes guardianship and we're out of your lives, and say you're willing to go to drug treatment. Grandma, when you think she's got her act together, go back to family court. Versus the other side, we're going to be real involved along with the juvenile court, and maybe we don't really have enough to support a case." (California investigative worker)

Alabama appears to differ from the other three study states in that if a relative is available and can care for a child, the child will not be taken into custody. The vast majority of children in study sites removed from their homes and placed with kin are in voluntary placements in each of the Alabama sites we visited. Respondents in Alabama still cited the level of risk to the child as a determining factor; however, it was discussed in relation to risk to the child in the kin's home (i.e., the relative's ability to protect the child from the offending parent), not whether the abuse or neglect allegation rises to the level of legal intervention. Central to practices in Alabama appears to be the agency's philosophy that keeping families "out" of the system is better for them.

"I won't take a child into custody if the relative is willing and able [to care for child]. I've only taken three kids into custody in two years. Ninety percent were placed with relatives or the situation resolved itself." (Alabama investigative worker)

"If we don't think the relative will protect the child from the offending parent or give adequate supervision, we may not place [with the relative]." (Alabama investigative worker)

"Only if relatives really push does state take custody [of a child] from the beginning [of the case]." (Alabama administrator)

"Workers tell them [the relatives] the advantages and disadvantages of being licensed. They tell them the burden of being a foster parent and that the agency will help them out, even if [they're] not licensed. The larger the sibling group, the more likely the relative will want to be licensed. Workers discourage licensing because of the stigma." (Alabama administrator)

"If he [the child] can be safe in his own home or with a relative, there would be no need for custody care. If we [the agency] make a recommendation for the child to go with a relative, the relative usually gets custody in the court hearing." (Alabama investigative supervisor)

"We really try to stay out of peoples' lives if we can. We want everyone to hopefully be self-sufficient and not have to depend on DHR [Department of Human Resources] continuing to be involved." (Alabama investigative worker)

Workers in Alabama also said that voluntary placements were the only way that children could be placed with kin immediately, because if a child is taken into custody, the child cannot stay with the relative until the relative becomes licensed. Licensing often takes many months, during which time the child would be in a non-kin foster home.

While some respondents in local agencies in the other three study states asserted the view that keeping children out of the "system" is better for families, this did not appear to be an agencywide philosophy. Some workers in these states pointed out that empowering families to make their own decisions is also a factor in whether voluntary placements are arranged. If, early on in the process (i.e., before or during an investigation), parents are cooperative and suggest that a relative can take the child while they seek help, many workers noted they would agree to such an arrangement. Some workers said that even if a report of abuse and neglect was substantiated, they may accept a voluntary agreement between the birth parent and kin if the future risks were low.

"Most of us feel that if we can stay out of it, it's better usually. Once we [agency staff] get involved, there are limitations, restrictions. [Without us] some families will begin to work things out on their own." (Indiana assessment worker)

"[A voluntary placement] would have to happen early on, before any court involvement. If mom wants the child to go live with Aunt Suzie, we would do the criminal checks and a child protective services records check and see if there's anything we would have opposing [a voluntary placement], but if [we're okay with that] plan, we could send to probate court." (Connecticut ongoing supervisor)

"I had a case where a mother admitted her substance abuse and she went for inpatient treatment and gave her kid to her grandmother. If we have the option, we'll do it without DCF involvement and just do an informal agreement. But there are people that discourage that here. We've been told to discourage it, and I personally don't agree with it. We don't need to be involved in every informal arrangement. We are involved in that we do an assessment to make sure grandmother is safe, and we are involved if we can provide any support or services. But if there is no need for legal intervention, and if I can keep the court out of it, I will." (Connecticut investigative supervisor)

"What you need to have [for an informal arrangement] is cooperation from the parent. But they see you [the agency] as the enemy. They don't understand that we do not want to take the kids. They see our role as negative: 'You are child protective services, which means you are here to take my child,' no matter how many times you tell them that you don't want to do this." (Indiana investigative worker)

"I think it gives the family a sense of power that they are taking care of their situation, taking care of their own problems, without an agency having to come in and give them this help. I think it empowers them." (California investigative worker)

"Sure, we place without custody. A mom can voluntarily say she wants kids with grandma and then we refer for services. The issue becomes, why were we called out? Can the child be protected? This [informal arrangement] doesn't happen often, but it's a way out for everybody. We have fixed a problem, maybe more as street workers than as case managers for the state." (Indiana investigative worker)

Some respondents noted that their agency is doing more voluntary agreements because it has become more difficult to prove abuse occurred. There is also some indication that agencies would like to do more voluntary placements and often explore the possibility. However, agency staff noted that most families do not have the capacity to make these sorts of arrangements themselves.

Agencies that use family group conferencing, a technique that involves the entire family in planning for the care of a child requiring protection, report that family meetings may increase the use of voluntary placements. A court official in California noted that family group conferences mean that many families never come into court because they work out an arrangement among themselves.

> "Yes, it [arranging a voluntary placement] can be a common occurrence. Can grandmother provide protection for the child? We use family unity [meetings] a lot and are increasing the number of meetings over the last few months. We have a family unity meeting before filing a petition in some cases to see if the extended family can help out." (California administrator)

A lack of agency resources was seen in some agencies as an incentive for making informal placements but in others as a reason for not opening a voluntary placement case. In agencies where foster care caseloads were high and resources low, workers suggested that voluntary placements may save foster care resources for those children most in need. At the same time, agencies vary in the extent to which they have resources for children not in state custody. In some agencies, workers noted that they had to place children in foster care to get support for kin and the children they care for.

> "Most agencies are understaffed, probably, and if a relative comes forward and wants to care for the child, we let them so that we can expend energy on those families where we have to force intervention." (Alabama administrator)

> "We really don't have time at this office to provide for voluntary cases. The only way to open a case is through dependency and [with the] court involved, a very official case. The other more voluntary cases we refer out for services." (California continuing worker)

Many workers also suggested that negative media attention has made their agencies more risk adverse and that they cannot rely on voluntary placements as much as they did in the past. Some workers noted that agency guidance had narrowed the circumstances under which voluntary placements would be acceptable.

> "We don't place with a relative without taking custody. We used to do that years ago, used to step back and let them deal with it. Our

policy is not to take the child without custody. We can do an informal adjustment. The case then remains open, with monitoring and services, but no CHINS [child in need of supervision]. These caregivers are not licensed." (Indiana adoption worker)

"What used to happen during an investigation was that it was really an avoidance of us taking responsibility. I'm speaking of a child very much at risk, abused or neglected. The easy way out, if you will, was to tell the relatives to go to probate [court] to obtain guardianship, when, in fact, we didn't know anything about the relatives or if the child would even go to the relatives. Now it happens only as a short-term solution, when mom's incarcerated or in a substance abuse program." (Connecticut supervisor)

Case-Specific Issues

Administrators, supervisors, and workers noted a number of case-specific issues that affect whether voluntary placements with relatives are arranged. It was clear from our discussions with workers in Alabama that their use of voluntary placements extends to all types of children, regardless of age or type of abuse or neglect. In the other states, older children are more likely to be placed with a relative in a voluntary arrangement. Many workers noted cases involving teenager-parent conflicts that led to voluntary placements.

"A lot of times there is a lot of hostility between a parent and teen and we're called in. After talking to everyone, it's just a normal teenager-mom fight. If [a] child wants to go with grandma for a few days, then we make a plan, see if things quiet down." (Indiana assessment supervisor)

"But you can see that there are some tensions in this family, and you can see that this mom and dad and teenager need a break from each other. You might ask what other supports they have, and maybe the mom and dad say that they think it would be good if she [the teenager] goes and spends the weekend with the grandma. That's a family arrangement, which is separate from a DCF-sanctioned placement." (Connecticut investigative supervisors)

"Most of the agency is very liberal when it comes to placement of teens, but when it comes to children under seven, you might find big differences between regions and supervisors on how they allow something like a voluntary placement to happen." (Connecticut administrator)

In addition to a child's age, other case characteristics, such as a why a child needed protection, may affect the decision to arrange a voluntary placement. For example, our study found that voluntary placement was more common when a child needed to be placed due to a parental incapacity or other non–abuse-related reason. The relationship between the birth parent and kin caregiver was also a factor in deciding whether to open a case or take custody of a child. Workers noted having to open cases in which kin do not get along with or are scared of birth parents.

"I've got one [case] now. The mother has medical issues. When I got the referral we put some things in place that didn't work, so after a lengthy discussion with the family, we decided to let the baby go with the maternal aunt. So I've been monitoring the case for about a month now, and the baby is doing really well without any legal intervention." (Indiana assessment worker)

"We don't do as many of these voluntary out-of-home placements where it's a situation of abuse or neglect. More of those we use when it's a medically fragile child or a psychiatric intervention [for the child] is required." (California investigative supervisor)

"Many times relatives will say, 'I'll take the kids but only if you do something. We need your help and protection from Mom.'" (California supervisor)

"We don't have to take children into custody when there's an agreement between mom and dad and relative. We'll just provide wraparound services. We have to take custody when [the] relative is scared that mom will come into their home. If birth parents are uncooperative with the relative placement, we'll take custody and possibly place with relatives anyway." (Alabama administrator)

Some respondents noted that there are times when the agency takes custody of a child to enable the relative to be eligible for services. In

Alabama, the main reason cited for taking custody of a child placed with kin was to provide foster care payments to kinship caregivers who were financially distressed. In California, workers mentioned that for the child to be automatically covered by MediCal (California's Medicaid program), the agency must take custody of the child. Workers also noted that birth parents may have an incentive to agree to a voluntary placement since they have to reimburse the agency for the cost if their child is placed in foster care.

"If they can afford to take care of the children without any help, then they would rather not be foster parents because of all the strict regulations, and even checking out their home is different if they're a foster parent because we have to hold kin foster parents to the same standard as we hold foster parents." (Alabama administrator)

"The agency has had to take custody before just so a grandmother can afford to keep the child. Money often makes a big difference." (Alabama administrator)

"Sometimes there is no difference between kin and non-kin. Kin want DHR to have custody as a hammer. Many of the grands [grandparents] are afraid of these kids, especially the ones that grew up in drug houses. Sometimes they say they cannot do this without more money and we will refer them to foster care." (Alabama foster care workers)

"We get reimbursement for certain services, and they [the birth parents] may have to pay back certain amounts of money for having kids in placement. You tell them they may save a little by not having a child in placement." (Indiana investigative worker)

Many workers said that voluntary placements may be used when kin are willing and able to care for a child but cannot pass the licensing criteria to become foster parents. Rather than placing the child with non-kin, workers noted they would place the child with kin voluntarily.

"Guardianships that go through probate court are basically if the family can't be licensed. Say they live in a two-bedroom apartment and kids with different ages share a bedroom, foster care and adoption [units] won't license a home like that." (Connecticut foster care supervisor)

"If we are working with a family and we know we can't license them, then we know that long-term foster care is not an option. Right from the beginning, we should just go to court, transfer guardianship, and get the hell out. Let these people live their life with these kids; that is permanent, solve the problem." (Connecticut foster care worker)

"For example, this grandmother was taking care of other children, and altogether she was caring for seven children in a two-bedroom apartment. Absolutely no way we could license her, so we just transferred the guardianship through the juvenile court. Not subsidized, because we could never, ever license her." (Connecticut foster care supervisor)

"When they don't want to follow through with the licensing, most of them agree to take legal guardianship of the children, and when they do that, then we can dismiss and come out of the situation." (Indiana foster care worker)

Workers also reported that they are often involved, not in arranging a voluntary placement, but in assessing a placement that was arranged by a birth parent or the police. It is not uncommon for the police to arrange for a relative to temporarily care for a child and then report the family to child welfare. Similarly, workers may begin a child abuse investigation and find that the child in question has already moved into the home of a relative. Workers are more comfortable accepting an arrangement that was made prior to their involvement than helping to arrange a voluntary placement. In addition, many workers suggested that their hands were tied in such situations—they could not remove the child from the relative because they could not prove the child was in danger.

"The bottom line is that if the plan has been made prior to our involvement, then the agency is covered. I've had cases where the police department gave the children to a relative at the time of removal, and child protective services must re-remove because a plan [between the relative and birth parent] was not made prior to the police department removal." (California administrator)

"The agency can't sanction a placement with a relative unless it's done legally. If the family makes arrangements on their own, then the case is not rising to the level where it warrants removal of the child. You must make sure you have a legal case to take custody of a child." (Connecticut investigative supervisor)

"Usually if families are that close, they take it upon themselves to find a solution before we [child welfare agency staff members] come into the picture. When a family is that together, they'll go down to probate court and get temporary guardianship and we'll never hear about it." (Connecticut investigative supervisor)

"My thing is, was the plan made prior? If the plan was made prior, then that's something we must respect and have to uphold, because as a parent that's your right." (California administrator)

"If a mother makes arrangements for a relative to pick the child up after a drug raid or arrest, [we] don't have to take custody of the child. [Even] when we're involved, it's not always necessary that we take the children into custody." (Indiana ongoing supervisor)

Influence of Risk and Resources on Agency Attention to Post-Placement Issues

In addition to providing information on the circumstances in which they may help arrange a voluntary placement, study respondents discussed how, if at all, the agency provided support and monitoring of these cases *post-placement*. The level and nature of ongoing attention paid to these placements varies significantly. Two main factors influence how agencies support and monitor these placements—the placement's level of risk and the availability of agency resources to support these families.

In Alabama, workers use voluntary placements for higher risk situations than do workers in other states. However, almost all of these placements are opened as active child protection cases. Workers assess all kinship homes to ensure that caregivers can provide safe and effective care, albeit based on standards considerably lower than those accepted for foster care licensure. Voluntary placements in Alabama are treated as in-home services cases and thus receive ongoing supervision and services.

In California, Connecticut, and Indiana, workers report that it is unlikely for the agency to open a case when a child is in voluntary kinship care. However, it appears that some local agencies have greater resources for voluntary placements, which may lead workers to open a case and provide services. When opening a case is an option, workers assess the ongoing risk of voluntary placement to determine whether to keep a case open and for how long, and whether and how to supervise the kinship home. Like the decision of whether to use kin voluntarily, workers are following unwritten rules to determine how to support and supervise these kin. Thus, practices vary considerably even within an office.

> "I think voluntary placements are very common at the emergency response stage. We make an assessment of the relative's ability to protect the child from the parent; we might even help the relative gain legal guardianship. The 30-day closure guideline for emergency response cases means the worker would leave the case open at least through the temporary guardianship hearing; sometimes they will open the referral and send it over to the voluntary unit, while we wait for the case to stabilize, then close it out. We don't close cases that we worry about. If they meet a certain level of risk, we leave the cases open." (California administrator)

> "Sometimes there is a voluntary placement, but we still open a case. Or, we can close the case and let them work it out themselves. Relatives sometimes ask us to keep cases open. We may choose not to open a case if it is substantiated but low risk. More often than not, we do open a case." (California supervisor)

Absence of Permanency Planning for Children in Voluntary Placement

Child welfare caseworkers and administrators acknowledged in all sites visited that the agency does not conduct traditional permanency planning when children are in voluntary placements. Even when the agency opens a case following a voluntary placement, unless the court is involved, caseworkers do not generally discuss termination of parental rights (TPR) or adoption.

Even in Alabama, where voluntary agreements are used for the vast majority of kin placements, the agency does not seek TPR and does not develop a written permanency plan. In some sites, workers noted that they help kin obtain temporary legal custody and this result represented the permanency outcome. In Alabama, parental approval to give kin temporary custody is typically a condition for a voluntary placement.

> "We don't do a permanency plan [for voluntary placements]. Foster care does permanency planning. Once they get with the grandma . . . it's safe, it's closed, it's done. It's unwritten permanency planning." (Alabama foster care worker)

> "It depends on whether or not the court is involved. A lot of times we place with a relative and after about three months, we may close the case with the courts but leave it open to us. So I don't think we look at permanency, in terms of TPR, as closely when the courts are out of the picture, as opposed to when the court is in the picture." (Alabama foster care supervisor]

> "[If the parent is not involved or capable of reunification] the goal is to remain with the relative with temporary custody because we don't follow through with adoptions and termination of parental rights if we have relatives. If the child is not in our custody, we usually don't consider adoption." (Alabama foster care supervisor)

Several Alabama kinship caregivers were upset that child welfare workers pushed them to accept temporary custody. They did not feel they had been told the truth about the options available to them.

> "They ask you to take custody so they can close the case. What they [DHR workers] do is they tell you that they have to remove the children from their home, [and] is there anybody willing to take custody? Once you take custody, it's closed. They give you no information about any alternatives. You could become a foster parent for this child, or you can take custody of this child, or you can adopt this child. Those are really the options that are offered. But they ask you to take custody because it gets the case closed and off their desk in a hurry." (Alabama caregiver)

In several sites, workers noted that they refer kin to probate court to obtain guardianship. A major barrier to obtaining guardianship, however, is the substantial court cost involved. In Connecticut, workers reported that in the past, they would recommend to kin voluntarily caring for children to go to probate court to obtain guardianship. This practice was prohibited by policy instituted following the death of a child placed with kin voluntarily, a child who had been referred to probate court for guardianship. However, in Connecticut, as well as in the other states examined, child welfare workers may be asked to assess the homes of kin seeking guardianship from the probate court.

> "We used to be able to tell them to go to probate court, but we can't do that anymore, it's against policy now. I've had relatives go to court, before and after we've gotten involved, and request that they want the child living with them. It makes cases easier for us if a grandparent or someone has already started the process of going to probate court and requesting that the court give them custody. The court then requests that DCF do a study to see if this family is appropriate for the child to go to. So we're getting it on the other end." (Connecticut investigative worker)

Support for Private Kin Seeking Assistance

Child welfare agencies vary considerably in how they support private kin who seek help from them. Depending upon the specific circumstances of the case, local policies, and the services available, caseworkers may open a voluntary services case, help kin petition for custody, or help them through adoption or guardianship proceedings. In almost half of the sites we visited, including all of the rural sites, workers or administrators noted that they sometimes make children wards of the state and license the kinship caregiver as a foster parent. This practice, however, is not without controversy.

> "Sometimes we'll [take custody of] the child, but a lot are 'orchestrated to get money.' This is discouraged, but it has been done. Some people do it as a manipulation tactic. We've had families that have done that; they say, 'If I don't get the special care rate, I might really need to consider having you come and pick him up.' There has been a long-standing discussion on whether or not there should be a child welfare case because of finances." (California administrator)

Workers in Bridgeport, Connecticut, commented that many private kinship caregivers are attracted by the foster care stipend to seek child welfare assistance. In Lake County, workers noted that a child is not abandoned if a relative agrees to care for a child, and thus they will not take custody of a child if private kin seek out child welfare assistance after they initially agreed to care for a child. Lake County workers also noted that they tell kin that if a child is made a ward, there is no guarantee that the child will be placed with them.

Summary and Discussion

When and how often child welfare workers rely on voluntary kinship care varies greatly across states. Furthermore, the use of voluntary kinship care varies among counties, among offices within a county, and among individual workers. In addition, child welfare agencies provide various types and levels of support to private kin who seek assistance from the local agency. This variation in agency practice toward voluntary and private kinship care reflects differing local visions of the role and scope of the child welfare system.

In most states, child welfare agencies view voluntary kinship care as an option to be used, on a fairly limited basis, when caseworkers believe that children face a low level of risk based on specific case circumstances. In our study, California, Connecticut, and Indiana are representative of this view of voluntary kinship care. None of these states has policies, procedures, or guidance that clearly articulate when workers should rely on voluntary kinship care. Workers in these states noted that they follow unwritten rules and commonsense social work practices to determine when voluntary kinship care is appropriate. On the one hand, caseworkers need flexibility to determine the best way to resolve a family situation based on the specifics of the case. On the other hand, the lack of policy or practice guidance leads to great variability in how caseworkers resolve cases having similar circumstances. While caseworkers use their professional judgment as to when children can safely remain with kin voluntarily, workers' decisions appear to be influenced by their personal opinions about the extent to which particular families should be involved with the child welfare system.

Besides variations in practice, states like California, Connecticut, and Indiana may, intentionally or not, use voluntary kinship care to influence birth parents and kin. If, after a substantiated incident of abuse or neglect, a caseworker suggests that the birth parents place a child with kin, the birth parents may believe that if they do not comply with this suggestion, their children will be placed in foster care. Most of the workers in the three states spoke cautiously about their use of voluntary kinship care, saying that they do not pressure birth parents to place their children with kin. They also reported that they do not place children in voluntary kinship care, but help birth parents decide the best solution to the crisis.

In contrast, Alabama is representative of a handful of states that use voluntary kinship care whenever possible. Believing that keeping children out of the foster care system is often best, workers and administrators in Alabama spoke openly about their use of voluntary kinship care as diversion from foster care. They see their approach to kinship care as a form of family preservation and question why a state agency should assume custody of a child who can safely be cared for by extended family. Critics of Alabama's approach suggest that they are abdicating at least part of their responsibility for caring for these children. Although children in voluntary kinship care in Alabama receive ongoing supervision, they are not supported by foster care payments and may not have access to the same services as foster children. Also, child welfare staff members do not conduct permanency planning for children in voluntary kinship care.

Foster children receive greater financial and service support than do poor children outside the child welfare system, and policymakers are concerned that the system provides private kin with an unintended incentive to seek out child welfare assistance. At the same time, caseworkers recognize that private kin often care for children who have been abused or neglected, but are able to avoid agency involvement by stepping forward before it is officially reported. Research has shown that children in private kinship care face socioeconomic risks similar to those that children in voluntary and kinship foster care deal with. Moreover, private kinship caregivers do not receive the same level of services as either voluntary or kinship foster caregivers, although they are eligible for many services (Ehrle et al. 2001).

Acknowledging the challenges facing private kinship care families, many state and local welfare and child welfare agencies have developed programs to provide these families with additional financial and service support. Still, as evidenced by the results of this study, there are questions about how to support kin who seek out child welfare assistance, including the question of the point at which agencies should deem as wards of the state children cared for by private kin.

Much of the ongoing debate about child welfare agencies' use and support of kinship care reflects a larger debate about the mission and scope of the child welfare system. Child welfare agencies respond to children who have been abused or neglected and protect them from future harm. Yet it is unclear when and how child welfare authorities should get involved when a previously abused or neglected child is living with kin as a result of family intervention. When does a family's private crisis become a public concern, and when does the public concern end? What responsibility do child welfare agencies have to assess kin's ability to protect a child? What responsibility do agencies have to monitor the well-being of children cared for by kin? When children are cared for by kin, what responsibility do agencies have to help birth parents address challenges they face so that they can parent again? Under what circumstances and for how long should child welfare agencies be responsible for providing financial support and services to children cared for by kin?

To answer these questions, child welfare agencies must determine whether to treat kinship care as an extension of the biological family or as a type of temporary substitute care. If kinship care is merely an extension of the biological family, then child welfare agencies have limited responsibility for children in kinship care. Child welfare agencies have no reason to intrude into private family matters unless children are at significant risk of abuse or neglect. What may be difficult to gauge is the risk a child in kinship care faces. Without ongoing monitoring, child welfare agencies cannot determine whether kin can prevent birth parents from maltreating their children, not to mention whether kin themselves are abusive or neglectful. But abuse and neglect are possible in all families, and child welfare agencies do not monitor all families. If child welfare is to treat kinship care as an extension of the biological family, then agencies have no reason to scrutinize kinship care placements without evidence of abuse or neglect by kinship caregivers.

If child welfare agencies view kinship care as a temporary substitute placement, then it seems that these agencies should be responsible for monitoring a child's well-being and planning for the child's permanency. Moreover, to the extent that we think financial assistance influences children's well-being, child welfare agencies should financially assist children in kinship care just as they would children in non-kin foster care.

Most states view and treat kinship care both as an extension of the biological family and as a temporary substitute placement, depending on how and if child welfare becomes involved and the ongoing risk children face. The challenge these states face is determining whether, after becoming involved in a family crisis, the child welfare agency needs to stay involved or whether kin can provide adequate safety for a child without agency involvement. Also, states must decide when to become involved when kin have been caring for a child but later seek out assistance. Child welfare agencies assume that when kin step forward privately or early in the process, children are better cared for and at lower risk. This assumption is based on common sense and not empirical evidence. Unfortunately, there is almost no research that assesses the risk of different kinship care arrangements and that offers guidance to child welfare agencies and staff in making these decisions.

NOTE

1. Florida, Kentucky, Ohio, South Carolina, Utah, and Virginia.

In Their Own Words

Kin Speak Out about Their Caregiving Experiences

Victoria Russell and Karin Malm

This chapter reports the stories told by kinship caregivers about their experiences caring for related children who were involved with child welfare agencies. While other chapters in this book use information collected from focus groups to draw conclusions about child welfare agency policies and practices with kin, this chapter seeks to illustrate the circumstances and experiences of kin from their own perspective. Kin spoke passionately about how their caregiving affected and was affected by larger family issues, the issues faced by the children in their care, their own issues and challenges, and their interaction with the child welfare agency and the courts.

We report the experiences of 25 of the 157 kinship caregivers who participated in focus groups during the spring and summer of 2001. The stories of kinship caregivers presented here are based on the transcribed notes of the focus groups. The names of the caregivers, children, and other identifying information have been changed or omitted to protect their confidentiality. We did not select the 25 stories based on how articulate the caregivers were about their experiences. Rather, we selected stories that appeared to be representative of the feelings and experiences of the 157 participants. Moreover, we present caregivers' experiences from their perspective, using their own words as appropriate. Thus, the information they provided about such issues as eligibility for services or agency procedures may not always be accurate, but is what they believed to be true.

The 25 stories are grouped into the four categories or themes that were discussed most frequently, namely family issues, child issues, caregiver issues, and interaction with the child welfare system. Many, if not most, of the stories address more than one theme, and we recognize that our choice of category for an individual story is somewhat arbitrary.

Family Issues

The following four stories told by kinship caregivers stress the influence of birth parents and other family members on the kinship care placement. Kinship caregivers commented on the challenges posed by the ongoing contact they have with birth parents and other relatives, as well as the ongoing contact that the children in their care have with their parents. These stories illustrate the difficulties that child welfare workers report in working with kin in the areas of case planning, supervision, and birth parent visitation.

Annie

Annie is caring for four nieces and nephews ranging in age from 8 to 18 years. Annie began caring for the children after they were abandoned—Annie's sister left the children at her mother's house and didn't come back. Annie's mother felt that she was too old to care for the children, and Annie's father was just recovering from a stroke, so Annie offered to take them. It was not an easy transition for the children or for Annie.

> "I am single. I didn't want kids; I worked. That was all I did was work. My job was my primary activity. Luckily, I had five rooms in my house, but I had to get beds for all of them. Three days after I took the kids, two of them got the chicken pox."

Annie took the children to help her parents out and ended up making a long-term commitment. One of the most difficult things for Annie and the children to deal with was the fact that the children were older when she began caring for them, and they loved and wanted to be with their mother:

"That was the hardest thing; they did not lose contact with their mother at all. There was a lot of animosity because she would show up and she would want to be mom. I would give them a set of rules to live by and she [the birth mother] would tell them they didn't have to. That was our biggest problem, and I think that was the reason why one of the children was incarcerated. A lot of the things that happened, I think, may not have happened if things were handled a little bit differently. She wasn't consistent; she would come in and then she would disappear for a couple of weeks, and then she would come back again. It was like that, basically the whole time.

"She just recently got to the point where she takes the youngest child on the weekends only, and she is suing for partial custody of the child. She is finally showing consistency. But the youngest one is the only one that goes and stays with her; the older ones don't want to do it, they are too busy. She has a hard time with that. She will say to me, 'Make them do it.' I can't make them. I have been trying to guide them in the right direction for four years. She wants to be their best buddy and then she wants me to discipline them when she gets mad at them. I tell them all that they have to try and forge a relationship because she will always be their mother."

Annie was determined that this situation was going to be temporary—lasting just until the children's mother could care for them again—but she feels the child welfare agency had a different agenda:

"Within the first two years they were really trying to push guardianship on me. And I kept saying, 'No, my job is to keep my nieces and nephews together until their mother is ready to take them back.' I don't need any kids; if I wanted them, mine would already be grown. I didn't mind stepping up when I had to, to help out, but me going into this was with the understanding that eventually they were going back with their mother."

Helen

Helen is rearing two grandchildren, ages 10 and 15, and a great-nephew, who is 8 years old. Helen began caring for her grandchildren almost immediately after they were born. Her great-nephew and his sisters had been abandoned by their parents and were living with their grand-mother (Helen's sister). When having all the children became too much for Helen's sister to handle, Helen volunteered to take the boy. Helen is happy to care for her grandchildren and great-nephew:

> "My kids are all grown and I am still young, so I look at this as my second generation of kids. But I love it; I look at it like I was so young when I had my kids that I didn't get the opportunity to play. So now, as old as I am, I really have a lot of fun playing with these kids. Some-times they think I am a little crazy, but they keep me young. I enjoy it. My philosophy of the whole thing is that there [are] a lot of kids out there who don't have an opportunity to be with somebody that will take care of them and love them and give them things. Yes, I could go out and work for me all the time, but that is no fun, because I am really not enjoying it or sharing it with anybody."

Helen doesn't have many problems in caring for her grandchildren and great-nephew. Her only real challenge is with visitation. The issue is not too much of a problem with her great-nephew; she just has to be clear about her expectations:

> "The mother is my niece and she is young, and I think she enjoys the fact that she doesn't have her kids and she can live her life and do what she pleases. And she knows that the kids are all okay (her other four kids are with her mother), so she will see them when she wants to; otherwise, she really doesn't bother. She will call on a reg-ular basis. At first there was no contact—for the first year—but now she is back in the picture and she sees him on Sundays for church. He would come home crying and really confused. I am very direct and very open, so I sat down and told him the way that it really was. Now, if he goes, he goes; if he doesn't, he doesn't, but he is okay with it. I really don't have a big problem with it. We communicate on a good level. I have made it very clear that when he comes to [the birth mother's] house, 'These are my rules, [the rules] also follow him to your house.' . . . She abides by my rules, but I am very hard and firm, and I don't have a problem with jumping into her face and telling her, 'You either do it my way or you don't see your child at all.' I don't care what [child welfare] says, I am responsible for this child. He has to have some kind of structure."

The visitation situation for her grandchildren is more of a problem. She has tried to keep her grandchildren away from their mother, but the children don't want to stay away:

"My other two, that's a problem. The 15-year-old loves her mother to death and her mother is nothing but a drug addict. I try very firmly to keep her [the grandchild] away from her mother, because her mother has done some things with her that really don't sit well with me. I tried explaining that to her [the grandchild] on the grounds that, 'Yes, that is your mother, but her lifestyle is not the right lifestyle for you to be around. I am not trying to keep you separated from her, but due to the circumstances at this time it is best that you stay away from her.' That is where I am having a major, major problem. The 10-year-old, about two years ago, got mad at me and said he was going to stay with his mother. I said, 'Fine.' I was tired of him saying that so I packed up all of his clothes and I dropped him off to his mother. He stayed about four days, then he called me, crying that he wanted to come home. He never has said that again."

Sherry

Sherry has been taking care of her 8-year-old grandson for the past five years. She began caring for him after she noticed that he was being abused. As she described it:

"I was watching my grandson several times a week for my daughter (for day care), and he was showing up with some nasty bruises. I finally called 911. My daughter had two black eyes, and her boyfriend was screaming at me, and my grandson was clinging to me. My daughter didn't want me to take care of him [the grandson] because I'd been the one to turn them in [to child welfare]. Most of the abuse came from the boyfriend, but some it might have come from my daughter."

Shortly after the child was taken into child protective custody, the child's father and paternal grandmother got involved in hopes of getting custody.

"The other grandma wanted to care for him, too, because she knew about the monthly payments you receive. But she didn't pass the criminal check and came up dirty on the drug test. Her son meanwhile had gotten dragged back to jail on other drug charges. I was the only one there with clean hands . . . pretty sad actually."

Sherry continued caring for her grandson, but had put off thinking about adoption until very recently. She had been hoping that her daughter and her ex-husband would take responsibility for their son.

"I've been waiting four years for my daughter and her ex-husband to get it together. My grandson's been waiting. I've put off adoption because I thought they'd both maybe get it together, but that was a big mistake in the long run. It just dragged the process out. He [the grandson] started acting out more at school. His parents would come by and visit and say, 'Oh, yeah, we're going to bring you home one day.' I didn't realize how bad it was for him until he started seeing a psychologist because he was doing all this stuff at school."

Finally, because Sherry didn't think it would be good for her grandson to wait any longer for his parents, she decided to pursue adoption. Soon after making this decision, she says, "all hell broke loose." The boy's paternal grandmother still wanted custody of him and started trying to bribe him during visits. Sherry says that everything got entangled and her grandson was right in the middle of the conflict—everyone suddenly wanted him. To solve the problem, everyone went to court: Sherry, the paternal grandmother, the parents of the little boy, the little boy and his attorney, the social worker, and the boy's psychologist.

According to Sherry, the adoption process so far has produced an effect opposite of what she was hoping for—it has made things worse for her grandson. And even though the child's psychologist and social worker thought it was a bad idea, the little boy's attorney succeeded in convincing the court to let the little boy decide what he wanted. Sherry believes that in doing so, the court made her grandson feel like he was in control. And because her grandson just wants to make everyone happy, nothing was decided. Her grandson told the court that he wanted to see everyone and the court decided against adoption. Sherry is still the child's guardian, but he continues to have visits with his parents and his other grandmother.

Melissa

Melissa has been caring for three of her grandchildren on and off for 12 years. She became her granddaughter's primary caretaker when her daughter was arrested for drugs. Melissa described her feelings at the time of the arrest:

> "I don't think you have time to think. You don't even think about the next hour. You just think about right then and there and what you are going to do to keep these children safe. It's not about the parents at the time anyway, it's about the children. With my daughter, I knew she was doing something wrong, but I couldn't put my finger on it. When it happened, I was angry, but you don't have time to focus on that, because you have to take care of that child. Don't want to show anger when you pick up the child because then they will sense that in you and you will have to reassure them. You have to be angry later on, once the kids have settled down. Say to children they are going to be okay, safe—that they are with grandma."

Even though Melissa had been angry with her daughter, she feels that it is very important to make sure that her granddaughter doesn't see her anger:

> "Regardless of what these parents have done, these children still love these parents. Deep down she loves her mother and is going to want a relationship with her. That is why we have to be very careful while we are caring for these kids not to bring these parents down to these kids because then you are going to end up with double trouble—you will have the parents to deal with and a child that is angry."

Though Melissa doesn't necessarily feel that reunifying the children with their parents is always a good thing, she feels that it is a reality. Kids will most likely be reunited with their parents. Because of that, Melissa wants to make sure she doesn't do anything to make reunification more difficult for her granddaughter than it needs to be.

Child Issues

The following eight stories illustrate the emotional challenges facing the children cared for by kin and how kinship caregivers deal with these challenges. One of the most common issues raised by kinship caregivers was the difficulty they faced in comforting children and making them feel at ease, while at the same time figuring out how to discipline them when they are unruly and rebellious. Many of the children cared for by kin face severe emotional and physical challenges as a result of exposure to drugs or alcohol, abuse, and neglect.

Darleen

Darleen has been rearing her 7-year-old nephew for four years, ever since he was sexually abused by his mother. In her words,

> "My reason for taking in my nephew is that his father [Darleen's brother] is irresponsible. He's not capable of taking care of a young boy. And [child welfare] would not allow him his parental rights. So I stepped in because it's my nephew. He's my blood. He needs to know where he belongs."

Darleen was working full-time and had a good job before she began taking care of her nephew. Because of the time commitment involved in caring for her nephew, she eventually lost her job:

> "When I first got involved with my nephew, I had a full-time job with medical benefits, working 56 hours a week. With the problems my nephew was having because he has attention deficit syndrome . . . the school and day care would call my job four times a day. It was out of control. I had to leave my job to get my nephew. So, finally, down the line I lost my job.
> "I was out of work for a year and a half. DCF [Department of Children and Families] did not bother to say to [me], '[We] will go with you to the unemployment office and fight for your unem-

ployment,' because they said I left my job for unspecific reasons, but they didn't give me any type of support. They could of at least written me a letter, with the DCF stamp on it . . . to even back me up, because I went to like five interviews for my unemployment, to try to get it, and I never got it."

In addition to lack of support from the child welfare agency after she lost her job, Darleen also struggled with its unhelpfulness when her nephew's behavioral problems escalated:

"When my nephew set my living room on fire, do you think DCF volunteered to replace my furniture or my carpet? And then when we took him to the hospital to get him evaluated, they said, 'If you don't take [the child] back home with you, and you let them put him in an institution, he might never come back.' I told the social worker straight up, 'Well, so what? When I wake up in the morning, I will still own my home and my life.' So I let them take him for a month."

Darleen spoke at length about feeling unsupported by the child welfare agency. After the fire, when her nephew came back to live with her, she still didn't get the support she needed:

"I did not get assistance with day care, I did not get assistance with having to go out to find another apartment so that I would have room for this child and his brother. They did not help me with anything."

Though frustrated with the child welfare system, Darleen is dedicated to caring for her nephew.

"I'll never forget the day I went to court to get my nephew. The DCF lawyer asked me 'What do you think you're going to gain by getting your nephew?' What am I going to gain? What do you think I'm going to gain? My nephew. I don't see anything else there. That's all I can possibly gain . . . the fact that I can have my nephew with me, show him love, and let him know that someone is there in his court. I feel as if they have taken his mother because they took her parental rights. They have taken his father. They separated him from his brother. There is nothing else he can lose. The kid needs to know he has somebody that is going to be constant. Now everything that he is used to having is no more."

Pauline

Pauline is 73 years old and has been caring for her two great-grandchildren, ages 9 and 13, for nine months. The children's grandmother (Pauline's daughter) had been caring for them, but eventually she asked Pauline to step in. Pauline didn't mind doing it because she had cared for her "grands" before, having reared them from infancy. To make room for the children in her small house, Pauline gave one child her bedroom, the other child the spare bedroom, and she moved into the dining room.

In general, Pauline doesn't have any major problems with the children or with child welfare. The process of becoming licensed didn't bother her, though it took a little longer than she would have liked. Now that she is getting regular payments, her only concern is making her great-grandchildren follow her rules. As she stated, "It hard to train other people's children." Though the children have tried to challenge her, Pauline is not worried. Recently, her great-granddaughter tried to physically push Pauline, and Pauline described the scene that followed when the two of them almost came to blows:

> "My great-granddaughter told me . . . 'You can't hit me.' I said, 'Try me.' I said, 'You are not going to hit me.' Oh, she tried to challenge me once—she certainly did—she run into me. I just took her and flipped her over on the bed. I didn't hurt her, but I let her know [she was] not going to run into me again."

Jorge and Rosa

Jorge and Rosa are caring for three nephews (ages 8, 12, and 14), their 15-year-old niece, and her 15-month-old baby. They have been caring for their nephews for about 10 months and their niece since she got pregnant when she was 13. Having grown up in non-relative foster care, Rosa wants to make sure the children remain with family. Jorge believes that caring for his niece and nephews is a family obligation and sees no other choice.

Jorge talked about discipline and the discrepancy between his beliefs about disciplining children and the child welfare agency's beliefs and mandates.

"It's not a factor of child abuse or nothing. But when we were growing up, if you got out of line, your parents put you in line. Now we do not have that option. We take away their privileges, no TV, no phone, no games, no nothing. Back then [when Jorge was growing up], how many kids didn't get a whipping? You hit them once and they got it. But nowadays, it's like they can do whatever they want. I mean, I'm not saying that all the kids are bad, that they all deserve a punishment, but those who do don't get it in time and that's where the problem occurs."

As he described it, Jorge and Rosa are caring for rebellious kids who had very little discipline growing up. Jorge feels that the kids he cares for do whatever they want because they know that if he hits them they can tell child welfare and Jorge will be the one at fault. This situation makes raising teens difficult for him.

Rosa is concerned that the children are not getting the counseling services they need to help them deal with their anger. In addition to adjusting to a new home and having to learn to abide by new rules, her nephews are always having to deal with being let down by their mother. Rosa recognizes that the children really want to be with their mother; as she put it, they keep "waiting and waiting to go home," but their mother isn't ready to take them back. Jorge and Rosa are willing to keep the children until they are age 18 but want more freedom to raise the children in the way they see fit. Jorge and Rosa also want more services to help the children in ways that they cannot.

Julia and Bill

Julia and Bill are caring for four grandchildren—ages 3, 10, 13, and 16—while the children's mother is in prison. Initially, three of the children were put into the foster care system and one child was placed with his biological father.

When asked why they had decided to obtain their foster parent license and care for their grandchildren, Julia and Bill told the following story. Their 10-year-old grandson, Jake, had been with his biological father for about six months when Jake's dad drove to Julia and Bill's house, dropped Jake off, and said that he never wanted to see or hear from him again. Not knowing what to do, Julia and Bill called child welfare to let the boy's social worker know what was happening and to let the agency know that they wanted their grandson to stay with them. Unexpectedly, Jake's social worker showed up at their house the next day to inform them that child welfare had found a licensed foster placement for him. When Jake heard that he would have to leave his grandparents, he panicked. He wrapped himself around his grandmother's legs and begged the social worker to let him stay. The social worker pulled him from his grandmother, however, and put him in the car. By this time, both Julia and Bill were beside themselves and promised their grandson that they would do anything they could to get him back.

Julia and Bill immediately began the steps needed to become licensed foster parents. They were worried about their grandson and the rest of their grandchildren, who were scattered in different placements and had little or no contact with one other. It took them about a year, but finally Julia and Bill met all the licensing requirements and their grandchildren came to live with them.

Being together again and in their grandparents' home has been a difficult adjustment for the children. Julia believes that they are settling in now, but at first they were in their own little worlds:

> "It was like they really got used to being in a shell, afraid to make a move, afraid to say something, afraid to eat. They were in their own little shell; they had to protect themselves and they didn't trust anyone. It took a long time for these kids to get out of that mode they [were] in. 'Don't be afraid to ask for a glass of water, to ask for a second helping. Don't be afraid of normal activity in a house'—but they were. You would think they were prisoners of war, afraid to make a move without being told to."

Though Julia and Bill feel that the children are starting to get used to the security of being with their grandparents, they are still having some trouble. As Julia described it,

> "If they see a car come in the yard, they are afraid somebody is there to take them away. They think that anytime they can be taken away again and that's a terrible feeling for a child."

Additionally, Julia and Bill believe that being separated from each other and in foster care traumatized the children. When Bill and Julia first started caring for the children, they would put the children to bed at night and in the morning the children would be sleeping on the floor in Bill and Julia's room. Things have improved. Now the children all start out the night sleeping in their own beds, and in the morning they are usually sleeping together on the living room floor. Julia is expecting to see more improvement soon and for them to "graduate back to [their] bedrooms."

Even though it was a difficult process, Julia and Bill are glad that they became licensed foster parents. They are happy to have their grandchildren with them and vow that they will never be separated from each other or from family again: "We're keeping them. . . . They [child welfare workers] are never going to take those kids or separate them again."

Margie and Ray

Margie and Ray are caring for their 6-year-old granddaughter, whose mother is addicted to drugs and whose father is in prison. Margie and Ray have raised six children of their own; their youngest just started college. When they found out that their granddaughter needed care, they were just starting to get used to life with no children. Margie keeps telling herself the situation is only temporary, but she loves her granddaughter and would rather keep her until she is an adult than have her return to the situation she had been living in. Margie and Ray are quite certain that their granddaughter is not their son's biological child but have chosen not to find out.

When their granddaughter first came to live with them, she was having a difficult time emotionally. Margie didn't feel that her granddaughter needed any counseling or special support at that time, just time to adjust to the security of being with her grandparents. However, Margie described an incident that made her very aware of the special care her granddaughter might need:

> "It'll always be with me that when she came, she came with nothing. I took her to the secondhand store, and she asked if everything costs something and I said, 'Yes.' She said, 'How are you going to pay for it?' and I said 'Remember, I have a job.' She was so excited when someone came to the house, she would take them to her dresser and show them that she had her own socks, a drawer full of her very own socks. She mostly wanted to wear white socks and I bought lots of packages of white socks, and she wanted to change

her socks several times a day. I'd let her change her socks whenever she wanted. She'd change her socks at least four times a day."

At first Margie and Ray were concerned, but now that their granddaughter has been with them for a while, she doesn't change her socks so much. Margie and Ray think that she feels much more secure. Their granddaughter's insecurity when she first came to live with her grandparents was highlighted when she went to visit her mother: when she came back, she found that Margie had rearranged the living room furniture. When the granddaughter saw the change, she got very upset. With that Margie and Ray realized that they "just need to keep things the same."

The couple didn't receive any services for the first six months they cared for their granddaughter. They now have access to services but confessed that they don't take advantage of everything available to them. Because they both work, their main concern has been child care; once they got that, they didn't really need much else. Also, Margie and Ray try not to bother the social worker too much because they know she is overwhelmed with other cases:

"Every time I've called and left a message, she's gotten back to us. I really can't complain. Once I learned her caseload, I said, 'Oh let me get off your nerves.'"

Maria

Maria and her husband are caring for two granddaughters, 2 months and 2 years of age, and are in the process of adopting both children. Maria's daughter and son-in-law are drug addicts. When Maria's daughter had her first baby, Maria cared for the baby a lot. Maria always felt that something was wrong, she just didn't know what. By the time the baby was 6 months old, Maria started noticing that the baby often had bruises and she cried a lot. Maria kept questioning her daughter and son-in-law, but kept getting the same excuses and stories. One day Maria noticed a bite mark on the child. When Maria confronted her daughter, she tried to make up a story, but Maria refused to believe it. Maria and her husband did not call child protection but tried to help the family themselves. They convinced their son-in-law to go to a drug rehabilitation program and convinced their daughter to move in with them.

Soon after their daughter and the baby moved in, she gave birth to a second baby, who was addicted to heroin. At this point, child protection became involved. The second baby was taken immediately into child protective custody and placed with a foster family trained to care for drug-addicted babies. Maria tells what happened:

> "The baby was born with drug addiction and she went to [a] special foster home for the first few days because she needed special care. I went to the nurses and asked them how to take care of the baby, so they decided to let me try. I had no experience with drug babies, but it's been working out. They gave me special training. The agency says it's something new, like an experiment, the first time. I was hoping not to fail. I got my little granddaughter last month and she's been with us since then."

Maria says she and her husband feel that they have a pretty good relationship with child welfare and are in the process of adopting their two granddaughters. They have gotten the services they needed for the children, and when they became caregivers, they were immediately given information about payment options and services.

Looking back, Maria doesn't know why she didn't figure out that her daughter and son-in-law were on drugs. She just thought they were tired and slept a lot because of work. Now she thinks that this was just her excuse for them. Now that she knows what was going on, she doesn't want her daughter or son-in-law to see the children anymore. She complies with visitation, but doesn't trust that they can take care of their children. Maria said her other three children are good parents to their children and asks herself why this daughter got involved with drugs.

Barbara

Barbara and her husband have been caring for her 9-year-old nephew for more than two years. She and her family had been making reports to the child welfare agency for years before the agency was able to remove her nephew and his siblings from their parents (Barbara's brother and his wife):

> "I have nine brothers and sisters and we were all always concerned about our one brother. We'd been calling child welfare over the

years about him and his wife, and there were a couple of emergency removals into foster homes, but the three children were always returned."

When the children came into custody for the last time, Barbara and her brothers and sisters got together to decide how their family could best help the children. Her nephew was originally placed with his uncle, but he molested one of his cousins in the home. Barbara was angry because she felt child welfare did not share enough information with the family on what abuse her nephew had experienced. The whole family then decided that Barbara and her husband would be best suited to care for their nephew, since all their own children were grown.

Barbara is happy to care for her nephew, but wants to make sure she has the continued support of the state:

> "My worker is trying to push us into adoption, but I'm scared to death about adopting him because he's got such high tendencies to be an offender because of the violence and sexual experiences. The worker keeps telling me I'll get federal aid, not to worry. I think they want the county out of control of this child, who is every day for me a challenge. When I see the phone machine blinking, my heart drops when I answer—[I fear] it's his school with another problem. But my husband and I love him and he has a heart of gold and he's so much fun to be around. He's changed our lives immensely in ways we never thought possible."

Barbara and her husband have made a long-term commitment to their nephew, but it was not an easy decision. They love him very much, but know that it is going to be a difficult road. She is grateful every day that her husband is as committed to her nephew as she is, even though her nephew is not her husband's blood relative. She is also thankful that they are taking this on as a married couple, because when one gets overloaded, the other can take over.

> "I couldn't imagine having all this love and going the extra mile if they weren't a relative. I don't think someone who is not related would take all those calls from school. He would have been in and out of foster homes by now."

Arlene

Arlene is 73 and began caring for her two grandchildren, a 2-year-old boy and a 3-year-old girl, because their parents are addicted to heroin. One day, the children's mother left them with Arlene and didn't return. Concerned that she was too old to care for two small children, Arlene called child welfare and asked them what she should do. The children stayed with Arlene for a short time and then were sent back to live with their parents.

The children had been with their parents for about three months when child protective services got a tip that the parents were using heroin. The police raided the hotel where the family was living and caught the children's father "shooting up." The children were removed immediately and taken into protective custody. The little boy tested positive for drugs; fortunately, the little girl did not. Arlene learned the children had been taken from their parents when she received a phone call on the night of the incident from the children's mother (who was in jail). Arlene went and picked up the children, and two weeks later the court awarded her guardianship.

Arlene has numerous frustrations with the child welfare system and with the courts. Because of the abuse and neglect perpetrated upon her grandson by his parents, he had a severe speech delay when Arlene first became his guardian. In addition, Arlene said that while she was caring for the children, their parents did very little to comply with the case plan or court orders. Even so, Arlene was told that she had to take her grandchildren for visitation. She was angry that, with all of the parental abuse, neglect, and unwillingness to change, it was still important to the courts and to child welfare that her grandchildren see the people who neglected them and injected her grandson with heroin.

Arlene was also disturbed by the lack of financial assistance she received. Her primary frustration was that she received only $285 per month from Temporary Assistance for Needy Families (TANF) to care for her two grandchildren. Meanwhile, the children's father received $1,000 per month in workmen's compensation—none of which he was required to give to his children. Despite her frustrations, Arlene was glad to care for her grandchildren:

"There are things they need to know. Whose hands are these? Whose feet are these? Need-to-know answers, who do I look like? They need to know about themselves. When they are in foster care, you don't know. You spend all this time then later trying to find out who you are—your identity. They want to know, 'What did I eat when I was little?' They need to know these things. It creates who they are—it makes them secure."

Caregiver Issues

The kinship caregivers participating in the focus groups faced numerous challenges themselves. Many spoke of the emotional toll and how much they needed counseling or other forms of emotional support. Many caregivers noted their advanced age and deteriorating health and questioned how long they could continue caring for their children. They also discussed the financial difficulties they faced caring for children they had not planned to raise.

Janice

Janice is a 51-year-old single grandmother who has been caring for two of her grandchildren, ages 3 and 10, for most of their lives. In telling her story, Janice described the difficult emotional process she, as a parent, went through as she tried to come to terms with the fact that her child was incapable of being a functional parent:

> "All of us see it coming and you go through a lot of mixed feelings. You go through anger, pity for the parent, trying to persuade them, and finally then it's there. By the time I made up my mind, I didn't have any time to be angry. I couldn't concentrate on my bad feelings because I have a job to do. I headed straight to court. . . . Got help from legal services, a volunteer lawyer. I have never been more persistent in my life than getting the best interests of these kids. I left behind my shame, embarrassment, and pride. I didn't care who knew it. I just wanted to give those kids a stable home, whatever I had to offer them."

Janice said that becoming a relative caregiver has not only changed her life but also had an impact on her 16-year-old daughter. Because Janice works, she has her daughter pick the grandchildren up on her way home from school and pays her to babysit.

Janice (who receives a $565 welfare payment each month to help her care for her grandchildren) noted how ironic it is that eligibility workers don't pay any attention to her concerns about child care or the general emotional well-being of her or her family, but will go into detail to make sure that she isn't overpaid.

Grace

Grace, who is 33, is caring for five nieces and nephews between the ages of 8 and 14 in addition to her own two children. Grace began caring for the children three years ago after her sister died. At the time, Grace was trying to put her life back together after her bad marriage ended. She was not in a place emotionally where she felt comfortable caring for seven children, but she felt she had no choice. Most of Grace's relatives had already raised their children and were either not willing or not able to care for her sister's kids. Grace took the children and hoped for the best.

> "I'm 33 and coming off a bad marriage, trying to get established for me and my own two kids. . . . I still feel the pressure today, because it is so extremely difficult. There is no one I can pass these kids on to. The fathers weren't present when my sister was alive, the grandparents don't come or call. At my age I feel enormous pressure trying to care for seven kids."

Grace said a number of times that the pressure of trying to care for all seven children on her own is overwhelming, and she doesn't get much help or sympathy from the child welfare or the social welfare agencies. She recently lost her job and is having a great deal of trouble making ends meet.

> "I am not asking for any special privileges, but income is a very important thing. I don't like the fact that you have to do food stamps and you have to do welfare and [child welfare] makes you feel beneath them. I feel like saying, 'Excuse me, I'm an intelligent woman, I cannot help the circumstances I've fallen into, so maybe we could generate a job with a little flexibility.'"

Grace doesn't know how she will continue to care for her own children and her nieces and nephews in the state she is in:

"I follow everything to the letter. I have problems because I'm a young woman, but I can't get counseling. I asked for a lot of assistance, counseling for myself. Child welfare told me that they don't provide that. I thought that that was so unfair. They said that their purpose was to make sure at all costs that these children are cared for. Well, if I am not sane and healthy, and I have custody of these children, how is that maintaining? All I am asking is that you provide somewhere for me to go to seek help. They [child welfare] tell me that you have to do it yourself. Okay, take into account I have just lost my sister, I have taken in her five kids, coming off a rocky marriage, do you think I have time to really be looking for some help for myself? [Child welfare] should cover this. I've had a very ugly ride with them."

Phyllis

Phyllis is 52 years old and is caring for three grandchildren, ages 2, 3, and 4, because the oldest grandchild was prenatally exposed to cocaine. Becoming a relative caregiver was shocking for Phyllis in a couple of ways. First, Phyllis didn't find out that her son and his wife were going to have a baby until they called Phyllis in a panic after her daughter-in-law went into labor. Before the shock of being a grandmother had subsided, Phyllis was given another shocking piece of news: her grandson was born addicted to cocaine and needed a caregiver. Phyllis offered to take care of the baby and has raised him ever since. Phyllis's son and his wife had two more children soon after the first. And because the couple didn't do what they were supposed to with the first baby, child welfare took both of these children into custody at birth.

When Phyllis began taking care of her first grandchild, she says she was given no support from the child welfare agency—"just directions." At the time, this didn't bother her because she believed that her caretaking would only be temporary.

"I thought I was helping out the parents. I thought it would be short term—that the mother would go to a program and get her life together and I'd get to be the grandmother and I'd visit them from time to time and live my life."

Unfortunately, it was not long before Phyllis realized that her son and his wife were in denial about their problems and refusing to get help. Shortly after Phyllis began caring for their second and then third baby, she realized that she needed help. For a year, Phyllis and her grandchildren were homeless and living in a hotel. She was working time-and-a-half just to make ends meet, and the only support she was given by child welfare was in the form of vouchers for clothing and food.

Finally, Phyllis was able to get help through a child welfare program, which now provides her with a monthly payment to help with the children. Phyllis and her three grandchildren now live in a small apartment and she's thinking about adopting the children.

Josephine

Josephine is 69 years old and is caring for two of her great-grandsons, ages 2 and 5. When introducing herself, Josephine had this to say: "Can you imagine a 69-year-old taking care of two little boys with so much energy? But I can't let them go to the system."

Josephine has been caring for her granddaughter's children off and on since the first child was born 10 years ago. Child protective services took the children into custody two years ago when the granddaughter gave birth to her youngest child and they found out that she was addicted to drugs.

As she describes it, Josephine felt a lot of pressure from her family to take in as many of the children as possible. When the children first came into custody, the family got together to figure out how to keep them with family and out of the system. While she is happy that the children are not in the system with strangers, Josephine is hoping that their stay with relatives is temporary and that her granddaughter will beat her addiction.

Josephine has no complaints about the child welfare agency at all. In general, she gets what she needs from them. Her main concern is caring for her great-grandchildren long term. At age 69, she can't imagine having to take care of teenagers in 10 years. She just wants either her daughter (the children's grandmother) or her granddaughter to get better and take responsibility for the children. Josephine's family has gotten together to talk about the long term, but they don't want to make any decisions right now—they want to wait to see if her granddaughter's drug treatment works. In the meantime, Josephine's family gives her moral support and encouragement.

Margaret

Margaret, a 78-year-old-licensed foster parent, has been caring for her 11-year-old great-grandniece for over a year. The "niece" came into child protective custody after being stabbed by her mother, and Margaret has known and cared for her niece intermittently since infancy. Margaret raised three children alone after being widowed and feels that she has had a lot of experience parenting. One of her sons lives just a few minutes away, and he helps her take care of her house and discipline her niece. Sometimes Margaret worries about money, especially when her foster parent payments don't come on time, but in general she says everything is fine.

Margaret made it very clear that she wants to care for her niece for as long as she is able but does not want to adopt her. A few months ago, Margaret had a meeting with her niece's social worker and a lawyer during which they asked Margaret if she was interested in adopting her niece. Margaret told them yes, but later changed her mind because she felt that she was too old. When she told the social worker about her decision, the social worker first asked Margaret if her family had pushed her to say no. When Margaret said that she had made the decision on her own, the social worker told her, "Well you know, you can't be a foster parent all the time!" Margaret is not sure what the social worker meant by this and is now worried that if she doesn't adopt, she will lose her niece.

Agency Interactions

As discussed in earlier chapters, kinship caregivers often do not fully understand the roles and requirements of the child welfare agency and typically do not receive services they need. Kinship caregivers' interactions with child welfare workers vary greatly, as shown by the stories that follow. Most kinship caregivers expressed dissatisfaction and distrust of the system and the caseworkers assigned to them. However, several caregivers praised their workers and found that, as caregivers, their needs were met.

Tanika

Tanika is caring for and in the process of adopting three nieces. Previously, Tanika had not realized that their mother (her sister) was using drugs until the doctor noticed that there was something different about the youngest child. The doctor tested her and found out she had drugs in her system. Tanika and her mother "didn't want to see the kids split up," so they took them in. And while desiring to care for the children, Tanika and her mother didn't think it would be right to adopt them. The agency, however, pressed them to do so. "They [child welfare] made it like we had to adopt them or someone else would adopt them," Tanika explained.

Though not happy about having to adopt her nieces, Tanika says otherwise she's had a pretty good experience with the child welfare system. Originally, she was caring for her nieces supported only by a welfare payment. Tanika's caseworker then suggested that she consider becoming a licensed foster parent. After checking into her background and into "her personal business," the child welfare agency quickly approved Tanika and she began receiving foster care payments after about a month.

Though she is a licensed foster parent, Tanika doesn't agree with and follow a lot of the rules she is supposed to obey. With regard to parental visitation, she explained,

> "My sister is clean two years since February; she is working, she does things for the kids. The rights have been terminated, but we're going to leave it at that—she sees her kids whenever she wants to with no problem. They [child welfare] said that she's not allowed to see them, but that's my sister, these are her kids, we're family, and she can see them whenever she wants to."

In addition to visitation, there are other rules set up for foster parents that Tanika doesn't agree with and therefore doesn't follow:

> "They tell you that you have to ask permission when you want to take that child on vacation? I do exactly what I want to. We go where we want to go."

Ruth

Ruth is caring for two nieces and two nephews between the ages of 9 and 15. Ruth was very clear about some of her concerns with kinship care:

> "With the federal government slowly erasing our welfare system, and child welfare not allowing relatives to get assistance to help their own family members, they [children] have to go into foster homes. The only ones left to take care of our black children, to compensate for the relatives who can't [care for them], are white people getting these big lucrative checks."

Ruth doesn't understand why child welfare agencies have enough money to pay foster parents to care for children but not enough to pay relatives. Answering her own question, Ruth contends that, at least in her county, the explanation is racial:

> "The bottom line is they think black folks are always begging and got our hand out. Like our sister said, black people used to take care of family and they [the government] don't want to take care of us. They're tired of us begging, and they don't want to give us nothing and that's why they don't. And the little they do give us, it's not enough to survive in 2001."

Dorothy

Dorothy and her husband have been caring for her 15-year-old granddaughter on and off since she was born. Recently, her niece asked her to care for three of her children, but because Dorothy's husband is recovering from a stroke, they had to say no. Dorothy feels that her caseworker is overworked and has a hard time returning Dorothy's phone calls. The family also has not received a lot of the services that her caseworker promised he would set up. A number of different people have made appointments to come to Dorothy's home to work with her granddaughter and then have never shown up.

Dorothy knows that child welfare workers are overwhelmed but really feels that they need to be more compassionate. She believes that one caseworker harassed her niece so much that she had a stroke:

"The [social worker] told her that she wasn't a fit mother and couldn't visit her children on Mother's Day and would fix it so she would not get her children back. All that stress, my niece was on a breathing machine and a heart monitor, and the worker just told her that she should get her fat butt off the couch."

Although her family has not had the best experience with child welfare, Dorothy is willing to deal with the aggravation so that her granddaughter can stay with relatives.

Janelle

Janelle is caring for four nieces and nephews. Three are in the custody of the state and one is in Janelle's custody. Their mother, who is Janelle's sister, is addicted to drugs. Two of the children were originally placed with Janelle and two were placed with their other aunt, Janice. Janelle says that everything was fine with the arrangement her family had made for the children until Janice began using drugs and the children were removed from her care. In the end, Janelle took the other two children also. She believes that it is good for children to be with family, not just for their well-being, but also for the good of her family as a whole:

"You look at the news and everything and there's something to having them with family. Plus my mother, she's 74 years old, she would just cry and pray and worry about the kids. This way she knows where they're at. I didn't have any reservations about taking the children, except for the teenagers. You see, I had three sons. We're family. It takes a village to raise a child."

Once Janelle and her family settled the children's living arrangements, everything fell into place. Janelle is very pleased with child welfare. She is regularly contacted by her caseworker, she gets the services she needs for her children, and she feels that the per diem she receives to help her care for the kids is sufficient. She says her experience has been

"very positive, professional. They [child welfare] contact me often, once a month. Came out [to the house] about three weeks ago . . . [I] told the caseworker that I want to get [the] oldest boy into some more intense counseling this summer. I've never had any problem with the caseworkers. Every one [I've had] has been very supportive; everyone [I've] had contact with [is] very professional."

Janelle is also very cognizant of her responsibilities as a relative caregiver:

"But you know as foster parents and relative caregivers, we have a responsibility. If it's urgent or something, you need to contact someone, go on up the line. Their workload is high; workers are in court Tuesday and Thursday, so I'll leave a message and my worker always calls back. It's our responsibility to call [our caseworker]. My worker calls every two or three weeks and asks, 'Do you need anything? Do the kids need anything?' It's just the individual caseworker, but it's our responsibility if we need to talk to someone. That's what they told us in the foster parent training classes."

Though Janelle is happy with her experiences with child welfare, and she understands and accepts her role as a relative caregiver, she does have significant challenges. She recalled a time when she was having trouble with one of her nephews after his visits with his mother. He would come home, act defiant, and say things like, "You're not my mother." Janelle spoke with the caseworker, who organized a meeting with the family:

"It got kind of heated, but she [the worker] let my sister know that she needed to be supportive and not manipulate the kid when she visits with them. Lots of times that's what we run into when we have visitation; the parent tries to sabotage what's going on with the kids if the kids are happy. The case conference got really heated and I was ready to say forget it. I was having trouble at my job, then [having] to come home and battle with them. Like I told them, 'I love you and I'm willing to take care of you, but you must respect my rules and that's the bottom line.' We got to the bottom of it."

Brenda

Brenda is caring for three grandchildren. She first became a relative caregiver when her first grandchild was born cocaine positive. Soon after

Brenda's daughter gave birth, child welfare called Brenda to ask if she would be willing to care for the baby and Brenda agreed. This child has major health problems and requires extensive and ongoing medical care. From the beginning, child welfare pushed Brenda to get legal custody of the baby and didn't explore other options with her. Brenda regrets not having been given more information:

> "I was not told at the time that I could have put him on foster care. Because he was disabled and all that, that could have really helped me; he could have really benefited from that."

Instead, Brenda received little in the way of financial support or services to care for her grandson and bore much of the financial burden for him herself.

When Brenda's daughter had her second child, child welfare called Brenda again and asked her to be the caregiver. She told the agency that she couldn't imagine how she could do it financially. What Brenda wanted was for her daughter to get her life together, stop using drugs, and take responsibility for her children. When Brenda refused to pick the baby up from the hospital, child welfare talked her into a compromise. Brenda agreed to allow her daughter and the new baby to move into her house for three months. If her daughter stopped using drugs and started taking responsibility for the children, Brenda would let her stay.

Before the three months were up, Brenda's daughter tested positive for drugs and moved out, leaving both of her children behind. By this time, Brenda had become attached to the second baby and couldn't let him go into the foster care system. Instead, she decided to keep him, regardless of her financial situation.

One day, Brenda was listening to the news and heard about a relative caregiver in a nearby county who was a licensed foster parent and was getting regular foster care payments. Brenda was surprised to learn of this possibility—no one at child welfare had ever mentioned it to her. She immediately called the agency and tried to get information about becoming licensed. Though she feels that she got the "run-around" for a while, after six months she finally got help. After completing the foster parent licensing requirements, Brenda began receiving monthly foster care payments. The assistance came just in time for the birth of Brenda's third grandchild.

Tamika

Tamika is 27 years old and has cared for her four brothers and sisters for the past seven years. Tamika started taking care of her siblings because their mother was addicted to drugs. When the children came into child protective custody, Tamika had just given birth to her own child. She decided that, since she was going to be at home with her own baby, she could care for her brothers and sisters as well.

Tamika has two primary concerns about the foster care system. First, she doesn't think the agency gives out enough information about the rights and responsibilities of relative caregivers. She believes that as a caregiver, you either have to ask for services or you go without. To illustrate this concern, Tamika told us that she had been caring for her siblings for four years before she found out that she could become licensed as a foster parent and receive monthly payments. Other than referring her to welfare, her child welfare caseworker had offered her only clothing and food vouchers. Tamika felt that this was not enough and is angry that she was given no information about licensing.

Once Tamika found out about the possibility of becoming licensed, it took another three years for her to complete all of the licensing requirements. Seven years after taking in her siblings, Tamika finally got her first foster care check. Though she now receives a regular payment, she still has to "beg" if she wants services for the children.

In addition to Tamika's frustration with the licensing process, she also feels the child welfare system distrusts her. To be licensed, Tamika had to submit to a drug test. This made her angry because she doesn't know any other foster parent who had to have a drug test. She thinks that she was targeted because she is young and lives in a housing project.

Janice

Janice is a 44-year-old grandmother who has been caring for her 6-year-old granddaughter since birth. She doesn't like the idea of anyone else caring for or adopting her granddaughter, believing that no one can "do for my kids what I can." To clarify why she is so wary of the "system," Janice told us about her involvement with child welfare when her daughter was a teenager:

"My daughter was a runaway and was giving me problems, so I put her in the system. The system wound up listening to my daughter more than they listened to me. My attorney told me it was virtually impossible to get her out of the system. But it was no fault of mine. I did get her back but then she wanted to fight, so I whacked her and she was right back in the system."

Janice doesn't want this kind of thing to happen with her granddaughter. Janice is caring for her granddaughter but does not have custody. She was told that if she wanted to get legal guardianship, child welfare would have to take the little girl out of her home for six months and conduct a formal investigation. Janice doesn't want to go through that and doesn't see why it is necessary:

"They [child welfare] do different things for different people. That's why my baby is 6 years old and I still don't have guardianship. They keep putting up 'brick walls.'"

Because she is not her granddaughter's legal guardian, Janice gets very few services. She currently receives a welfare payment but knows that her granddaughter needs counseling and welfare won't cover it. Janice has been able to get child care for her granddaughter, but has done this under her daughter's name. Janice worries about her difficult situation, and wonders if it is all her fault for not getting guardianship.

Joanie

Joanie is a 50-year-old widow who is raising her 2-year-old grandson. Joanie became his caregiver after it was discovered that her son and his wife were not properly caring for their child. Though suffering from significant physical and mental disabilities, Joanie's son and his wife were living on their own at the time the baby was born. After the baby stopped gaining weight, child welfare got involved. Following a divorce, Joanie's son moved in with her to help care for the baby.

Joanie is not worried about her ability to care for her grandson, although he also has physical and mental disabilities. However, she is worried about what the child might be missing out on by growing up with an older caregiver:

"I wanted him to have a young mom that could get out and run in the yard and keep up with him, you know—do the things that I did with my son when he was growing up."

When asked whether she had thought about becoming a licensed foster parent, Joanie replied that she wants to keep custody of her grandson. If she became licensed, child welfare would have custody. Also, she is quite satisfied with the support she receives from the agency. At the beginning, she didn't feel listened to, but now she gets what she needs, including child care when she needs it, and her son is in counseling and goes to parenting classes.

Joanie admits that caring for both her son and grandson is very challenging, but adds,

"Whether rich or poor, there's always love with family . . . the easy thing to do is put them in foster care; it is harder to keep them."

9

Kinship Care

Paradigm Shift or Just Another Magic Bullet?

Rob Geen

Other researchers have recently described child welfare agencies' reliance on kin as foster parents as a paradigm shift (Hegar 1999; Jackson 1999). Thomas Kuhn introduced the concept of paradigm shifts in his landmark book, *The Structure of Scientific Revolutions*, where he defined paradigms as "universally recognized scientific achievements that for a time provide model programs and solutions to a community of practitioners" (1970, viii). A paradigm shift, Kuhn asserts, follows a period of scientific revolution during which the professional community gathers enough evidence to discard an earlier paradigm and assembles enough new evidence to support a new paradigm. During a scientific revolution—as a new paradigm arises, and before an older one is discarded—a professional community finds itself in a period of paradigm conflict.

Child welfare has rhetorically, and largely programmatically, accepted kinship care as a new paradigm. Yet, from a research perspective, this is not a true paradigm shift; the professional community has not assembled enough new evidence to support a new paradigm and thus should be squarely in the middle of a paradigm conflict. Because child welfare has accepted a new paradigm without the insights generated from a scientific revolution, the field finds itself unable to effectively identify policy and practice changes needed to support this new paradigm.

The child welfare field has, in fact, a history of embracing new theories or programmatic approaches and implementing them without significant research evidence of their effectiveness—a "magic bullet" approach. Moreover, lacking an understanding of how and when a new approach can be effective, the field accepts the assumption that a new approach will be beneficial for a wide segment of the child welfare population. The 1980s family preservation movement may be the most notable example of this magic bullet approach. Faced with significant criticism about the number of children removed from their parents' homes and placed in foster care, the child welfare field experienced a pendulum swing away from foster care to much greater emphasis on family preservation. Moreover, the field was captivated by the notion that, given enough investment in families, foster care placements could be prevented. Begun in the 1970s, intensive family preservation programs, which were designed to serve children who were "at imminent risk of placement," enjoyed tremendous momentum in the 1980s. Energized by the reported success of the Homebuilders program in Tacoma, Washington, states quickly began to replicate versions of the intensive family preservation model. States and programs were then surprised to find that subsequent evaluations of family preservation programs showed little impact on foster care placements. At this point, few states have retained their intensive family preservation programs, and those that have kept such programs have narrowed the population for which services are targeted or have provided less intensive services, and have moved away from foster care prevention as the main goal.

Embracing new paradigms based on limited information is not unusual, particularly in the social sciences, which are less exact than the physical sciences. However, child welfare may be even more prone to adopting approaches not fully tested because of the intense public scrutiny it faces and the harsh criticism it has received. New models and quick-fix solutions are attractive to politicians and agency administrators eager to respond to the public uproar over children killed by parents or foster parents, children lost in the system, or children remaining in foster care for many years.

I would argue that too many in the child welfare field are embracing kinship care as a magic bullet as well. While the federal government and almost every state give preference to kin, no single study to date concludes that children placed with kin fare better in the long term than children placed in non-kin foster care. This is not to say that there is not reason to believe that children will benefit from kinship care; we just do not have the evidence. There *is* considerable evidence that kinship care placements are more stable, and stability, all other things being equal, is beneficial for a child's well-being. We also know that children in kinship care are more likely to be placed with siblings and to maintain contact with birth parents, siblings not placed with them, and other relatives.

If we have reason to believe that children will fare better in kinship care, then why is it a problem that child welfare agencies falsely believe that kinship care represents a paradigm shift? This is a dilemma because we do not understand this new paradigm well enough to implement it. We should be in the middle of a paradigm conflict—a period marked by significant investigation that will lead us to either embrace the new paradigm, throw it out, or, most likely, embrace it conditionally. Instead we have accepted the new paradigm without the benefit of a research base. In a detailed review of the existing literature, Maria Scannapieco (1999) noted that "kinship care research is in its infancy" (152). This sentiment has been echoed by almost every researcher who has examined kinship foster care (Berrick 1998; Geen and Berrick 2002; Gleeson 1999; HHS 2000).

In an environment devoid of evidence, persuasive arguments can be made on sheer conjecture. For example, many experts have argued that we have a system that permits kin to receive greater financial assistance from the child welfare system than from the public welfare system, providing a powerful incentive for birth parents to give up their children and kin who are caring for children privately to enter the child welfare system. The study described in this book found little evidence to support this claim.

In essence, because the field skipped its scientific revolution, it is now trying to implement policy and practice changes with minimal guidance from research. While I personally embrace the new kinship care paradigm, it is not a panacea for the ills of the child welfare system. Based on my experiences on this and other studies, I am convinced that kinship care is both underused and overused. Certain state policies and practices make it difficult for some kin who could provide excellent care for a child to be licensed as a foster parent. However, largely because of the lack of non-kin foster care homes, local agencies are relying on some kin who are providing marginal care and who would not be used if additional resources were available. Yet I do not believe we have the knowledge to know when kinship care should be used. At the same time, the field cannot wait until it has complete knowledge to act—policies and practices that are not consistent with the new paradigm must be examined and altered based on what is known.

It is my hope that this book will help inform policy and practice. But even more so, I hope this study motivates other researchers to explore the wide range of issues raised by the new kinship care paradigm, issues that in an ideal world would have been explored during a scientific revolution that preceded the new paradigm. Key findings from the study, as detailed in the previous chapters, are summarized below, and some of the many questions that remain unanswered or require additional examination are identified. Based on my experience from this and previous studies, I then recommend policy, programmatic, and practice changes that would help agencies make better use of the valuable resource of kinship care.

Summary of Findings and Unanswered Questions

While child welfare agencies recognize the benefits of using kin as foster parents and acknowledge that kinship care is unique from non-kin foster care in many important ways, these agencies have not yet altered local policies and practices to take advantage fully of the benefits kin can offer. In the preceding chapters, the findings of a large-scale qualitative study of frontline practices have illustrated how existing foster care policies and practices, developed almost entirely with non-kin foster care in mind, may fail children placed in kinship care.

Identification and Recruitment of Kinship Caregivers

When a child must be removed from his or her parent's home, caseworkers first look to see whether there is a noncustodial parent that can safely care for the child. Caseworkers report making greater efforts in recent years to identify, locate, and assess noncustodial fathers. The next preferred placement choice for children is another relative. Agencies are actively seeking out relatives to act as foster parents, and several factors have increased the level of effort they are making to identify relatives, including the Adoption and Safe Families Act (ASFA). Respondents noted that local authorities' preference for kin varied and was influenced by a number of factors, including the extent to which agencies and workers value the extended family, specific agency policies, the courts' philosophy, and a lack of non-kin foster homes. Caseworkers in all sites were quick to point out that while relatives are given preference, their primary responsibility is the safety of the child. Thus, while caseworkers look to kin first, preference for kin is contingent on their ability to adequately care for a child.

Identifying kin can be problematic. While workers routinely ask birth parents to identify relatives, the practice is fraught with difficulties. Many parents are reluctant to identify relatives. Workers also regularly ask the children being placed, if they are old enough, to identify relatives they are close to, but many children identify relatives who may not be appropriate.

At the same time, a number of factors influence whether kin will be willing to take on the role of caregiver. These factors include the status of the relative's relationship with the birth parent, the characteristics or number of children, the obligation to family, the length of stay, the services offered initially, the kin caregiver's relationship to the child, and pressure from family or the child welfare agency. When kin express willingness to act as caregivers, caseworkers must then assess whether kin can provide an adequate level of protection and an appropriate standard of care. Moreover, caseworkers identified a number of reasons why children may initially be placed with non-kin foster parents, including delays related to licensing requirements and specifically criminal and child abuse and neglect background checks.

The findings related to identifying and recruiting kin to act as foster parents clearly demonstrate that caseworkers are acting with little agency guidance or direction. While workers generally use similar approaches to identify kin, how workers decide whether or not to place a child with an identified kin appears to vary considerably. This study leaves many questions about the recruitment of kin unanswered. For example, to what extent should child welfare staff members try to convince kin to accept children who must be removed from their homes? One could argue that kin who need to be convinced to take a child are not all that committed and may not provide the love and attention that workers are seeking for the children. On the other hand, one could argue that kin who eagerly accept children may not fully understand what they are getting into. Workers need to identify the reasons kin are reluctant to take a child and then assess whether these reasons raise questions about kin suitability. While this study identified some of the reasons why kin may be hesitant, more research is needed to understand kin's decisionmaking process and how this may be affected by caseworker practice. It is important to assess the extent to which agencies are pressuring kin to take children, and whether kin who accept children as a result of such pressure provide high-quality care. Future research should examine whether children placed with kin who felt pressured to take a child have less placement stability because these kin are not able or willing to provide long-term care.

This issue highlights a larger and more basic question that future research must answer—When is kinship care the best alternative for a child? Because much of the limited research on kinship care has compared kin and non-kin foster care, we have almost no information about factors related to kinship care that may affect children's outcomes. What is it about kinship care that we believe promotes a child's well-being, and are these qualities universal to kinship care or dependent upon other factors? For example, experts argue that kinship care is beneficial because it is less traumatic to the child than non-kin foster care. Aside from the fact that we lack proof of this assertion (see below), there is reason to question whether this is always the case. How does the prior relationship that kin had with a child needing placement affect the trauma and future outcomes that the child experiences? How does the relationship between the kin and the birth parent affect the child's experience? Is kinship care equally effective for all types of children needing placement, or are there certain characteristics—for example, age, sex, birth order, and special needs—that affect whether a child will do well in kinship care? The benefits of kinship care may also be affected by the length of time that a child requires placement.

Similarly, there may be many factors related to kin that influence whether they will be effective caregivers. In our study, caseworkers reported that their placement decisions were primarily based on the level of safety and standard of care that kin could provide. Because kin often face economic challenges and have greater contact with abusive birth parents than non-kin foster parents have, some have questioned whether kin can provide an adequate level of safety and standard of care. In addition to being very difficult to measure, it is uncertain how workers should weigh their assessments of the safety and standard of care kin provide with the supposedly inherent benefits of kinship care placements.

Licensing and Payment

Federal policy allows states considerable flexibility in setting foster home licensing standards and determining how to apply these standards to kin. While federal courts require states to offer foster care payments to certain kin (those who meet non-kin licensing standards and who care for title IV-E–eligible children), states can decide how to financially support other kin caring for children in state custody. This flexibility has led most states to adopt different foster home licensing and payment policies for kin than they have developed for non-kin foster homes.

Moreover, local interpretation and implementation of state licensing and payment policies vary considerably. In policy, all of the study states require kin to be licensed to care for a foster child. However, in several locations it is common for judges to order a child placed with an unlicensed kinship caregiver. In policy, all four states report that they allow children to be placed with kin before licensure. In practice, localities vary considerably, not only in their willingness to place a child with a yet unlicensed kinship caregiver, but also on the requirements that these kin must meet and the financial assistance they will be offered before they are licensed.

In policy, three of the four study states report that they grant for kin waivers of certain licensing standards that are required of all non-kin foster parents. In practice, the one state that reported not waiving licensing standards for kin (California), in fact, allows counties some discretion in waiving standards or requesting a state waiver. In this and the other study states, the processes for getting a waiver, the frequency with which workers pursue waivers, and the standards that may be waived vary greatly among the localities studied and even within localities among different workers and supervisors.

The debate about the licensing of kinship foster homes has unfortunately focused on if or under what circumstances kin should be held to the same standards as non-kin foster parents. Licensing standards have been used primarily as a proxy for safety. Instead, the debate should focus on how to ensure the safety of *all* foster children, whether placed with kin or non-kin foster parents or in group settings, and whether licensing standards are effective in this pursuit.

When I look at states' foster home licensing standards and realize that my house, where I am raising two children of my own, may not—without a number of changes—meet the standards in some states, I question how accurately these licensing standards measure safety. Children's safety is as much, if not more, a function of the quality of the parenting they receive than a function of the potential dangers of their physical environment. There are foster parents who have met strict licensing criteria who are found to be abusive themselves or who do not adequately keep foster children out of harm's way. Meanwhile, there are parents living in substandard housing or dangerous neighborhoods who effectively educate and monitor their children's activities to ensure their safety.

Most states' foster home licensing standards appear to focus more on measuring what is easy to measure, what can be defended in appeals of licensing actions (for example, such quantifiable items as square footage), and what is needed to limit liability (such as criminal or child abuse and neglect histories) than on what leads to a safe and nurturing placement for a child. I see three main reasons why this is so. The first is the difficulty and expense associated with conducting more thorough assessments. Such assessments would require a much greater amount of caseworker time and would require that caseworkers be carefully trained to make good assessments. Such assessments might also have the expense of limiting the number of persons willing to undergo such evaluation to become foster parents. Such assessment would also have a political cost. The greater the subjectivity of an assessment process, the greater the media scrutiny would likely be in the event a child in foster care is abused or neglected.

Second is the legal aspect of licensing by a governmental agency. A license is considered a property right of the licensee under administrative law. A license must be granted if the applicant meets the criteria specified in law or rule. Objective, easily measured criteria are easier to defend in administrative or court proceedings.

The third and main reason why states' licensing standards are the way they are is that we really do not know how to effectively assess a home to ensure safety and nurturing. Future research to examine the factors that are predictive of a safe and nurturing foster home, both kin and non-kin, is greatly needed. Such research is essential for child welfare agencies to better assess potential foster parents, to design foster parent training curricula, and to monitor existing foster homes.

In addition to licensing disparities, we found that local practices for paying kinship caregivers vary. For example, two of the study sites in Indiana do not offer foster care payments to kin until they are licensed, yet one does. In Alabama, where the vast majority of cases use kin to divert children from the foster care system entirely, the three study sites appear to vary considerably in their propensity to take a child into custody and offer kin foster care payment. Looking just at kin who participated in focus groups in the four study states, it is remarkable how often these kin, who are often struggling financially as a result of their caregiving, do not receive foster care payments for a significant period of time or ever.

Why do so many kin in Alabama fail to receive foster care payments, and how prevalent are these causes in other states? If Alabama is typical of other states that have more than one assessment "option" for kin and offer different levels of financial support, then many kin either may not be informed about the availability of foster care payments or may be discouraged from taking the steps necessary to obtain payments. If the findings from Indiana and Connecticut are generalizable, then many kin do not complete the required steps for getting foster care payments. Future research could help identify why kin do not complete required steps and how local agencies can alter requirements or better assist kin in meeting these requirements.

In the debate about payment of kin, the question of why kin do not receive foster care payments has taken a back seat to the question of whether kin should be offered such payments at all. Whether and how much financial assistance one wants to offer to kin who care for foster children depends primarily on what the assistance is meant to do. If a foster care payment is intended to convince people to become foster parents, then one could argue that kin need not be paid the same as non-kin, since they probably need less incentive to take a foster child. If a foster payment is meant as a reward for taking a foster child, one could argue that kin who act as foster parents should not be paid for caring for a related child, since such care is part of their familial responsibility. I believe that a foster care payment is intended, at least in part, to ensure that a child for whom the state is responsible is cared for adequately. Under this assumption, if financial assistance to foster parents affects the quality of care provided to children, then there is no legitimate reason for providing kin less financial support if they care for a child in state custody. This assertion raises the questions of how foster care payment levels are determined and how different levels of payment impact the outcomes and well-being that foster children experience.

While foster care payments are intended to help care for a foster child, I do not believe that states set their foster care payment rates with much consideration of what is truly required to care for a child. The media image of parents taking foster children for the money is not accurate in the majority of cases. Most of the foster parents I know or have spoken with expend a much greater sum of money on their children than the state provides them. Because kinship caregivers often have limited incomes, not only do they depend upon financial assistance more than most non-kin foster parents do, but also they may have limited ability to supplement the financial assistance with their own resources.

Few studies have assessed how the level of financial assistance provided to foster parents affects the quality of care provided or the well-being of foster children.[1] Not only would such research help inform the debate about payment to kinship foster parents, it would inform child welfare agencies' decisions on where to allocate limited resources.

The question of whether to offer kin foster care payments is intertwined with the larger debate over how to support kin caring for children outside of the child welfare system (private and voluntary kinship care arrangements). The issue of financial support of kinship care and the service system (welfare or child welfare) that should be responsible for kinship care families may have received more attention than any other issue related to kinship care. As a result, this issue is addressed in greater detail below.

Casework Practices with Kinship Foster Parents

This study confirmed prior research showing that child welfare workers have different casework practices with kin and non-kin foster parents. Despite the fact that kin are typically unprepared for their roles as foster parents, caseworkers often fail to provide kin with needed information, may provide misleading information, and report difficulties communicating with kin. Workers recognize the potential benefits of involving kin in case planning, given that many kin have prior knowledge of the child in care, yet report that kin often are not involved or are less involved than non-kin foster parents.

Similarly, workers report that kin are less likely to follow agency rules and procedures, yet workers often provide less supervision of kinship care placements. Workers rely much more on kin than non-kin foster parents to supervise birth parent visits with children in their care. Children in kinship care appear to enjoy more frequent and flexible contact with their birth parents than do children in non-kin foster care, but workers raised concerns about the ability of kin caregivers to effectively supervise visits.

Non-kin foster parents choose to be involved with child welfare agencies and are trained to understand and expect that caseworkers will be highly involved in assessing the well-being of foster children and making decisions about their care. Kin's lack of preparation, and fear and mistrust of the child welfare agency, can make case planning and supervision quite challenging.[2] While this study has raised and described these issues, it has done little to offer solutions. Future research needs to identify strategies that child welfare agencies can employ to better engage kin, birth parents, and extended family members in case planning. One strategy that has received widespread acclaim is family group decision-making (FGDM). While FGDM appears promising, it has not been rigorously evaluated so that program designers are informed not only if it is successful, but also how local agencies can adapt the model to meet local needs and circumstances.

To enhance casework practices with kin, local agencies need to determine how to engender trust and openness among kin. Public agencies may have great difficulty in achieving this. Some administrators have noted the difficulty in being responsible for removing a child *and* for helping the parent get the child back. Kin may be more likely to trust and work cooperatively with private agencies that are part of their community. Even though they are under contract to the child welfare agency, kinship caregivers appear to respond more favorably to private agencies than to public agencies (Geen et al. 2001). Future research should include evaluations of private agency kinship care programs to determine their effectiveness as well as the programmatic features that are key to their success.

In addition to pointing out that kinship foster parents do not always meet licensing standards, critics of kinship care question its safety because of the improper access that birth parents may have when their children are placed with kin. While this study suggests that birth parents are more likely to have unscheduled and unsupervised visits with their children when they are placed with kin, this fact does not mean that such placements lead to greater abuse by birth parents. This issue will not go away until research examines the extent to which kinship care exposes children to the risk of abuse or neglect from their birth parents as a result of unsupervised visitation. Moreover, future research needs to examine how agencies can identify kin who will protect children from abusive birth parents and how agencies can better support kin in this effort.

Providing Services to Children in Kinship Foster Care

Service delivery practices are also different when children are placed in kinship care. Workers offer fewer services to kin than to non-kin foster parents. In fact, some workers acknowledge that they have higher expectations of kin or that they do not want kin to become dependent upon the public agency. However, most workers acknowledge that, for a variety of reasons, their agency simply fails to adequately meet the needs of kin. In addition, kin request fewer services of caseworkers than do non-kin foster parents. Kin do not know what to ask for, are afraid to ask out of fear of appearing unable to care for a child, or may simply want to avoid public agency intrusion. Finally, many kin face barriers to accessing services. They are often unable to obtain support when they seek it out because of eligibility constraints, lack of familiarity with community resources, or waiting lists for services.

Despite research on the characteristics of kinship foster parents and the services they are offered, request, and receive, we still have limited information on kin's service needs. Research should both explore the services that kin need to meet the needs of the children in their care and the support kin need themselves to be effective caregivers. Kin may need additional assistance in caring for children, especially in the beginning, since they are typically thrown into their caregiving responsibility with little or no warning. Research should identify, from kin's perspective, what their immediate needs are and how agencies can either provide assistance directly or help kin access community services.

There is also scant research on the consequences of kin caregiving. Future study should examine the burden that caregiving places on kin as well as the sources of that burden. Research should consider how the burden affects kin as well as the children in their care and how services or support can alleviate the burden. Also necessary is research assessing the impact of kinship care on other children in the kin caregiver's home.

Permanency Planning with Kinship Foster Parents

Child welfare agencies often approach permanency planning differently when children are placed with kin. While ASFA has increased the focus on achieving permanency quickly, children placed with kin often remain in long-term foster care without termination of parental rights (TPR) occurring. Birth parents may be significantly less motivated to complete case plan requirements when their children are placed with kin. In addition, guardianship as opposed to adoption is the most common permanency outcome with kin as well as the outcome most stressed by caseworkers. While more relatives are willing to adopt than is typically believed, there are many reasons—including financial disincentives—why kin may *not* be willing to adopt.

Permanency can mean many different things from the multiple perspectives of those involved in a foster care case, including the foster child, the kinship caregiver, the birth parent, and the child welfare agency. Testa (2001) notes that there is conflict between the traditional meaning of permanency as "lasting," which is rooted in the psychology of bonding and attachment, and the meaning rooted in law that defines permanency as "binding." A child is most likely not concerned about how binding a placement is, but wants to feel that they have a home that is forever. Similarly, kinship caregivers and birth parents may be prepared for a permanent (lasting) placement yet may be reluctant to agree to a more binding agreement. By contrast, child welfare agencies are stressing, albeit to varying degrees as this study shows, that adoption should be the first option for all children and only after adoption has been ruled out should guardianship, a less binding option, be considered. Future research should explore whether kinship care, regardless of permanency outcomes, offers children a lasting relationship. Essential in this analysis should be children's perceptions of whether the relationship is lasting. In one of the few studies that have examined this issue, Testa and Cook find that "neither adoption nor guardianship makes much practical contribution over and above the bonds of kinship to the continuity of these family relationships" (2001, 27).

Research should look further into whether binding agreements result in more lasting relationships. How do the rates of adoption disruption differ from those of guardianship? Research must also assess how subsidies and post-permanency services affect both adoption and guardianship disruptions.

To the extent that a binding relationship is preferred, future analysis should explore more fully the reasons why some kin are reluctant to adopt. Do kin understand the differences between adoption and guardianship? To what extent do kin refuse to adopt due to financial disincentives, such as those noted in this study? One of the strongest and most troubling findings from this study is that kinship care may reduce the motivation of birth parents—in particular, substance-abusing parents—to complete required case plan activities in order to be reunified with their children. Future research needs to assess whether, in fact, kinship care reduces birth parents' motivation, and if so, what it is about kinship care that has this effect. If validated, this finding could have important policy and practice implications for both child welfare agencies and substance-abuse treatment providers. Future research should also examine other ways in which kinship care may affect birth parents, including noncustodial fathers, post-permanency.

Using Kin as a Diversion from Foster Care

This study found that, while often not openly discussed, voluntary placements with kin are fairly common. In Alabama, the vast majority of children placed with kin are placed voluntarily. The primary reason to take custody of a child placed with kin in Alabama is to provide additional financial support to kinship caregivers. In California, Connecticut, and Indiana, agency guidance and culture may support the use of voluntary placements, but on a much more limited basis. The use of voluntary placements in these states varies greatly, both among and within states, as well as among and within individual offices within a state. Workers balance a voluntary placement's potential risk to a child with the desire not to intrude into the private arrangements made by families.

Agency support and supervision of voluntary placements varies greatly. The level of risk and available agency resources often determines how voluntary placements are treated. Alabama uses voluntary kinship care placements for relatively high-risk situations, and then will open a case on the child and provide ongoing support and supervision. In the other three study sites, workers typically do not open a case or provide much support to voluntary placements, but they also do not use such arrangements for high-risk situations.

Few other researchers have discussed, let alone studied, child welfare agencies' use of kin as a diversion from foster care. Certainly more research is needed to identify the circumstances under which child welfare agencies are relying on kin voluntarily. What would have happened to children placed in voluntary kinship care had this option not been available? Would they have remained in the parents' care? Would they have been taken into state custody and placed in foster care, possibly with kin? And, of course, research is needed to evaluate whether, both in the short term and long term, these placements are good for children. A key concern about these placements is the extent to which kin can protect children from birth parents without an order of protective custody. A benefit of these placements is that they may minimize the stigma and intrusion of the child welfare agency.

To what extent are kin being coerced to accept children voluntarily? Most of the kinship caregivers in Alabama interviewed for this study were not aware that kin could act as foster parents and receive financial assistance in that capacity. Most felt, accurately or not, that if they had not accepted the children in their care, the state would have taken custody of the children and placed them in non-kin foster care. In 1989, the Ninth Circuit Court found in *Lipscomb v. Simmons* that children have a constitutional right to associate with relatives and that states' failure to use kin as foster parents denies children that right. Financial support arguments aside (see discussion below), one could question whether states that use kin to care for children who would otherwise be taken into state custody are violating the rights of kin caregivers by not informing them of their right to act as a foster parents for the related child and receive additional financial assistance and services.

Several researchers have commented on the difficult decision that child welfare agencies must make in response to private kinship care families who seek out assistance. For example, James Gleeson, reporting on the experiences of Illinois, a state that at one time brought many private kinship care children into protective custody, comments:

> Lessons from Illinois and other states suggest that taking children into state custody unnecessarily should be avoided and that diversion efforts can be facilitated through family conferences, mediation, and other non-adversarial approaches to assisting families with decision making. This is not to say that all informal kinship care arrangements are safe or permanent or support the child's well-being. It is clear, however, that if the only service available to vulnerable children and their families is formal kinship care, demand for this placement service will grow (Gleeson 1999, 47).

Additional research is needed to understand the circumstances under which kin privately take over child rearing of related children. Research should also examine the circumstances under which kin seek out assistance from child welfare agencies. Much of the debate on kinship care has focused on the financial incentives or disincentives created by the significantly different levels of assistance provided by welfare versus foster care payments. To what extent would the kinship care debate change if the majority of kin seeking help from child welfare authorities were shown to be, as I suspect, more interested in nonfinancial assistance than foster care payments?

Additional Research Needs

The most fundamental research gap, and the reason I am not comfortable accepting kinship care as a paradigm shift, is evidence that kinship care has a positive impact on children. I am not aware of a single well-designed, controlled, longitudinal study that the field can depend on to support the efficacy of kinship care in comparison with other forms of foster care.[3] Again, while such a study would demonstrate the benefits of kinship care, studies that assess the impact of kinship care on children's well-being are needed for several reasons. First, demonstrating the efficacy of kinship care would likely change the tone if not the content of the debate from one of concern about how kinship care is different from traditional foster care to a focus on how to make the most of kinship care. Second, studies examining the impact of kinship care on children's well-being may identify not only circumstances under which kinship care is more likely to benefit the child, but also circumstances under which kinship care may not be in children's best interest. Third, such studies can identify agency policies or practices that either limit or accentuate the benefits kinship care can provide.

In addition to evaluating the impact of kinship care on children's well-being, future research should examine its impact on kinship caregivers themselves (as discussed above), birth parents, and extended families. Studies on birth parents should examine the relationship between birth parents and their children before, during, and after placement. Research should examine the use of kinship foster care when abusive or neglectful birth parents are substance abusers, victims of domestic violence themselves, or incarcerated. Child welfare agencies need guidance in how to better engage birth parents and how kinship care affects the case planning process. Studies should include both mothers and fathers, including noncustodial parents.

Existing research has largely overlooked the impact of the broader extended family on kinship care placements. Extended family members can be an important source of support for kinship caregivers and have a big impact on children's well-being. Kin who become foster parents of a related child report that they are often ostracized from extended family members, who side with the birth parent and blame the kinship caregiver for taking the child. Future research should assess the involvement of extended family members and the impact of this involvement, both positive and negative, on kinship caregivers and the children in their care.

Finally, kinship care research to date has focused almost exclusively on African-American children and caregivers. Future inquiries should examine the use of kinship care, both privately and publicly, among whites as well as other racial and ethnic minorities, including Native American, Latino, and Asian families, including immigrants.

Policy and Practice Recommendations

While this study was meant to be exploratory and the sites selected are not representative of kinship practices nationally, it has identified challenges created by the uniqueness of kinship care that all child welfare agencies probably face. Drawing on the findings from this study, I suggest policy and programmatic changes that child welfare agencies may want to consider and I identify areas in which increased training would assist caseworkers and kinship caregivers.

Policy Changes and Guidance

Because of a limited research base, child welfare agencies have minimal information to inform development of kinship care policies. This study, in fact, illustrates the wide variation in caseworker practices that results from a lack of specificity in policy. While caseworker decisions must be made on a case-by-case basis, agencies can do a better job of helping guide caseworkers and supervisors by identifying factors to include in the decisionmaking process. In addition, agencies should review existing policies to ensure that they are not inadvertently limiting kin's access to services or supports.

- *Develop guidance to help workers make informed decisions about when to place children with kin.* Decisions about where to place a child need to be made on a case-by-case basis by workers and supervisors, but agencies can identify factors, unique to kinship care, that should be considered in the decisionmaking process.
- *Prevent appropriate kin from being denied the opportunity to be foster parents.* States should examine foster parent licensing standards and waiver policies, ensuring that they are sufficient to guarantee the safety of foster children, but not so overly prescriptive as to deny persons (kin and non-kin) who can be effective caregivers the

opportunity to become foster parents. Moreover, agencies may want to consider allocating funds to assist otherwise appropriate kin who are unable to meet certain safety requirements due to a lack of resources (for example, the purchase of smoke detectors and fire extinguishers) or to complete needed home repairs. In addition, agencies may be able to more effectively recruit kin to act as foster parents if they, from the initial contact, assure kin that they will receive needed support services, such as child care, tutoring, and counseling.

- *Examine policies to determine if kin are being inadvertently denied services they may need to care for a child.* When supportive services are linked to licensing, most kin will fail to receive support since many are not licensed and those that are may take a long time to complete the licensing process. Workers also identified a need for greater clarity in child welfare agency policies about the services that may be available for kin.

- *Rethink financial assistance policies for kin who agree to care for foster children permanently.* There is no rational justification to deny ongoing financial assistance to relatives who cannot meet adoption or guardianship requirements, yet still allow these same kin to care for children permanently. How can kin be an acceptable adoptive parent but not be an acceptable subsidized adoptive parent? If being unable to meet requirements means that kin are somehow not acceptable caretakers, then they should not be permitted to have permanent custody. If they *are* acceptable caretakers, then they should not be denied ongoing financial support—such denial only serves to punish the children.

- *Do a better job of articulating how a legal change in permanency affects the responsibilities of the kinship caregiver and the rights of the birth parents.* Both the adoption and the guardianship process are difficult for kin (not to mention workers) to understand, and kin may simply get anxious over the word *adoption.* Agencies may want to work with their state courts to design a permanency option that is culturally sensitive to concerns of kinship caregivers but allows for greater stability than guardianship is at least perceived to have. In addition, greater caregiver commitment, regardless of how it is measured, should not be rewarded with less assistance.

- *Rethink permanency planning practices for children in kinship care.* Agencies may want to experiment with methods to better assess kinship caregivers' commitment as well as how permanent kinship care children feel, rather than focusing solely on legal permanence.

Program Development

Child welfare agencies need to identify programmatic changes that could improve their ability to use kin effectively. Many agencies have acknowledged the different needs of kinship caregivers and have begun to develop innovative strategies to serve these caregivers better.

- *Be innovative in identifying kin.* Because birth parents may not reliably identify kin, child welfare agencies should take advantage of any available resource to identify, locate, and assess kin early in the process, including using the Federal Parent Locator Service developed as part of the child support enforcement system, examining a child's school records, and talking with neighbors, clergy, teachers, or other members of the community with whom the child or family has a connection.
- *Continue and improve efforts to recruit non-kin foster parents.* Acknowledging the benefits that kinship care can provide and actively seeking out available kin does not in any way diminish the need for non-kin foster parents.
- *Experiment with new approaches to engage kinship care families.* Family group conferencing programs (also called family group decisionmaking) that bring the entire family network together to plan for the care of a child constitute a promising approach that many agencies have instituted. In some locations, workers noted that court reports include a section for kinship caregivers to provide feedback and request assistance, and this has helped kin feel part of the decisionmaking process.
- *Explore ways to bring kinship foster parents together more.* In many localities, experienced foster parents are recruited to mentor new foster parents. This approach may also work well with kinship foster parents. In addition, non-kin foster parents benefit greatly from participation in foster parent associations. Therefore, child welfare agencies are increasingly helping to develop kinship caregiver support groups. Support groups not only provide an opportunity for kin to share experiences with one another, but they also can be an effective way to educate kin about the child welfare system and services available to them.

Worker Training

Caseworkers acknowledged that working with kin is different from working with non-kin foster parents, yet few workers receive information or training on how to approach kinship caregivers differently. I suggest the following:

- *Develop worker training on how best to communicate with kin and use them in case planning.* The results of this study indicate that workers clearly understand the unique circumstances of kinship care placements and acknowledge the benefits that kin can offer in case planning. Yet workers also acknowledge having difficulty establishing and maintaining effective working relationships with kin.
- *Be more flexible in working with kin.* Workers in some local agencies noted that they were able to get kin to participate in case planning by holding meetings in the evening or on weekends and at locations more convenient to kin, such as local community agencies or churches.
- *Educate workers on resources available to support kin foster parents.* Workers admitted that they have limited knowledge of community resources and often rely on foster parents for information with which to advise kinship caregivers. Moreover, many workers appear confused about the eligibility criteria and the application process for a variety of public services for which kin should be eligible.
- *In larger jurisdictions, consider specialized caseloads or units that deal primarily with kinship care.* Because of the unique challenges faced by kin, workers may need special skills and/or information to effectively work with kin. Moreover, given the frequent changes in policy and community resources available to kin, specialized workers or units are more likely to keep abreast of such changes.

Kin Training

Unlike their conditions for non-kin caregivers, many child welfare agencies do not require kinship caregivers to complete any formal training to be a foster parent. Since kin are caring for a specific child they usually already know, kin may not need to complete the same training that non-kin foster parents complete. Yet the most common recommendation from workers and administrators participating in this study on improving kinship care practice was to provide kin with better information and training.

- *Develop strategies to better inform kinship caregivers of what is expected of them as foster parents and what they can expect from the agency and the courts.* Because kin typically step in to help during a crisis, it is unlikely that they will be well informed at first. Thus agencies must work intensively with kin during the early stages of a placement to get them "up to speed." Simply referring kin to foster parent training is unlikely to help, given that workers found that kin were unlikely to attend such training. Kin may not respond well to offers of "training," but may be interested in orientation or support group meetings, and during these meetings kin can receive needed information.
- *Educate kin on services available.* Agencies must do a better job of informing kin of the services available from the child welfare agency, other public services kin may be eligible for and how to apply, and services available from community agencies.
- *Provide information and guidance to kin on how to monitor birth parent visitation.* Kin need guidance on following court orders, what to look for in the interaction between birth parents and children, and providing feedback to caseworkers. Some locations pay kin to supervise visitation, and kin may be more open to training when they are paid and see supervision of visitation as an added responsibility.
- *Prepare both kin and the children to manage the ongoing relationship they will have with birth parents.* Child welfare agencies need to acknowledge that many birth parents will continue to be involved in their children's lives when kin take guardianship or even adopt. Agencies may also want to consider providing some limited but ongoing supervision of these children post-permanency.

Beyond Research: The Philosophical Debate over Financial Assistance

Whether and how kinship care can promote the safety, permanency, and well-being of foster children are largely empirical questions that future research can address. I believe the policy changes recommended above, based on the study findings described in the book, will help child welfare agencies do what they can to help children in kinship foster care achieve positive outcomes. States should examine and eliminate illogical inconsistencies in their policies for financially assisting kin who agree to take permanent responsibility for foster children. And kin caring for children in foster care should not be denied foster care payments.

Yet, to this point, I have not made policy recommendations about financial support for kinship care families more generally. In contrast to other issues related to kinship care, the debate about how and when to financially support children cared for by kin, both with and without child welfare involvement, is a philosophical one and part of the larger debate about the role of society in serving children without parents. Thus, before I make recommendations for policy changes related to financial support of kinship care, it is necessary to outline the philosophical basis for current policies.

Government Responsibility Based upon Children's Status

The government's response to children separated from their parents, as evidenced by legislative history and judicial decisions, appears directly related to the level of legal responsibility that public agencies assume for a nonparental placement or setting. The greater the legal responsibility, the greater the financial assistance provided and the greater the level of oversight and intrusion into the lives of children and families.

CHILDREN LIVING WITH PARENTS. Parents have a constitutional right and responsibility to rear their own children, and the courts have carefully guarded these rights. Thus, government's responsibility to care for children who live with their parents is minimal. While government offers assistance to parents in financial distress, its legal authority to question parents' child rearing is limited to responding to allegations of child abuse or neglect.

CHILDREN IN PRIVATE KINSHIP CARE. Government affords kin the same level of privacy and child rearing authority as it affords parents, with intrusion limited to investigation of child abuse or neglect.[4] The reasons for the arrangement and the care of the relative child are not the state's concern unless the child's safety is jeopardized. Yet federal legislation does recognize that some caregivers are not legally required to support a child and thus kin are eligible to receive child-only payments for related children, even if their own income would otherwise make them ineligible for federal aid.[5]

CHILDREN LIVING IN FOSTER CARE. Government assumes the greatest responsibility for foster children, since these children are typically in court-ordered state custody. The state has the duty to ensure that basic needs of these children are met, including food, clothing, shelter, medical care, and education. In addition, the state assumes the responsibility of addressing parental inadequacies or arranging for an alternative permanent living arrangement for children. In turn, states provide the greatest amount of oversight for foster children, the highest level of government financial support, and a wide array of services. Some may argue, however, that kin caring for foster children should not be equally compensated as non-kin foster parents because of their familial obligation to care for a related child. Legally, however, government's responsibility for foster children is the same whether they are placed with kin or non-kin.

Because we have tied government assistance to legal responsibility, the level of assistance provided to children in foster care is significantly greater than the support provided to children in private kinship care. While children in private kinship care may in theory be entitled to assistance in instances where children in parent care are not (when kin are non-poor), the level of assistance is small, and in practice, non-poor kin rarely access benefits. In essence, poor kinship caregivers are treated no differently than poor single parents. Yet many would argue that government is more obligated to support kinship caregivers who step in when a child needs care than it is obligated to support single parents.

The Paradox of Financial Assistance

Identifying populations that society feels a greater obligation to assist creates a paradox for policymakers. By selecting a group that is more deserving of assistance, such policies provide an incentive to become a member of such a group. Thus, providing greater assistance to kin who care for children in state custody than kin who care for children privately provides kin the unintended and undesirable incentive to seek out child welfare assistance. Similarly, providing greater assistance to kin than to birth parents creates an incentive for parents to turn their children over to kin to rear. At the same time, identifying a population to provide greater assistance to provides government agencies an incentive to limit the size of such a population, since public resources for social services are limited. In regard to kinship care, states have a financial incentive to limit the number of children for whom they have legal responsibility by, for example, using voluntary placements.

This paradox is not unique to kinship care and, in fact, parallels criticisms made of our nation's welfare system. David Ellwood describes this problem in our welfare system as an "assistance-family structure conundrum," where "higher benefits to single parents may encourage families to split up and young, unmarried women to have babies. . . . Both the need for aid and the negative incentives of providing it are clear. That is why it can be such a vexing conundrum" (1988, 21–23). Ellwood poses a solution, however: "The further we move toward a system that makes judgments about the causes of poverty . . . the less bothersome the conundrums seem to be" (43). Ellwood notes that welfare would be the perfect antipoverty policy if poverty were caused only by the lack of money. By understanding the causes of poverty, he argues that welfare becomes only a small part of the safety net for disadvantaged families.

Kinship care is not caused by a lack of money, nor is lack of money the primary concern of many kin. Thus addressing the needs of kin primarily through our welfare system seems misguided. Similarly, kinship care does not necessarily place a child in need of protective supervision. Therefore, addressing the needs of kin *only* through the child welfare system would also be misguided. Part of the solution to designing a public policy approach to kinship care is understanding why kin are caring for children, the needs kin have as a result, and how best to meet these needs. Some kin may only have financial needs that may be best addressed through welfare. Many more kin will need services to help them care for their related children. Most will have a combination of both. An effective kinship care policy would better match kin needs with public support and match state intrusion and oversights with safety concerns. Kin who need greater financial assistance than is offered under welfare or who need services to help care for a related child should not seek out child welfare involvement to get the support they need.

Welfare's Inability to Serve Kin

An obvious, easily implemented approach to meeting the financial needs of kinship care families (private, voluntary, and foster), and one that is likely to be somewhat successful, is to ensure that these families receive the supports for which they are already eligible. Only one in four children in kinship care is supported by a foster care or Temporary Assistance for Needy Families (TANF) payment. Only two in five children in low-income kin families receive food stamps. Similarly, two in five children in kinship care receive Medicaid health coverage (Ehrle and Geen 2002a).

The chapters above documented a number of reasons why kin foster parents may not receive services from child welfare agencies. Private kinship care families may also fail to receive services for which they are eligible for a number of reasons. Many kin report that they are not aware that they are eligible for benefits. Because kinship care families are a relatively small group in comparison with poor parents, they are often overlooked by program administrators and policymakers. Outreach materials that discuss services available to "parents" may be ignored by kinship caregivers. Even if kinship caregivers are aware of the services for which they are eligible, the stigma they feel from accepting welfare assistance may keep them away. Finally, studies have found that kinship caregivers who apply for public assistance are sometimes mistakenly denied assistance by eligibility workers who are not aware that kin are eligible to receive these services.

While improved outreach and training of workers would certainly help kinship care families access public assistance, I do not believe that our welfare system is designed to meet the needs of kinship care families. Our existing welfare system is primarily designed to assist young, low-income mothers with no or minimal financial assets. With recent reforms, the system provides time-limited assistance and makes assistance dependent upon employment or work activities. The system is designed to provide income support to poor families, but it significantly limits benefits, at least partially to make welfare an unattractive option. Moreover, the welfare system was not designed with older caregivers in mind.

While all kin are generally eligible to receive child-only welfare benefits, and child-only recipients are generally not subject to work requirements or time limits, many are not eligible to receive benefits for themselves due to either their level of assets or their income (which is often low, but not low enough to meet TANF eligibility standards). The difference between a child-only grant and a family grant is typically not that substantial. However, because many kin can only receive child-only grants, they are often not eligible for several other supports that are linked to TANF family grant receipt. These may include food stamps, energy assistance through the Low-Income Home Energy Assistance Program (LIHEAP), child care assistance, and free meals for school-aged children through the school lunch and school breakfast programs.

The existing welfare system obviously makes little sense for low-income aged kinship caregivers who are seeking assistance for themselves and their children. We do not expect aged caregivers to work (and many states do not require aged caregivers to work under existing policies). The reasons why welfare was reformed to provide time-limited assistance and a work incentive do not apply to aged kin. Furthermore, aged kin should not be held to the same eligibility requirements for welfare benefits. Many aged kin have assets that make them ineligible to receive welfare payments. However, since these kin are closer to retirement than most single mothers, if not already retired, I do not believe we should expect them to use their assets to care for a related child.

While we may expect that younger low-income kinship care providers should work, the existing welfare system is not appropriate, even for these younger kin caregivers. Should our welfare policies take the same approach with a 50-year-old grandmother who agrees to take care of her infant grandchild as with an 18-year-old mother? I do not think so. While younger than aged caregivers, 50-year-old kinship caregivers are still much closer to retirement than young mothers and thus should not face the same asset restrictions that our welfare system currently imposes. Similarly, since they are older, it is reasonable to expect kinship caregivers to save a greater portion of their income for retirement. Thus, compared with younger welfare mothers, a greater share of kin caregivers' income should be disregarded when considering the level of welfare benefits provided.

Meeting Kin's Financial Needs—A New Approach

So how should we meet the financial needs that result from kin caring for a related child? Let's start with children in state custody. Kin who care for children in foster care should be eligible for foster care payments, and these payments should remain higher than the assistance provided to children in private kinship care. While offering higher payments to children in foster care may provide an incentive for kin to enter the child welfare system, offering less to foster children simply because they are cared for by relatives seems unfairly punitive. Moreover, foster parents are responsible for more than private kinship caregivers and should be compensated for such. Foster parents are expected to meet with caseworkers, attend court dates, help arrange visits with birth parents, and ensure that foster children receive needed services, such as therapy. In essence, it costs more for a kin to care for a foster child, even if the needs of that child are the same. In addition, if states raise the financial assistance provided to kin outside of foster care, as I suggest below, then kin will have less of an incentive to seek out foster care.

To meet the needs of children not in state custody (private and voluntary arrangements), states could make several changes (and some states already have) to their TANF system.[6] First, states need to address kin's immediate financial needs. There are many expenses that kin face in taking in a child, such as clothing, diapers, car seats, cribs, and furniture. States should make available to kin a one-time, per-child payment to assist with this transition. There is precedence for this in our existing welfare system. Many states make available emergency payments and others provide increased payments in September to assist parents in meeting costs associated with children returning to school. Second, states should significantly increase the assets that kin may have and still be eligible to receive a TANF family grant. Many kin have worked hard for years and put themselves on a path toward self-sufficiency. Through no fault of their own—to the contrary, as a result of their altruism—they may be diverted from this path as a result of the caregiving responsibility if they must use assets accumulated for retirement to care for a related child. Third, at least for aged caregivers and probably for all kin, TANF benefits should not be time-limited, since the policy objective is not to provide an incentive for kin to work. Fourth, for older if not all kin, income disregards should be significantly increased; kin should be allowed to have income that allows them to save for retirement. Fifth, two-parent kinship care families should be eligible for income support, particularly families headed by aged kinship caregivers.

Finally, I believe that kin should receive greater financial assistance than parent welfare recipients receive. In no state are welfare benefits sufficient to raise a child. In 1997, in fact, states' maximum welfare benefits averaged 34 percent of the federal poverty level.[7] Remarkably little is written about why state welfare benefits are this low. Discussions with welfare experts suggest that there are three basic reasons for the low welfare benefits, reasons that are not applicable for kinship care families. First, states cannot afford to provide higher welfare benefits. While this may be true, kin parents are a relatively small population, so the cost of increasing benefits to this population would be more manageable. Second, there is a lack of political will to give welfare families greater support. The general public blames welfare families for their plight and does not see them as deserving of greater support. While the general public may feel that kin, particularly grandparents, are somewhat to blame for having raised a child who is unable to parent, most citizens would see kin as more deserving than welfare parents. Finally, welfare benefits are intentionally kept low so as not to provide incentives for low-income families to become dependent on public assistance. States want low-income families to have an incentive to work. In addition, individual states may not want to increase their benefit levels for fear of attracting more low-income families to establish residency in the state. Policymakers must still be concerned about the fiscal incentives kin have. However, because kin are voluntarily accepting the responsibility of taking care of a child, there may be less concern about their motivation. Moreover, policymakers must also be concerned about the incentive kin have to turn a child over to child welfare so that children can be supported by a foster care payment. While this proposal to increase benefit levels for kin may be controversial, there is evidence that states can afford it and that there is enough political will to implement such an approach. Several states have created kinship payments through their TANF system that provide a greater level of support than is provided by child-only payments, though less than would be available if a child was taken into custody and supported with a foster care payment (Andrews et al. 2002). Officials in at least some of these states argue that these higher payments are cost effective, as the state is having to take custody of fewer children and thus not making foster care payments and incurring child welfare administrative costs.

While changing welfare eligibility requirements and benefit levels will significantly help meet kin's financial needs, one additional change is needed: kin should not be served by the same agency workers who provide welfare benefits. All children who live with kin, regardless of whether they were abused or neglected, have experienced the trauma of being separated from their parents. These children likely need services beyond financial assistance. The welfare system is neither designed nor equipped to understand and respond to the needs of these children and families. Moreover, the stigma associated with receiving welfare will continue to keep some kin from seeking assistance. Child welfare agencies are better equipped to assess and meet the needs of kinship care families. While child welfare agencies also suffer from a poor public image and even greater stigma than do welfare agencies, in recent years, many child welfare agencies have expanded their delivery of voluntary family support services, often relying on community-based agencies that are trusted by kinship care families. In addition, making child welfare agencies responsible for all kinship care children may allow for a more systematic assessment of which children require protective supervision. Just to be clear, *I am not suggesting that private kinship care families become part of the child protective services caseload.* When there are no safety concerns, there is no reason for child protective services agencies to intrude in the lives of these families. However, child welfare agencies can and do provide a function that extends beyond child protective services. Assisting private kinship care families fits within the larger child welfare mission, certainly more than it fits within the mission of our welfare system. And if child welfare agencies can tap into the capacity of the community-based agencies (including faith-based organizations) that are known and trusted by residents, they will be more successful in encouraging kinship caregivers to access the assistance they need.

I am well aware that these suggestions do not solve the paradox described above of providing greater support to certain kin or greater support to kin than birth parents. However, it is doubtful that providing greater support to private kin will have a great impact on the use of kinship care. The placement of a child in kinship care is a two-way transaction; both the kin and the parent have to agree. It seems unlikely that providing additional benefits to kin will convince both kin and parents that such an arrangement is now in their best interest. At the same time, additional policy changes could be considered to reduce unintended incentives for children to be passed around simply to get higher benefits. For example, kin who apply for benefits could be required to take legal guardianship of the children in their care. More diligent child support enforcement could reduce the incentive for birth parents to give children to kin.

Kinship caregivers are a valuable resource. They are also a resource we largely take for granted, because whether or not we offer them much government assistance, kin are dedicated to ensuring that children who cannot be cared for by their own parents are loved and made to feel part of a family. As policymakers continue to develop strategies to assist kinship care families, I hope they focus less on theoretical incentives that lack empirical support and more on identifying and meeting the needs of children cared for by kin.

NOTES

1. A study by Berrick and Needell (1999) found that children placed with kinship foster parents in California who received foster care payments remained in foster care longer than those placed with kin supported by a TANF grant. Likewise, few studies have systematically assessed the impact of foster payment rates on recruitment of foster parents.

2. This fear may be well founded. Involvement with child welfare agencies could result in enforcing rules that the family believes are unnecessary, involvement in services or treatment not wanted by the family, removal of the children due to noncompliance, or termination of parental rights.

3. In fact, one of the few longitudinal studies of the well-being of children in kin and non-kin foster care found little difference in their adult functioning (Zuravin, Benedict, and Somerfield 1993).

4. However, the constitutional rights of parents are so strong that state or local governments may limit kin's authority to rear related children by requiring parental consent for such things as medical care or enrollment in school.

5. 1950 Social Security Act Amendments.

6. Of course, states could simply scrap their TANF-funded system of support for kin and replace it with a new kinship payment system, which could also be TANF funded, but not be bound by TANF requirements and guidelines. While this may be the best approach in the long run, I suggest what I believe is a more realistic strategy, at least politically, in the short term.

7. Even if you add in food stamps benefits, state financial assistance averages only 62 percent of the standard of need.

Study Description

Rob Geen and Cynthia Andrews Scarcella

The study upon which this book is based involved intensive case studies of local kinship care policies and frontline practices in 13 counties or cities representing four states during the spring and summer of 2000. These study sites included Jefferson (Birmingham), Mobile, and Talladega counties in Alabama; Los Angeles, San Diego, Santa Clara (San Jose), and Santa Cruz counties in California; Bridgeport, Hartford, and Torrington, Connecticut; and Lake (Gary), LaPorte, and Marion (Indianapolis) counties in Indiana. We selected four states with different state policies for licensing and paying kinship foster parents. Based on the Urban Institute 1999 kinship care policy survey,[1] Alabama provided kin who wished to care for children in state custody with the option of not becoming licensed and supporting these kin with Temporary Assistance for Needy Families (TANF) child-only payments instead of foster care payments. California offered foster care payments to kin who became licensed only if they cared for a child that was IV-E eligible.[2] Connecticut assessed kin based on standards different from those used for non-kin foster parents, but still provided kin with foster payments. Indiana assessed all kin and non-kin foster parents based on the same licensing standards.

In each state, we selected sites where child welfare agencies placed large numbers of children in kinship foster care. These sites were the larger, more urban counties in the states. In addition, we selected one rural county in each state to assess whether kinship care practices might be different in these communities. For logistical reasons, these rural counties were selected because of their proximity to the urban counties visited. In addition, we selected rural counties that placed enough children in kinship care to make our assessment of local policies and practices relevant to participants.

Data Collection

In each of the 13 study sites, we interviewed child welfare administrators and court personnel or judges (or both) and conducted focus groups with child welfare supervisors, caseworkers, and kinship caregivers. Where appropriate, we also conducted focus groups with other child welfare staff working with kin in addition to local kinship care providers. Separate focus groups were held with caseworkers and supervisors responsible for investigating child abuse and neglect reports and for working with children removed from their homes and placed in foster care with kin. We asked local child welfare administrators to identify 8 to 10 caseworkers or supervisors for each focus group who had experience working with kin and who had been employed with the child welfare agency for at least two years. We also conducted separate focus groups with licensed and unlicensed kinship caregivers. In each site, we asked the child welfare agencies and/or local kinship care providers to identify and recruit 20 kinship caregivers to participate in two focus groups.

A team of two Urban Institute researchers conducted each interview or focus group. At least one senior researcher with extensive prior experience conducting interviews and focus groups participated in each visit. The junior researchers who participated all had prior interviewing experience and most had prior experience facilitating focus groups. All researchers attended a one-day training session to practice interviewing and focus group facilitation techniques. Researchers used semistructured protocols to conduct the one-on-one and small group interviews. Protocols that allowed more flexibility were developed and used for the focus groups. All focus groups and small group interviews were audiotaped. For the individual interviews, one researcher was assigned the task of taking notes, and verbatim notes were taken to the extent appropriate and possible.

All caseworker and supervisor focus groups were held at local child welfare agency offices, and most were conducted during lunch, which was provided. Focus groups were held in child welfare agency conference rooms or at the offices of nonprofit agencies that work with kinship caregivers. Most of the caregiver focus groups were held in the evening and dinner was provided; a few occurred during breakfast, which was provided. In some sites, child care was also provided. Focus groups generally lasted an hour and a half. The kinship caregivers who participated in the focus groups each received a $20 compensation for their time and expenses.

In all, we conducted 41 focus groups with 235 caseworkers and 30 focus groups with 137 supervisors. The average caseworker focus group (5.7 members) was larger than the average supervisor focus group (4.6 members), since several locations had a limited number of supervisors. Approximately the same number of investigation workers and supervisors (103, 48) participated in the focus groups as did foster care workers and supervisors (107, 55). The remaining workers and supervisors either had generic caseloads (i.e., served families at all points in the system) or performed specific functions in which they worked with kin (e.g., family unity workers and licensing workers). Despite our requirement that workers and supervisors have at least two years of child welfare experience to participate in the focus groups, many had relatively short tenures; supervisors, not surprisingly, had longer tenures on average. Approximately 44 percent of workers and 30 percent of supervisors had no more than three years of child welfare experience. An additional 23 percent of workers and 15 percent of supervisors had between four and six years of experience. The tenure of workers varied significantly by state, with Indiana having the most tenured workers and supervisors and Alabama having the least. In all states, the vast majority of workers and supervisors were female (an average of 83 and 74 percent, respectively).

In all, we conducted 25 focus groups with 157 kinship caregivers. The size of the focus groups (an average of 6.3 caregivers) allowed kin sufficient time to recount personal experiences as well as provide opinions on issues raised by the facilitator or other focus group participants. The majority of participating kin were grandparents (51 percent were grandmothers, 10 percent were grandfathers) of the children in their care. An additional 24 percent of caregivers were aunts (19 percent) or uncles (5 percent). The majority of caregivers were African American (59 percent). Of the remaining caregivers, 25 percent were white, and 4 percent were Hispanic. The number of Hispanic caregivers is lower than what would have been expected if the caregivers had been selected randomly because we asked child welfare staff to only recruit English-speaking caregivers, since all of the focus groups were conducted in English. Most caregivers were over age 50 (59 percent) and were unmarried (53 percent, 18 percent single, 24 percent divorced, and 11 percent widowed). Approximately one-third of the caregivers were caring for one child, while 38 percent were caring for three or more children.

Human Subjects

The Urban Institute's Internal Review Board (IRB) approved the study's human subjects procedures to protect those participating. All focus group participants were required to sign a consent form before the focus groups began. Kinship caregivers were invited to complete a short questionnaire about their caregiving situation, but were clearly informed that this exercise was voluntary and would not affect their participation in the focus group or their payment. All participants were informed that the focus groups were being recorded and that the audiotapes would be transcribed. Participants were assured that, while direct quotes from the focus groups would be reported, no comment would be attributed to a specific person. In addition, participants were given the option to have the tape recorder turned off for a period of time if they wanted to make a comment that they did not want recorded.

Analysis and Reporting

The audiotapes were transcribed and the transcribed notes from the focus groups as well as notes from the other interviews were coded for analysis using Nud*ist content analysis software. Two researchers coded notes from the first site visits for training purposes to ensure intercoder reliability. Analysis focused on identifying differences of experience or opinion across states; across sites within states; between administrators, supervisors, and workers; between workers and caregivers; and between urban and rural sites. Direct quotes from administrators, workers, and caregivers included in this paper were selected to be representative of the opinions voiced. Moreover, we present caseworker opinions and caregivers' experiences based on their perspective. Thus, the information participants provided about such things as eligibility for services or agency procedures may not be accurate, but it is what they believed to be true.

Description of Study Sites

Alabama

Alabama Family Services is a division of Alabama Department of Human Resources. It is a state-administered child welfare system with county regional offices. In 2000, there were 21,965 reports of abuse and/or neglect made to Alabama Family Services, and of these, 6,932 were substantiated (DHHS 2002). Furthermore, 5,044 children were in foster care as of March 29, 2002, and approximately 3 percent of these children were living with a kin caregiver (Alabama Kinship Care State Fact Sheet 2002).

Alabama gives preference to relatives for placement. Following a child abuse and neglect investigation, if it is determined that a child cannot remain in his or her parents' home, Alabama's child welfare policy requires caseworkers to seek out kin to care for the child. A relative is defined as an individual related by blood, marriage, or adoption—a definition broader than the definition used to determine eligibility under TANF.

In Alabama, kinship care providers are assessed based on the same standards as non-kin foster parents, but the child welfare agency may modify or waive the age requirement on a case-by-case basis. For example, if one spouse is over age 21, the other may be under 21. Children may be placed with relatives after a criminal background check, a child abuse and neglect registry check, a home study, and income verification have been completed. These kin are eligible to receive a foster care payment of approximately $230–$266, a TANF child-only grant of approximately $111–$194 (depending on the number of children), and, if eligible, another payment, such as survivor's benefits or Supplemental Security Income (SSI). Kin must complete all the licensing requirements within 180 days. If the kinship caregiver does not meet the requirements in the specified time frame, the home may be approved as a relative placement site only (not foster care) and possibly receive TANF. Once kin meet all of the licensing requirements, they are eligible to receive a foster care payment of approximately $250 or another payment, such as survivor's benefits or SSI.

Child welfare workers in Alabama may help arrange for a child to be placed with a kinship care provider without seeking adjudication. Kin caring for a child who has not been adjudicated as abused or neglected are not required to meet specific standards and are eligible to receive a TANF child-only grant of approximately $111–$194 (depending on the number of children) or another payment, such as survivor's benefits or SSI. The relative may petition for custody, or the parent may sign an agreement for the relative to care for the child.

During 2000–2001, in more than 75 percent of kinship cases, the state chose not to file for termination of parental rights (TPR) for children in kinship foster care for 15 of 22 consecutive months. Alabama state policy allows children to remain in long-term foster care with kin on a case-by-case basis. Placement with a relative may be considered a compelling reason not to terminate parental rights. There is no minimum age for the child or length of time the child has lived with the relative to permit long-term foster care. When the relative is willing to commit to the child long term but cannot afford to do it without assistance, or is not willing to adopt, long-term foster care is acceptable.

Seven locations in Alabama are involved in a kinship pilot program called the Kinshare program. The program provides financial and supportive services to relative caregivers to prevent at-risk children from entering a foster care placement. Services through this program include counseling, child care, food assistance, respite care, special needs payments, and emergency intervention services.

Site visits were conducted in three Alabama counties: Mobile, Jefferson, and Talladega. Mobile County, with a population of 399,843 in 2000, is an urban area that is 63 percent white non-Hispanic/Latino, 33 percent African American, and 1 percent Hispanic or Latino.[3] Per capita personal income for the year 2000 was $21,914.[4] As of January 2001, there were 320 children supervised by Mobile County Family and Children Services who were cared for by relatives; of these, 101 were cared for by licensed kin foster parents. Additionally, 74 of the children (and 31 families) were involved in the Kinshare program.

Jefferson County, Alabama, is an urban area (Birmingham) with a population of 662,047 in 2000. It is 57 percent white non-Hispanic/Latino, 39 percent African American, and 2 percent Hispanic or Latino. Per capita personal income for the year 2000 was $30,638. As of September 2000, there were 935 children in care, 13 of whom were placed with relatives.

Talladega County, Alabama, is a rural area with a population of 80,321 in 2000. It is 67 percent white non-Hispanic/Latino, 32 percent African American, and 1 percent Hispanic or Latino. Per capita personal income for the year 2000 was $18,740. As of 2001, there were 436 open CPS cases and 27 children living in licensed relative foster homes. In addition, there were 60 children living in nonlicensed relative homes (and most were not in the custody of the Department of Children and Families [DCF]).

California

California Children and Family Services is a division of the state's Department of Social Services and is administered by 58 county offices. The county child welfare offices have considerable flexibility in determining child welfare policy. In 2000, California had 243,755 reports of abuse and/or neglect, of which 72,844 were substantiated (DHHS 2002). As of January 2001, 93,539 children were in out-of-home placements in California, and 37 percent of those were living with kin (California Kinship Care Fact Sheet 2002).

If a child abuse and neglect investigation determines that a child cannot remain in his or her parents' home, California's child welfare policy requires caseworkers to seek out kin to care for the child. Grandparents, aunts, uncles, or siblings are given preference for placement. California's definition of kin includes only those related by blood, marriage, or adoption—the same definition the state uses to determine eligibility under TANF. In California, kinship care providers are required to meet the same standards as non-kin foster parents must meet. Children may be placed with kin after a criminal background check, a child abuse and neglect registry check, and a home study have been completed. These kin are eligible to receive a TANF child-only grant of approximately $87 per month. Kin must complete all the requirements under this option within 72 hours. If they do, they are eligible to receive a federally funded payment of approximately $473 per month if the child is IV-E eligible or the TANF child-only grant of approximately $87 per month.

California has established the Kinship Support Services Program (KSSP) for kinship caregivers in eligible counties (counties with more than 40 percent of foster children in kinship care). The program provides support services to kinship caregivers and their families who are part of or at risk of becoming a part of California's foster system.

In California, child welfare workers may help arrange for a child to be placed with a kinship care provider without seeking adjudication. In such circumstances, kin are assessed based on a criminal background check, child abuse and neglect registry check, and a home study. Kin who are caring for a child who has not been adjudicated as abused or neglected are eligible to receive a TANF child-only grant of approximately $87 per month.

California state policy allows children to remain in long-term foster care with kin in cases where the kin caregiver does not choose to adopt due to familial or cultural factors but needs a subsidy to care for the child. Subsidized guardianship is offered to kinship care providers willing to permanently care for children for whom reunification or adoption is not possible. California's Kinship Guardianship Assistance Payment (KinGAP) program now allows children to exit the system via a state-subsidized legal guardianship and the child welfare case is terminated. There is no minimum age for the child to qualify. However, the child must have been in the same relative placement for at least one year. The average payment amount per child is $473 per month. Services are not offered in addition to the payment; however, in counties that have a KSSP project, these families can access KSSP services.

Site visits were conducted in four California counties: Los Angeles, San Diego, Santa Clara, and Santa Cruz. Los Angeles County had a population of 9,519,338 in 2000. An urban area, it is 31 percent white non-Hispanic/Latino, 10 percent African American, and 45 percent Hispanic or Latino. Per capita personal income is approximately $29,522. Children and Family Services workers supervise 38,273 out-of-home placements, and 18,308 (48 percent) involve relative homes.

San Diego County had a population of 2,813,833 in 2000. It is an urban area that is 55 percent white non-Hispanic/Latino, 6 percent African American, and 27 percent Hispanic or Latino. Per capita personal income for the year 2000 was $32,910.

Santa Clara County had a population of 1,682,585 in 2000. It is an urban area that is 44 percent white non-Hispanic/Latino, 3 percent African American, and 24 percent Hispanic or Latino. Per capita personal income for the year 2000 was $55,677. In February 2001, there were 1,049 relative homes caring for kin, representing approximately 39 percent of all placements.

Santa Cruz County had a population of 255,602 in 2000. It is a suburban area that is 66 percent white non-Hispanic/Latino, 1 percent

African American, and 27 percent Hispanic or Latino. Per capita personal income for the year 2000 was $37,866.

Connecticut

The Connecticut Department of Children and Families is a state-administered child welfare system. The commissioner of DCF is appointed by the governor and is advised by a statewide advisory council (whose members are also appointed by the governor). There are five regional offices (Southwestern, South Central, Eastern, North Central, and North Western) and nine suboffices. In 2000, there were 29,850 reports of abuse and/or neglect made to Connecticut DCF, and of these approximately 11,001 were investigated and substantiated (DHHS 2002). In all, 6,624 children were in foster care on the last day of 2001, and approximately 18 percent of these children were living with a kin caregiver (Connecticut Kinship Care State Fact Sheet 2002).

In Connecticut, preference for placement is given to relatives. A relative is defined as an individual related by blood, marriage, or adoption, the same definition used by the state's TANF program. Connecticut also has special study homes—special studies deal with those foster parents who have a relationship with the child but are not related (for example, godparents, teacher, family friend, or neighbor). Workers are required to seek out kin when it is determined that a child must be removed from the home.

Kinship care providers are assessed based on the same standards as non-kin foster parents; however, the state may waive training on a case-by-case basis. Kin may receive individualized training specific to their needs. The child can be placed with a relative after a criminal background check, a child abuse and neglect registry check, and a basic assessment/home visit have been completed. Kin then have 90 days to complete the remaining requirements, which include an application, physicals, confidentiality and disciplinary agreements, a financial statement, references, a home visit, animal shots, an income check, a child care plan, and compliance with home regulations. Each child is required to have a specific bedroom and his or her own bed; if a child is sharing a bedroom, it must be shared with a child of the same sex, and there can be no more than four children to a bedroom.

After kin have been provisionally licensed, they are eligible to receive the standard board payment of $684 per month and the same foster care services that non-kin foster parents receive. The caseworker must provide the same amount of supervision to kinship care providers as they provide to non-kin foster parents. There are no kin-specific programs or specific training available to kin (or to caseworkers). However, according to a Waterbury administrator, in the case *Juan F. v. O'Neill,* the court found DCF in violation of a consent decree by not providing the same services to relative and non-relative caregivers. The court ordered the agency to treat all caregivers the same. Starting in July 2001, the legislature was scheduled to create 39 positions within DCF dedicated to supporting relatives.

Connecticut's policy regarding licensing kin has changed since 2000. Before July 1, 2001, all kin were "certified." The requirements for certification were similar to the health and safety standards of foster care but not as stringent (especially the income requirement), and relatives did not have to participate in any training. Many workers noted that some relatives who had previously been certified could not pass the stringent licensing requirements. One Bridgeport administrator commented that those relatives who were previously certified may remain certified; however, their board payment must be paid by the state. Despite the licensing changes, many of the interviewees noted an increased use of relatives because of a shortage of non-kin foster homes. While caseworkers do not *help* place a child without taking custody, many caseworkers noted that they do advise parents and relatives that they can transfer custody to the relative through probate court.

In approximately 51 to 75 percent of the time, Connecticut does not file for TPR after a child placed with a relative has been in foster care for 15 of 22 consecutive months. Connecticut attributes this high percentage to its subsidized guardianship program. The program is offered to kinship care providers willing to permanently care for children for whom reunification or adoption is not possible. The subsidy is offered to any child placed with a licensed relative for at least 12 months who has been under the custody of the public agency for 12 months, and where adoption is not the plan. While relatives who are certified are able to apply for the subsidized program, they may not all be eligible. Payment per child through this program averages $650–$735 a month, depending on the age of the child. The payment is made with state funds, and the program also offers medical coverage and referrals to a range of other services, such as home-based treatment and day care.

The city of Hartford is served by the North Central Region of the Department of Children and Families. Hartford DCF workers estimated that kinship caregivers are used as resources in approximately 50 percent of the cases. In the city of Hartford, 152 relative homes house 229 children and 23 special study homes house 32 children. The North Central Region DCF supervises a total of 639 relative homes with 630 children placed in these homes. In 2000, the city of Hartford had a population of 121,578, while the population of Hartford County was 857,183 (Connecticut Department of Economic and Community Development 2001). The county is an urban area that is 73 percent white non-Hispanic/Latino, 11 percent African American, and 12 percent Hispanic or Latino. Per capita personal income for the city for 2001 was $18,007, and for the county was $29,930.

Bridgeport is served by the Southwestern Region DCF. Like Hartford, Bridgeport DCF workers estimated that kinship caregivers are used as resources in approximately 50 percent of the cases. In 2000, the town of Bridgeport had a population of 139,529 people, and the county (Fairfield) a population of 882,567. The county is urban and is 73 percent white non-Hispanic/Latino, 10 percent African American, and 12 percent Hispanic or Latino. Per capita personal income in 2001 for the town of Bridgeport was approximately $20,848, and for the county was approximately $42,304 (Connecticut Department of Economic and Community Development 2001).

An administrator in the city of Torrington estimated that relatives are used as placements for about one-third of their foster children—about 122 of 275 foster homes in all. Torrington is a part of Litchfield County and is served by the Northwestern Region DCF. The town (population 35,202 in 2000) is located in a rural area. The county (population 182,193 in 2000) is 95 percent white non-Hispanic/Latino, 1 percent African American, and 2 percent Hispanic or Latino. Per capita personal income for Torrington in the year 2001 was $26,035, and for the county was $32,206 (Connecticut Department of Economic and Community Development 2001).

Indiana

The Indiana Bureau of Family Protection and Preservation (BFPP) is part of the Division of Family and Children Services within the state's Family and Social Services Administration. BFPP administers child protective services, foster care, adoption programs, Healthy Families Indiana, youth services, and domestic violence and treatment programs. In 2000, there were 42,979 children reported as victims of abuse or neglect; of these reports, approximately 24,686 were substantiated. Furthermore,

11,305 children were in foster care on the last day of the state fiscal year 2000, and approximately 13 percent of these children were living with a kin caregiver (Indiana Family and Social Services Administration 2002).

Indiana's child welfare policy gives preference to kin who come forward to care for a child who has been abused or neglected, assuming that the potential caregivers meet necessary state requirements. The state definition of kin includes those related beyond blood, marriage, or adoption, and is broader than the definition used to determine eligibility under TANF. Workers are required to seek out kin to care for a child when it has been determined that a child must be removed from the home.

In Indiana, all kinship care providers must meet the same standards that non-kin foster parents must meet, but the child welfare agency may modify or waive non-safety standards for kinship care providers on a case-by-case basis. The child may be placed with the relative after a criminal background check and a child abuse and neglect registry check have been completed. There is no specific time frame during which kin must complete the remaining licensing requirements, and if the relative cannot meet the requirements, the court must be notified, and a decision will be made whether the child can stay in the unlicensed placement.

Provisionally licensed kin are eligible to receive a TANF child-only grant and may be eligible for other payments, such as survivor's benefits or SSI. Once relatives have met all of the licensing requirements, they are eligible to receive the standard board payment of $512 per month, a TANF child-only grant, and, if eligible, other payments, such as survivor's benefits or SSI. Such relatives are also eligible to receive the same services that non-kin foster parents receive. If the child is ordered by the court to stay with a relative in an unlicensed home, county money is used to make the board payment. It should also be noted that kin must be licensed under this option in order to get an assisted guardianship subsidy.

In Indiana, child welfare workers sometimes help arrange for a child to be placed with a kinship care provider without seeking adjudication. These kin must complete a criminal background check and child abuse and neglect registry check. Also, if possible, the worker will visit the relative's home. Kin caring for a child who has not been adjudicated as abused or neglected are eligible to receive a TANF child-only grant and, if eligible, other payments, such as survivor's benefits or SSI. In 2002, Indiana rarely chose not to file for TPR after a child had been in kinship foster care for 15 of the previous 22 months; it failed to file in fewer than 25 percent of cases. State policy does not allow children to remain in long-term foster care with kin. Subsidized guardianship is offered to kinship care providers willing to permanently care for children for whom reunification or adoption is not possible, so long as the child was not adjudicated as abused or neglected. It is offered if the child is seriously disabled, is 13 years of age or older, or is a member of a sibling group in which one child is at least age 13. It is also offered in special circumstances as long as kin will be able to provide care to the child without the agency's continuing involvement. The average payment amount per child is $514 per month and is funded through TANF funds. Services such as counseling can be offered in addition to the payment. Ongoing supervision is provided, but only once a year.

Lake County, Indiana, had a population of 484,564 in 2000. It is part of an urban area that is 61 percent white non-Hispanic/Latino, 25 percent African American, and 12 percent Hispanic or Latino. Per capita personal income for 2000 was $26,661.

LaPorte County had a population of 110,106 in 2000. Situated in a rural area, its residents are 85 percent white non-Hispanic/Latino, 10 percent African American, and 3 percent Hispanic or Latino. Per capita personal income for 2000 was $24,581.

Marion County had a population of 860,454 in 2000. It is part of an urban area that is 69 percent white non-Hispanic/Latino, 24 percent African American, and 4 percent Hispanic or Latino. The county's per capita personal income for 2000 was $30,780.

NOTES

1. State kinship care policies have changed significantly since 1999. The Urban Institute conducted a follow-up survey of states' kinship care policies in 2001 to coincide with this study of local policies and practices.

2. IV-E eligibility refers to the ability of the state to obtain federal reimbursement for certain foster care expenses under title IV-E of the Social Security Act. Children are IV-E eligible if they came from a home (the birth parent's home) that was eligible for welfare benefits.

3. All state demographic information was obtained from U.S. Census Bureau county quick fact sheets (www.census.gov).

4. With the exception of Connecticut, regional per capita personal income estimates were obtained from the Bureau of Economic Analysis (www.bea.gov).

References

AFCARS. 1998. Unpublished analysis of Adoption and Foster Care Analysis and Reporting System (AFCARS) data, U.S. Department of Health and Human Services.

Ainsworth, M. D. S. 1985. "Patterns of Infant-Mother Attachments: Antecedents and Effects on Development." *Journal of Urban Health: The Bulletin of the New York Academy of Medicine* 61 (9): 771–91.

Alabama Kinship Care State Fact Sheet. 2002. http://www.cwla.org/programs/kinship/statefactsheets.htm. (Accessed September 23, 2003.)

Altshuler, S. 1998. "Child Well-Being in Kinship Foster Care: Similar To, or Different From, Non-related Foster Care?" *Children and Youth Services Review* 20 (5): 369–88.

Andrews, C., R. Bess, A. Jantz, and V. Russell. 2002. *Collaboration between State Welfare and Child Welfare Agencies.* Washington, D.C.: The Urban Institute. *Assessing the New Federalism* Policy Brief A-54.

Barth, R., M. Courtney, J. Berrick, and V. Albert. 1994. *From Child Abuse to Permanency Planning.* New York: Aldine de Gruyter.

Beeman, S., and L. Boisen. 1999. "Child Welfare Professionals' Attitudes toward Kinship Foster Care." *Child Welfare* 78 (3): 315–37.

Beeman, S., E. Wattenberg, L. Boisen, and S. Bullerdick. 1996. *Kinship Foster Care in Minnesota.* St. Paul, Minn.: University of Minnesota School of Social Work, Center for Advanced Studies in Child Welfare.

Benedict, M., and R. White. 1991. "Factors Associated with Foster Care Length of Stay." *Child Welfare* 70 (1): 45–58.

Benedict, M., S. Zuravin, and R. Stallings. 1996. "Adult Functioning of Children Who Lived in Kin versus Nonrelative Family Foster Homes." *Child Welfare* 125 (5): 529–49.

Berrick, J. D. 1998. "When Children Cannot Remain at Home: Foster Family Care and Kinship Care." *The Future of Children* 8 (1): 72–87.

Berrick, J. D., and B. Needell. 1999. "Recent Trends in Kinship Care: Public Policy, Payments, and Outcomes for Children." In *The Foster Care Crisis: Translating Research into Policy and Practice,* edited by P. A. Curtis, G. Dale Jr., and J. C. Kendall. Lincoln: University of Nebraska Press and the Child Welfare League of America.

Berrick, J. D., R. Barth, and B. Needell. 1994. "A Comparison of Kinship Foster Homes and Foster Family Homes: Implications for Kinship Foster Care as Family Preservation." *Children and Youth Services Review* 16 (12): 33–63.

Berrick, J. D., M. Minkler, and B. Needell. 1999. "The Policy Implications of Welfare Reform for Older Caregivers, Kinship Care, and Family Configuration." *Children and Youth Services Review* 21 (9–10): 843–64.

Berrick, J. D., B. Needell, and R. P. Barth. 1995. "Kinship Care in California: An Empirically Based Curriculum." Unpublished report for the Child Welfare Research Center, University of California at Berkeley.

———. 1999. "Kin as a Family and Child Welfare Resource: The Child Welfare Worker's Perspective." In *Kinship Foster Care: Practice, Policy and Research,* edited by R. L. Hegar and M. Scannapieco. New York: Oxford University Press.

Bonecutter, F., and J. Gleeson. 1997. "Broadening Our View: Lessons from Kinship Foster Care." *The Journal of Multicultural Social Work* (special issue on permanency planning) 5(1–2): 99–119.

Boots, S. W., and R. Geen. 1999. "Family Care or Foster Care? How State Policies Affect Kinship Caregivers." Washington D.C.: The Urban Institute. *Assessing the New Federalism* Policy Brief A-34.

Bowlby, J. 1988. *A Secure Base.* New York: Basic Books.

Brooks, D., and R. Barth. 1998. "Characteristics and Outcomes of Drug-Exposed and Non–Drug-Exposed Children in Kinship and Non-relative Foster Care." *Children and Youth Services Review* 20 (6): 475–501.

Burnette, D. 1997. "Grandparents Raising Grandchildren in the Inner City." *Families in Society* 78 (5): 489–501.

California Kinship Care State Fact Sheet. 2002. http://cwla.org/programs/kinship/statefactsheets.htm. (Accessed September 23, 2003.)

Chipungu, S., and J. Everett. 1994. "The Power of Information: Exchange Patterns between African-American Foster Parents and Child Welfare Workers." *Journal of Multicultural Social Work* 3 (3): 17–33.

Chipungu, S., J. Everett, M. Verduik, and J. Jones. 1998. *Children Placed in Foster Care with Relatives: A Multi-State Study.* Washington, D.C.: U.S. Department of Health and Human Services.

Connecticut Department of Economic and Community Development. 2001. "2001–2002 Connecticut Town Profiles." http://www.ct.gov/ecd/cwp/view.asp?a=1106&q=251020. (Accessed September 23, 2003.)

Connecticut Kinship Care State Fact Sheet. 2002. http://cwla.org/programs/kinship/statefactsheets.htm. (Accessed September 23, 2003.)

Cook, R., and J. Ciarico. 1998. Unpublished analysis of kinship care data from the *National Study of Protective, Preventive and Reunification Services Delivered to Children and Their Families,* U.S. Department of Health and Human Services, Children's Bureau.

Courtney, M. 1994. "Factors Associated with the Reunification of Foster Children with Their Families." *Social Service Review* 68 (1): 81–108.

Courtney, M., and B. Needell. 1997. "Outcomes of Kinship Foster Care: Lessons from California." In *Child Welfare Research Review*, vol. 2, edited by J. D. Berrick, R. P. Barth, and N. Gilbert. New York: Columbia University Press.

Davis, I., J. Landsverk, R. Newton, and W. Ganger. 1996. "Parental Visiting and Foster Care Reunification." *Children and Youth Services Review* 18 (45): 363–82.

DiLeonardi, J. n.d. "Kinship Care, Permanency Planning and Substance Abuse." Distributed by Lifelink-Bensenville Home Society, Bensenville, Ill.

Dubowitz, H. 1990. "The Physical and Mental Health and Educational Status of Children Placed with Relatives, Final Report." Baltimore, Md.: University of Maryland Medical School.

Dubowitz, H., S. Feigelman, and S. Zuravin. 1993. "A Profile of Kinship Care." *Child Welfare* 72 (2): 153–69.

Dubowitz, H., S. Feigelman, D. Harrington, R. Starr, S. Zuravin, and R. Sawyer. 1994. "Children in Kinship Care: How Do They Fare?" *Children and Youth Services Review* 16 (1–2): 85–106.

Ehrle, J., and R. Geen. 2002a. *Children Cared for by Relatives: What Services Do They Need?* Washington, D.C.: The Urban Institute. *Assessing the New Federalism* Policy Brief B-47.

———. 2002b. "Kin and Non-kin Foster Care—Findings from a National Survey." *Children and Youth Services Review* 24: 55–78.

Ehrle, J., R. Geen, and R. L. Clark. 2001. *Children Cared for by Relatives: Who Are They and How Are They Faring?* Washington, D.C.: The Urban Institute. *Assessing the New Federalism* Policy Brief B-28.

Ellwood, D. T. 1988. *Poor Support: Poverty in the American Family.* New York: Basic Books.

Emick, M.A., and B. Hayslip, Jr. 1996. "Custodial Grandparenting: New Roles for Middle-Aged and Older Adults." *International Journal of Aging and Human Development* 43 (2): 135–54.

Everett, J., S. Chipungu, and B. Leashore, eds. 1997. *Child Welfare: An Africentric Perspective.* New Brunswick, N.J.: Rutgers University Press.

GAO. See U.S. General Accounting Office.

Gaudin, J., and R. Sutphen. 1993. "Foster Care vs. Extended Family Care for Children of Incarcerated Mothers." *Journal of Offender Rehabilitation* 19 (34): 129–47.

Gebel, T. 1996. "Kinship Care and Non-relative Foster Care: A Comparison of Caregiver Attributes and Attitudes." *Child Welfare* 75 (1): 5–18.

Geen, R., and J. D. Berrick. 2002. "Kinship Care: An Evolving Service Delivery Option." *Children and Youth Services Review* 24 (1–2): 1–14.

Geen, R., P. Holcomb, A. Jantz, R. Koralek, J. Leos-Urbel, and K. Malm. 2001. *On Their Own Terms: Supporting Kinship Care Outside of TANF and Foster Care.* Washington, D.C.: U.S. Department of Health and Human Services, Assistant Secretary for Planning and Evaluation.

Giarrusso, R., D. Feng, O. Wang, and M. Silverstein. 1996. "Parenting and the Co-parenting of Grandchildren: Effects on Grandparents' Well-Being and Family Solidarity." *International Journal of Sociology and Social Policy* 16: 124–54.

Gleeson, J. 1999. "Kinship Care as a Child Welfare Service." In *Kinship Foster Care: Policy, Practice, and Research,* edited by R. L. Hegar and M. Scannapieco. New York: Oxford University Press.

Gleeson, J., and L. Craig. 1994. "Kinship Care in Child Welfare: An Analysis of States' Policies." *Children and Youth Services Review* 16 (12): 7–31.

Gleeson, J., and C. Hairston, eds. 1999. *Kinship Care: Improving Practice through Research.* Washington, D.C.: Child Welfare League of America.

Gleeson, J., F. Bonecutter, and S. Altshuler. 1995. "Facilitating Permanence in Kinship Care: The Illinois Project." *Kinship Care Forum.* New York: National Resource Center for Foster Care and Permanency Planning, Hunter College School of Social Work.

Gleeson, J., J. O'Donnell, and F. Bonecutter. 1997. "Understanding the Complexity of Practice in Kinship Foster Care." *Child Welfare* 76 (6): 801–26.

Goerge, R. 1990. "The Reunification Process in Substitute Care." *Social Service Review* (September): 422–57.

Grigsby, R. K. 1994. "Maintaining Attachment Relationships among Children in Foster Care." *Families in Society* 75 (5): 269–76.

Grogan-Kaylor, A. 1996. "Who Goes into Kinship Care? A Study Examining the Factors Influencing the Placement of Children into Kinship Care." Unpublished.

Harden, A., R. Clark, and K. Maguire. 1997. *Informal and Formal Kinship Care. Volume I: Narrative Reports.* Washington, D.C.: U.S. Department of Health and Human Services.

Hegar, R. L. 1999. "Kinship Foster Care: The New Child Paradigm." In *Kinship Foster Care: Policy, Practice, and Research,* edited by R. L. Hegar and M. Scannapieco. New York: Oxford University Press.

Hess, P. 1987. "Parent Visiting of Children in Foster Care: Current Knowledge and Research Agenda." *Children and Youth Services Review* 9 (1): 29–50.

HHS. See U.S. Department of Health and Human Services.

Hornby, H., D. Zeller, and D. Karraker. 1996. "Kinship Care in America: What Outcomes Should Policy Seek?" *Child Welfare* 75 (5): 397–418.

Iglehart, A. 1994. "Kinship Foster Care: Placement, Service, and Outcome Issues." *Children and Youth Services Review* 16: 107–22.

Indiana Family and Social Services Administration. 2002. "Division of Family and Children Selected Assistance Programs Demographic Trend Report: 2001 State Fiscal Year." Indianapolis: Indiana Family and Social Services Administration.

Jackson, S. M. 1999. "Paradigm Shift: Training Staff to Provide Services to the Kinship Triad." In *Kinship Foster Care: Policy, Practice, and Research,* edited by R. L. Hegar and M. Scannapieco. New York: Oxford University Press.

Jantz, A., R. Geen, R. Bess, C. Andrews, and V. Russell. 2002. *The Continuing Evolution of State Kinship Care Policies.* Washington, D.C.: The Urban Institute.

Johnson, I. 1994. "Kinship Care." In *When Drug Addicts Have Children,* edited by D. Besharov and K. Hanson. Washington, D.C.: Child Welfare League of America.

Kinship Care Advisory Panel. 1998. "Summary of Proceedings: Kinship Care Advisory Panel Meeting." U.S. Department of Health and Human Services, Administration for Children and Families, Washington, D.C., October 5–6.

Korbin, J. 1991. "Cross-Cultural Perspectives and Research Directions for the 21st Century." *Child Abuse and Neglect* 151 (1): 67–78.

Kuhn, T. 1970. *The Structure of Scientific Revolutions,* 2d ed. Chicago: University of Chicago Press.

Kusserow, R. 1992. *State Practices in Using Relatives for Foster Care.* Washington, D.C.: U.S. Department of Health and Human Services, Office of the Inspector General.

Landsverk, J., I. Davis, W. Ganger, R. Newton, and I. Johnson. 1996. "Impact of Child Psychosocial Functioning on Reunification from Out-of-Home Placement." *Children and Youth Services Review* 18 (4–5): 447–62.

Leashore, B., H. McMurray, and B. Bailey. 1997. "Reuniting and Preserving African-American Families." In *Child Welfare: An Africentric Perspective,* edited by J. Everett, S. Chipungu, and B. Leashore. New Brunswick, N.J.: Rutgers University Press.

LeProhn, N. 1994. "The Role of the Kinship Foster Parent: A Comparison of the Role Conceptions of Relative and Non-relative Foster Parents." *Children and Youth Services Review* 16 (1–2): 65–81.

LeProhn, N., and P. Pecora. 1994. "The Casey Foster Parent Study: Research Summary." Seattle: The Casey Family Program.

Link, M. 1996. "Permanency Outcomes in Kinship Care: A Study of Children Placed in Kinship Care in Erie County, New York." *Child Welfare* 75 (5): 509–28.

Minkler, M., E. Fuller-Thomson, D. Miller, and D. Driver. 2000. "Grandparent Caregiving and Depression." In *Grandparents Raising Grandchildren,* edited by B. Hayslip and R. Goldberg-Glen. New York: Springer Publishing.

Minkler, M., K. M. Roe, and M. Price. 1992. "The Physical and Emotional Health of Grandmothers Raising Grandchildren in the Crack Cocaine Epidemic." *The Gerontologist* 32 (6): 752–61.

National Commission on Family Foster Care. 1991. *A Blueprint for Fostering Infants, Children, and Youths in the 1990s.* Washington, D.C.: Child Welfare League of America.

Needell, B., D. Webster, S. Cuccaro-Alamin, M. Armijo, S. Lee, and A. Brookhart. 2001. *Performance Indicators for Child Welfare Services in California.* Center for Social Services Research, School of Social Welfare at UC Berkeley. http://cssr.berkeley.edu. (Accessed September 23, 2003.)

Pecora, P., N. LeProhn, and J. Nasuti. 1999. "Role Perceptions of Kinship and Other Foster Parents in Family Foster Care." In *Kinship Foster Care: Policy, Practice, and Research,* edited by R. Hegar and M. Scannapieco. New York: Oxford University Press.

Sawyer, R. J., and H. Dubowitz. 1994. "School Performance of Children in Kinship Care." *Child Abuse and Neglect* 18 (7): 587–97.

Scannapieco, M. 1999. "Kinship Care in the Public Welfare System: A Systematic Review of the Research." In *Kinship Foster Care: Policy, Practice, and Research,* edited by R. Hegar and M. Scannapieco. New York: Oxford University Press.

Scannapieco, M., R. Hegar, and C. McAlpine. 1997. "Kinship Care and Foster Care: A Comparison of Characteristics and Outcomes." *Families in Society: The Journal of Contemporary Human Services* (September–October): 480–88.

Shlonsky, A. R., and J. D. Berrick. 2001. "Assessing and Promoting Quality in Kin and Nonkin Foster Care." *Social Service Review* 75 (1): 60–83.

Shore, N., K. E. Sim, N. S. LeProhn, and T. E. Keller. 2002. "Foster Parent and Teacher Assessments of Youth in Kinship and Non-kinship Foster Care Placements: Are Behaviors Perceived Differently across Settings?" *Children and Youth Services Review* 24: 55–78.

Solomon, J., and J. Marx. 2000. "The Physical, Mental, and Social Health of Custodial Grandparents." In *Grandparents Raising Grandchildren: Theoretical, Empirical, and Clinical Perspectives,* edited by B. Hayslip Jr. and R. Goldberg-Glen. New York: Springer.

Sonenstein, F., K. Malm, and A. Billing. 2002. *Study of Fathers' Involvement in Permanency Planning and Child Welfare Casework.* Washington, D.C.: U.S. Department of Health and Human Services, Assistant Secretary for Planning and Evaluation.

Spar, K. 1993. *"Kinship" Foster Care: An Emerging Federal Issue.* Report to U.S. Congress. Washington, D.C.: Congressional Research Service.

Stack, C. 1974. *All Our Kin: Strategies for Survival in a Black Community.* New York: Harper and Row.

Takas, M. 1992. "Kinship Care: Developing a Safe and Effective Framework for Protective Placement of Children with Relatives." *Children's Legal Rights Journal* 13 (2): 12–19.

Testa, M. 1997. "Kinship Foster Care in Illinois." In *Child Welfare Research Review,* vol. 2, edited by J. D. Berrick, R. P. Barth, and N. Gilbert. New York: Columbia University Press.

———. 1999. "Kinship Care and Social Policy." In *First National Roundtable on Implementing the Adoption and Safe Families Act: Summary of Proceedings.* Englewood, Colo.: American Humane Association, Children's Division.

———. 2001. "Kinship Care and Permanency." *Journal of Social Service Research* 28 (1): 25–43.

Testa, M., and R. Cook. 2001. *The Comparative Safety, Attachment, and Well-Being of Children in Kinship Adoption, Guardian, and Foster Homes.* Paper presented at the Fall Research Conference of the Association for Public Policy Analysis and Management, Washington, D.C., November 1–3.

Testa, M., and N. Rolock. 1999. "Professional Foster Care: A Future Worth Pursuing?" *Child Welfare* 78 (1): 108–24.

Testa, M., and K. S. Slack. 2002. "The Gift of Kinship Foster Care." *Children and Youth Services Review* 24: 55–78.

Testa, M. F., K. L. Shook, L. S. Cohen, and M. G. Woods. 1996. "Permanency Planning Options for Children in Formal Kinship Care." *Child Welfare* 75: 451–70.

Thornton, J. L. 1991. "Permanency Planning for Children in Kinship Foster Homes." *Child Welfare* 70 (5): 593–601.

U.S. Department of Health and Human Services. Administration on Children, Youth and Families. 2000. *Report to the Congress on Kinship Foster Care.* Washington, D.C.: U.S. Government Printing Office.

———. 2002. *Child Maltreatment 2000.* Washington, D.C.: U.S. Government Printing Office.

———. 2003. *The AFCARS Report.* http://www.acf.hhs.gov/programs/cb/publications/afcars/report8.pdf. (Accessed September 23, 2003.)

U.S. Department of Health and Human Services. Office of the Inspector General. 2002. *Recruiting Foster Parents*. Washington, D.C.: U.S. Department of Health and Human Services.

U.S. General Accounting Office. 1999. *Kinship Care Quality and Permanency Issues*. Washington, D.C.: U.S. General Accounting Office.

Wilson, L., and J. Conroy. 1999. "Satisfaction of Children in Out-of-Home Care." *Child Welfare* 78 (1): 53–69.

Wulczyn, F., and K. B. Hislop. 2001. "Multi-state Foster Care Data Archive." Unpublished data, Chapin Hall Center for Children, Chicago.

Wulczyn, F., K. Brunner, and R. Goerge. 1997. *An Update from the Multi-state Foster Care Data Archive*. Chicago: Chapin Hall Center for Children.

Young, V. 1970. "Family and Childhood in a Southern Negro Community." *American Anthropologist* 72 (2): 269–88.

Zimmerman, E., D. Daykin, V. Moore, C. Wuu, and J. Li. 1998. *Kinship and Non-kinship Foster Care in New York City: Pathways and Outcomes*. Prepared for the City of New York Human Resources Administration and Administration for Children's Services. New York: United Way of New York City.

Zuravin, S., M. Benedict, and M. Somerfield. 1993. "Child Maltreatment in Family Foster Care." *American Journal of Orthopsychiatry* 63 (4): 589–96.

Zwas, M. 1993. "Kinship Foster Care: A Relatively Permanent Solution." *Fordham Urban Law Journal* 20: 343–73.

About the Editor

Rob Geen is a senior research associate specializing in child welfare and related child, youth, and family issues at the Urban Institute. His child welfare research has included studies of child abuse and neglect investigation and substantiation, family preservation and family support services, foster care, independent living programs for foster youth, adoption, and the impact of welfare reform on child welfare systems. His previous research on kinship care includes three national surveys of states' kinship care policies, a research synthesis included in the U.S. Department of Health and Human Services' *Report to Congress on Kinship Care*, a study of alternative kinship care programs established outside of welfare and foster care, and analyses of national data on the well-being of children in kinship care and the services they receive.

About the Contributors

Roseana Bess is a research associate at the Urban Institute's Population Studies Center, where her research focuses on social services and child welfare–related issues, specifically the financing of services and collaboration between agencies. Ms. Bess has also had direct service experience as a case manager in New York City working with families at risk of having their children placed in foster care.

Karin E. Malm is a research associate at the Urban Institute's Population Studies Center, where her research focuses on such child welfare program areas as abuse and neglect, family preservation, foster and kinship care, and adoption. She is currently managing a study examining agencies' policies and practices involving noncustodial fathers of foster children. Before joining the Urban Institute, Ms. Malm directed an assessment study of collaboration between child welfare agencies and domestic violence organizations.

Victoria Russell is a research associate at the Urban Institute's Income and Benefits Policy Center, where she studies implementation of the TANF program. Currently, Ms. Russell is the co-manager of the Welfare Rules Database, a publicly available, longitudinal database tracking states' AFDC/TANF rules. Her past work includes research on welfare reform's financial impact on child welfare agencies and its effect on kinship care policies and programs within these agencies.

Cynthia Andrews Scarcella is a member of the Population Studies Center at the Urban Institute, where she specializes in research on child welfare, adoption, and related child and family well-being issues. She has been involved in numerous child welfare policy research projects, including research on state kinship care policies, child welfare financing, opportunities for collaboration between the welfare and child welfare systems, and consumer perception of adoption services at public child welfare agencies. Ms. Scarcella recently completed a brief on the economic, health, and social characteristics of children in grandparent care.

Amy Jantz Templeman was formerly a research associate at the Urban Institute's Population Studies Center, where she specialized in research on child welfare, kinship care, and related child and family well-being issues. She was involved in many child welfare policy research projects, including research on states' kinship care policies, child welfare financing, alternative kinship care programs, and consumer perception of adoption services at public child welfare agencies. Ms. Templeman currently serves as an HIV/AIDS educator with the Peace Corps in the Republic of Malawi.

Index

administrative case reviews (ACRs), 110
adoption, 178, 206, 216, 222. *See also* permanency planning
  financial deterrents to, 171–174
  vs. guardianship, 159–162
  willingness to adopt, 168–171
Adoption and Safe Families Act (ASFA), 10–12, 27–28, 65, 159, 163, 177
  Final Rule of January 2000, 10, 11, 14–16, 65
  HHS guidance on implementing, 154–155
Adoption Assistance and Child Welfare Act, 1, 9–10
African Americans, 2, 19
age
  of children, 57–58
  of foster parents, 7
  of relatives, 53–54
agencies. *See* child welfare agencies
Aid to Dependent Children (ADC), 64–65
Aid to Families with Dependent Children (AFDC), 65
Alabama, 31–32, 71–73, 78, 180, 184, 192, 197, 239, 244, 265–267. *See also specific topics*
Alabama Family Services, 265

Alabama Low-Income Kinship Programs, 147–148
assessments, 180
  expense associated with conducting, 238
  limitations, 238
assistance-family structure conundrum, 254

behavior problems, children with, 42–43
birth parents, 204–205
  caretakers' relationship with, 39–40, 59, 133–134, 202–203
  managing, 251
  impact of permanency placement on rights of, 248
  licensing as protection from, 73
  motivation, 164–167
  proximity to the home and community of, 56–57
  relative's history with, 39
  taking into consideration the preferences of, 57
  visitation/access to children, 51, 117, 126, 223, 240, 241
  how to monitor, 251
  kin may prevent, 123–125

birth parents, visitation/access to children (*continued*)
    need to be clear about boundaries, 122–123
    relatives allowing inappropriate, 120–122
bonding between relative and child, degree of, 54

California, 75–80, 161, 267–269. *See also specific topics*
California Children and Family Services, 267
case planning, involving kin in, 108–112, 127, 250
case reviews, administrative, 110
casework practices with kinship foster parents, 95–97, 240–241
    and kin's understanding of what is expected of them, 98–103
caseworkers, 95–98, 125–127, 234–235. *See also* supervision
    guidelines regarding when to place children, 247
    supervising visitation, 114–118, 123–125
        feedback caseworkers receive, 118–123
    what they tell kin foster parents, 103–108, 250
child abuse and neglect, 6, 15, 51, 82, 205, 217
child abuse and neglect registry check, 68
child care, cost and availability of, 49–50
child care assistance, 131–132
child-only payments/grants, 69, 143, 255–256, 272
child protective services (CPS), 106, 107
    background checks, 76–77
child welfare agencies, 12, 14–15, 129, 144, 215–216, 258–259. *See also* services
    agency support, 244
    kin's interaction with, 222–230
    lack of support from, 208–209
    policies of, as denying services, 151
    what caregivers can expect from, 251
child welfare policy, 9
children
    objections to possible placements, 57–58

taking into consideration the preferences of, 57
class, 18–19. *See also* poverty
communication with kin. *See* caseworkers, what they tell kin
concurrent planning, 28
Connecticut, 74, 78–80, 196, 269–271. *See also specific topics*
    subsidized guardianship program, 270
Connecticut Department of Children and Families (DCF), 269–271
constructive removals, 14
court hearings, 110–111
courts, what caregivers can expect from, 32–33
courts' *vs.* agencies' philosophy toward kinship care, 32–33
criminal background checks, 68, 76–77
criminal history, 82
custody. *See* permanency planning

demographics of children in kin and non-kin arrangements, 5
discipline, 210–211
    physical, 100–101
diversion, 182. *See also* voluntary kinship care placements
drug abuse, 77, 207, 214–215, 217, 226–228

educating kin on the services available, 251
educational needs, support in meeting children's, 133
elderly foster parents, 7
Ellwood, David, 254
emergency placements, 75
emotional challenges facing children, 208
emotional problems, children with, 42–43
employment, 7

family
    defined, 55
    extended
        impact on kinship care placements, 246–247
family foster care agencies (FFAs), 137

family group decisionmaking (FGDM), 186–187, 241, 249
family issues, 202–208
fathers
    absent, 28
    agencies efforts to identify and locate, 30
    placement with, 27–30
federal policy development, 8–11
financial assistance for kin, 92–93, 131–132. *See also* federal policy development; government responsibility; payment; state kinship care policies
    failure to take steps required to obtain, 87
    history, 64–66
    inadequacy, 239–240
    for kin who agree to foster children permanently, 248
    and kin's willingness to care for child, 48–49
    philosophical debate over, 251–260
    produced incentive to seek it out, 253–254
financial requirements
    to care for child, 239–240
    new approach to meeting kin's, 256–260
financial situation of relative caregiver, 52–53
foster care
    desire to keep children out of traditional, 46–47
    government responsibility for children living in, 253
    lack of non-kin, 33–34
    long-term, 155–159
    as traumatic, 30–31
    using kin as diversion from, 244–245
foster care diversion. *See* diversion
foster homes, reasons for lack of, 61–62n.2
foster parent associations, 140
foster parents, efforts to recruit non-kin, 249

government responsibility, based on children's status, 252–253
grandparents, 133

willingness to care for children, 44–45
guardianship programs/subsidized guardianship. *See* permanency outcomes; permanency planning

Health and Human Services (HHS)
    guidance on implementing ASFA, 154–155
high-risk situations, 192–193, 244. *See also* safety

identifying and recruiting kinship caregivers, 25, 60–61, 234–236
    being innovative in, 249
    state policies for, 26–27
identifying relatives, 34–38
    late in the case process, 162–164
Illinois, 245
Indian Child Welfare Act of 1978, 9
Indiana, 74–75, 78, 161, 271–273. *See also* specific topics
Indiana Bureau of Family Protection and Preservation (BFPP), 271
informal arrangements/adjustments, 2–3, 182. *See also* voluntary kinship care placements

Juan F. v. O'Neill, 270

kin. *See also* kinship foster parents; relatives; specific topics
    coerced to accept children voluntarily, 245
    definitions, 27, 54–56
    factors influencing ability to be caregiver, 235
    feeling obligated to care for children, 45–46
    impact of caregiving on, 8
    level of effort to find and place children with, 30–34
    non-related, 54–55
    preparation for caring for children, 129–130
    pressured into caring for children, 47–48
    prior relationship with child, 54, 96–97

kin (*continued*)
   on their caregiving experiences,
     201–202
     agency interactions, 222–230
     caregiver issues, 218–222
     child issues, 208–218
     family issues, 202–208
   understanding of what is expected of
     them, 98–103
kin *vs.* non-kin foster parents
   advantages and disadvantages of,
     95–96
   needs of, 130–134
Kinshare program, 266
kinship foster care. *See also specific topics*
   defining, 2–3, 27
   factors contributing to growth in, 4
   formal *vs.* informal, 2–3, 182. *See also*
     voluntary kinship care place-
     ments
   history, 2
   impact on children, 246
   number of children in, 3–6
   ongoing debate over, 13–20, 198
   paradigm shift *vs.* magic bullet
     approach, 231–233
   terminology, 2–3
   unevenly used across the states, 4
   viewed as extension of family *vs.* sub-
     stitute care, 198–199
kinship foster families
   belief in their self-sufficiency, 138–139
kinship foster parents. *See also* kin; *spe-
     cific topics*
   bringing them together, 249
   expectations of, 135–136, 251
   vs. non-kin foster parents, 6–8,
     130–136
   preventing appropriate kin from being
     denied chance to be, 247–248
Kinship Guardianship Assistance Program (KinGAP), 268
Kinship Support Services Program
   (KSSP), 148–149, 267, 268

licensing, 228, 236–240. *See also* federal
   policy development; state kinship
   care policies

   defined, 63
   of fictive kin, 55
   payment based on, 69–70
   and placements with unlicensed kin,
     71–76
   provisional, 68
licensing standards, 63–64, 66–68, 90–93
   barriers kin face in meeting, 76–79
   focused on limiting liability, 238
   kin and non-kin held to same *vs.* dif-
     ferent, 83–84, 91
   opinions about, 80–86
licensure, placement before, 73–76
Lipscomb v. Simmons, 245
low-income kinship programs, 147–148

MediCal, 190
mental problems, children with, 42–43
Miller v. Youakim, 9, 65

paper removals, 14
parental rights, 248. *See also* termination
   of parental rights
parents, birth. *See* birth parents
paternal relatives, placement with, 27–30
paternity issues, 28
payment, 63–64, 90–93, 236–240. *See also*
   financial assistance for kin
   barriers kin face in receiving, 86–88
   debate over, 14–15
   opinions about, 88–90
permanency, defined, 243
permanency outcomes. *See also* adoption
   kinship care and, 164
     and birth parent motivation,
      165–167
   long-term, 175–176
permanency placement, 10, 16–17, 28.
   See also adoption
   impact on caregiver's responsibilities
     and birth parents' rights, 248
permanency planning
   absence of, for children in voluntary
     placements, 193–195
   kinship care and, 153–156, 176–178,
     248–249
     adoption *vs.* guardianship, 159–162

identification of relatives late in the case process, 162–164
long-term foster care, 156–159
with kinship foster parents, 242–244
Personal Responsibility and Work Opportunity Reconciliation Act (PRWORA), 10
placement decisions, factors considered in, 50–58. *See also specific factors*
placements
  informal, 2–3, 182. *See also* voluntary kinship care placements
  length of, 40–42, 72. *See also* permanency
  with non-kin, initial, 58–59
policy changes and guidance, 247–249
poverty, 181. *See also* low-income kinship programs
  factors contributing to, 6–7
pre-approval placements, 68
private kinship care, 252–253. *See also specific topics*
  defined, 3
probate court, 194–195
probationary placements, 75
program development, 249
programs targeted to kin, 147–150. *See also* services
protection offered by kin, level of, 51

race, 18–19
recreational opportunities, providing, 133
recruitment. *See* identifying and recruiting kinship caregivers; identifying relatives
relative agreements, 182. *See also* voluntary kinship care placements
relatives. *See also* kin
  asking children for names of, 37
  motivation and willingness to care for kin, 38
    factors influencing, 38–50
  preference for, 30–34
  standard of care provided by, 52–53
research, limits of existing, 20
research needs, 246–247
resources available to kin foster parents, 250

reunification with parents, 17, 28, 99–100, 164, 207–208
  parents' efforts toward, 17
  relatives' willingness to work toward, 57
  visitation and, 117
risk. *See also* safety
  level of, 192–193, 244
runaway teenagers, 58

safety checks, 11
safety concerns, 11, 15–16, 32, 97, 127, 183. *See also* birth parents
San Diego Kinship Support Services Program (KSSP), 148–149
school, proximity to child's, 56
services. *See also* child welfare agencies; programs
  assumption that kin foster parents don't need, 135–136
  barriers kin face in accessing, 143–147, 248
  for children, 241–242
  concerns about dependency on, 136–137
  having to wait for, 146
  for kin foster families, 12–13, 129–130, 150–152
    are offered only to those who express need, 135
    fewer are offered, 134–138
    fewer are requested, 138–142
  kin unaware of the availability of, 140, 251
sibling groups, difficulty placing, 43–44
sleeping arrangements, 81
Social Security Act, 9
  1950 amendment to, 9, 64
  title IV-E of, 65, 273n.2
socioeconomic status. *See* class; low-income kinship programs; poverty
space requirements, 77–78
state kinship care policies, 8, 11–12
supervision. *See also* caseworkers, supervising visitation
  of children, 112–114
    in kinship *vs.* traditional foster care, 96–97
  of voluntary placements, 180, 244

supervisors and licensing standards, 86. *See also* licensing standards
Supplemental Security Income (SSI), 173

teenagers
    kin's reluctance to care for, 42
    placed with relative they object to, 57–58
Temporary Assistance for Needy Families (TANF), 9, 13, 55, 69, 72, 87–88, 255, 260n.6, 265, 267, 272
    suggested changes in, 257–258
termination of parental rights (TPR), 10, 154–158, 165, 193–194
training (requirements)
    for caseworkers, 151, 250
    for kinship caregivers, 67, 78–79, 151, 250–251
    types of, 83
trust and openness among kin, engendering, 241

Urban Institute, 12, 26, 154, 155, 180–181, 262
    Internal Review Board (IRB), 264

visitation. *See under* birth parents; caseworkers
voluntary kinship care, defined, 3
voluntary kinship care placements, 70–73, 179–182, 196–199. *See also specific topics*
    absence of permanency planning for children in, 193–195
    agency issues, 183–188
    case-specific issues, 188–192
    defined, 179
    risk, resources, and agency attention to post-placement issues, 192–193
    support for private kin seeking assistance, 195–196
    when they may occur, 182–183

waivers for licensing standards, 65–67, 79–80
    purposes, 79
welfare system. *See also* child welfare agencies; Temporary Assistance for Needy Families
    inability to serve kin, 254–256
well-being of children, 17–18